CONTENTS

Smoothies and Breakfast Recipes

Keto Green Smoothie

Serves: 2
Prep Time: 10 mins
Ingredients

- 2 tablespoons flax seed meal
- 2 cups frozen spinach
- 2 tablespoons chia seeds
- 1 scoop whey protein
- 5 cubes ice + 3 cups water

Directions

1. Put all the ingredients in a blender and blend until smooth.
2. Pour into 2 glasses and serve immediately.

Nutrition

Calories: 116 Carbs: 6g Fats: 4g Proteins: 13.6g Sodium: 54mg Sugar: 0.7g

Bacon and Eggs

Serves: 12
Prep Time: 15 mins
Ingredients

- ½ teaspoon dried organic thyme
- 24 organic bacon slices
- 7 oz full-fat cream cheese
- 12 hard-cooked organic large eggs, peeled, yolks removed, and sliced lengthwise

Directions

1. Preheat the oven to 400 degrees F and grease a baking dish.
2. Mix together the cream cheese and thyme in a small bowl and put aside.
3. Fill the egg white halves with the cream cheese mixture. Then cover them with the remaining egg white halves.
4. Tightly wrap each egg with 2 bacon slices.
5. Place the wrapped eggs in the baking dish and transfer tothe oven.
6. Bake for about 30 minutes.
7. Serve hot straight from the oven.

Nutrition

Calories: 326 Carbs: 1.4g Fats: 26g Proteins: 20.9g Sodium: 988mg Sugar: 0.4g

Creamy Keto Cinnamon Smoothie

Serves: 1
Prep Time: 10 mins
Ingredients

- ½ cup water + few ice cubes
- ½ cup coconut milk
- ½ teaspoon cinnamon
- ¼ cup vanilla whey protein
- 1 tablespoon MCT oil
- 1 tablespoon ground chia seeds

Directions

1. Put all the ingredients in a blender and blend until smooth.
2. Pour into a glass and serve immediately.

Calories: 406 Carbs: 11.3g Fats: 45.6g Proteins: 9.4g Sodium: 32mg Sugar: 4.3g

Scrambled Eggs with Mushrooms and Cheese

Serves: 4
Prep Time: 20 mins
Ingredients

- 4 tablespoons butter
- 8 eggs
- 4 tablespoons Parmesan cheese, shredded
- Salt and black pepper, to taste
- 1 cup fresh mushrooms, chopped finely

Directions

1. Mix together eggs, salt, and black pepper in a bowl and beat well.
2. Melt butter in a non-stick pan and add the beaten eggs.
3. Cook for about 5 minutes, and add Parmesan cheese and mushrooms.
4. Cook for another 5 minutes, stirring occasionally,
5. Because the dish will be hot after cooking, wait about 3 minutes before eating it with your hands.

Nutrition
Calories: 203 Carbs: 1.2g Fats: 17.5g Proteins: 11.2g Sodium: 217mg Sugar: 0.8g

Peanut Butter Chocolate Smoothie

Serves: 1
Prep Time: 5 mins
Ingredients

- 1 tablespoon unsweetened cocoa powder
- 1 cup unsweetened coconut milk
- 1 tablespoon unsweetened peanut butter
- 1 pinch sea salt
- 5 drops stevia

Directions

1. Put all the ingredients in a blender and blend until smooth.
2. Pour into a glass and serve immediately.

Nutrition
Calories: 79 Carbs: 6.4g Fats: 5.7g Proteins: 3.6g Sodium: 235mg Sugar: 1.6g

Cream Cheese Pancakes

Serves: 4
Prep Time: 12 mins

Ingredients

- 2 eggs
- ½ teaspoon cinnamon
- 2 oz cream cheese
- 1 teaspoon granulated sugar substitute
- ½ cup almond flour

Directions

1. Put all the ingredients in a blender and pulse until smooth.
2. Transfer the mixture into a medium bowl and put aside for about 3 minutes.
3. Grease a large non-stick skillet with butter and add ¼ of the mixture.
4. Tilt the pan to spread the mixture, and cook for about 2 minutes until golden brown.
5. Turn the pancakes over onto the other side and cook for about 1 minute.
6. Repeat with the remaining mixture in batches and top with your choice of berries.

Nutrition
Calories: 170 Carbs: 4.3g Fats: 14.3g Proteins: 6.9g Sodium: 81mg Sugar: 0.2g

Chocolate Coconut Keto Smoothie

Serves: 1
Prep Time: 10 mins
Ingredients
- 2 tablespoons unsweetened cocoa powder
- ¾ cup full-fat organic coconut milk
- 10 drops liquid coconut stevia
- 2 scoops collagen protein
- 4 ice cubes

Directions
1. Put all the ingredients in a blender and blend until smooth.
2. Pour into a glass and serve immediately.

Nutrition
Calories: 500 Carbs: 12g Fats: 38g Proteins: 26g Sodium: 120mg Sugar: 3g

Coconut Chia Pudding

Serves: 4
Prep Time: 25 mins
Ingredients
- 1 cup full-fat coconut milk
- ¼ cup chia seeds
- ½ tablespoon honey
- 2 tablespoons almonds
- ¼ cup raspberries

Directions
1. Mix together coconut milk, chia seeds, and honey in a bowl and refrigerate overnight.
2. Remove from the fridge and top with raspberries and almonds to serve.

Nutrition
Calories: 158 Carbs: 6.5g Fats: 14.1g Proteins: 2g Sodium: 16mg Sugar: 3.6g

Raspberry Avocado Smoothie

Serves: 2
Prep Time: 10 mins
Ingredients
- 1¼ cups water
- 1 ripe avocado, peeled and pit removed
- 3 tablespoons lemon juice
- ½ cup frozen unsweetened raspberries
- 2 scoops stevia

Directions
1. Put all the ingredients in a blender and blend until smooth.

2. Pour into 2 glasses and serve immediately.

Nutrition
Calories: 227 Carbs: 12.8g Fats: 20g Proteins: 2.5g Sodium: 11mg Sugar: 2.3g

Morning Hash

Serves: 2/Prep Time: 30 mins
Ingredients
- ½ teaspoon dried thyme, crushed
- ½ small onion, chopped
- 1 tablespoon butter
- ½ cup cauliflower florets, boiled
- ¼ cup heavy cream
- Salt and black pepper, to taste
- ½ pound cooked turkey meat, chopped

Directions
1. Blend the cauliflower florets in a chopper and keep aside.
2. Put butter and onions in a skillet and sauté for about 3 minutes.
3. Add chopped cauliflower and sauté for about 3 more minutes.
4. Add turkey and cook for about 6 minutes.
5. Stir in heavy cream and cook for about 2 minutes, stirring constantly.
6. Dish out to serve or refrigerate it for about 3 days for meal prep. You just have to heat it in the microwave while reusing it.

Nutrition Calories per serving: 309 Carbohydrates: 3.6g Protein: 34.3g Fat: 17.1g
Sugar: 1.4g Sodium: 134mg

Spanish Scramble

Serves: 2/Prep Time: 20 mins
Ingredients
- 3 tablespoons butter
- 2 tablespoons scallions, sliced thinly
- 4 large organic eggs
- 1 Serrano chili pepper
- ¼ cup heavy cream
- 2 tablespoons cilantro, chopped finely
- 1 small tomato, chopped
- Salt and black pepper, to taste

Directions

1. Combine together cream, eggs, cilantro, salt and black pepper in a medium bowl.
2. Put butter, tomatoes and Serrano pepper in a pan on medium heat and sauté for about 2 minutes.
3. Add egg mixture in the pan and cook for about 4 minutes, continuously stirring.
4. Garnish with scallions and dish out to immediately serve.
5. You can refrigerate this scramble for about 2 days for meal prepping and reuse by heating it in microwave oven.

Nutrition Calories per serving: 180 Carbohydrates: 2g Protein: 6.8g Fat: 16.5g Sugar: 1.1g Sodium: 231mg

Cheese Waffles

Serves: 2/Prep Time: 20 mins
Ingredients
- ½ cup Parmesan cheese, shredded
- 2 organic eggs, beaten
- 1 teaspoon onion powder

- 1 cup mozzarella cheese, shredded
- 1 tablespoon chives, minced
- ½ teaspoon ground black pepper
- 1 cup cauliflower
- 1 teaspoon garlic powder

Directions
1. Combine all the ingredients in a bowl and keep aside.
2. Grease a waffle iron and heat it.
3. Pour half of the mixture into the waffle iron and cook until golden brown.
4. Repeat with the remaining half mixture and dish out to serve.
5. You can refrigerate these waffles up to 4 days for longer use for meal prepping. Place the waffles in a container and slide wax paper between each waffle.

Nutrition Calories per serving: 149 Carbohydrates: 6.1g Protein: 13.3g Fat: 8.5g Sugar: 2.3g Sodium: 228mg

Spinach Frittata

Serves: 2/Prep Time: 45 mins
Ingredients
- 1½ ounce dried bacon
- 2 ounce spinach, fresh
- 1½ ounce shredded cheese
- ½ tablespoon butter
- ¼ cup heavy whipped cream
- 2 eggs
- Salt and black pepper, to taste

Directions
1. Preheat the oven to 360 degrees F and grease a baking dish.
2. Heat butter in a skillet and add bacons.
3. Cook until they become crispy and add spinach.
4. Stir thoroughly and keep aside.
5. Whisk together eggs and cream in a bowl and pour it in the baking dish.
6. Add bacon spinach mixture on to the baking dish and transfer in the oven.
7. Bake for about 30 minutes and remove from the oven to serve.
8. You can refrigerate this frittata for about 2 days for meal prepping and reuse by heating it in microwave oven.

Nutrition Calories per serving: 592 Carbohydrates: 3.9g Protein: 39.1g Fat: 46.7g Sugar: 1.1g Sodium: 1533mg

Keto Oatmeal

Serves: 2/Prep Time: 20 mins
Ingredients
- 2 tablespoons flaxseeds
- 2 tablespoons sunflower seeds
- 2 cups coconut milk
- 2 tablespoons chia seeds
- 2 pinches of salt

Directions
1. Put all the ingredients in a saucepan and mix well.
2. Bring it to boil and allow it to simmer for about 7 minutes.
3. Dish out in a bowl and serve warm.
4. For meal prepping, you can put all the seeds in a jar and mix them well, so it would be quicker for you to make your oatmeal.

Nutrition Calories per serving: 337 Carbohydrates: 7.8g Protein: 4.9g Fat: 32.6g Sugar: 4.1g Sodium: 98mg

Cheese Rolls

Serves: 2/Prep Time: 20 mins

Ingredients
- 2 ounce butter, thinly sliced
- 8 ounce cheddar cheese slices

Directions
1. Arrange the cheese slices on a board and cover each slice of cheese with butter.
2. Roll it up and serve as a nutritious breakfast.
3. You can cover these cheese rolls with a plastic wrap and freeze for meal prepping. Heat them in a microwave to reuse them.

Nutrition Calories per serving: 330 Carbohydrates: 0.7g Protein: 14.2g Fat: 30.3g Sugar: 0.3g Sodium: 434mg

Buttered Eggs

Serves: 2/Prep Time: 30 mins

Ingredients
- ¼ teaspoon black pepper, ground
- 2 eggs
- 2½ ounces butter
- ¼ teaspoon salt

Directions
1. Boil the eggs in a pot and allow them to simmer for about 7 minutes.
2. Remove the eggs from the pot, peel and chop them.
3. Add butter and season with salt and black pepper.
4. Mix well and serve to enjoy.
5. For meal prepping, you can add different herbs and chili flakes to add a good taste.

Nutrition Calories per serving: 635 Carbohydrates: 0.9g Protein: 11.7g Fat: 66.2g Sugar: 0.7g Sodium: 1113mg

Baked Eggs

Serves: 2/Prep Time: 10 mins

Ingredients
- 2 eggs
- 2 ounce cheddar cheese, shredded
- 3 ounce ground beef, cooked

Directions
1. Preheat the oven to 390 degrees F and grease a baking dish.
2. Arrange the cooked ground beef in a baking dish.
3. Make two holes in the ground beef and crack eggs in them.
4. Top with cheddar cheese and transfer the baking dish in the oven.
5. Bake for about 20 minutes and remove from the oven.
6. Allow it to cool for a bit and serve to enjoy.
7. For meal prepping, you can refrigerate these baked eggs for about 2 days wrapped in a foil.

Nutrition Calories per serving: 512 Carbohydrates: 1.4g Protein: 51g Fat: 32.8g Sugar: 1g Sodium: 531mg

Blueberry Smoothie

Serves: 2/Prep Time: 15 mins

Ingredients
- 1 cup fresh blueberries
- 1 teaspoon vanilla extract
- 28 ounce coconut milk
- 2 tablespoons lemon juice

Directions
1. Drop all the ingredients in a blender and blend until smooth.

2. Pour it in the glasses to serve and enjoy.
3. Meal prep tip: If you want more filling smoothie you can add more coconut milk in it. You can also use yogurt. If you want it to be more liquid add some water in it.

Nutrition Calories per serving: 152 Carbohydrates: 6.9g Protein: 1.5g Fat: 13.1g Sugar: 4.5g Sodium: 1mg

Quick Keto Pancakes

Serves: 2/Prep Time: 30 mins
Ingredients
- 3 ounce cottage cheese
- 2 eggs
- ½ tablespoon psyllium husk powder, ground
- ½ cup whipped cream
- 1 ounce butter

Directions
1. Mix together all the ingredients in a bowl except whipped cream and keep aside.
2. Heat butter in the frying pan and pour half of the mixture.
3. Cook for about 3 minutes on each side and dish out in a serving platter.
4. Add whipped cream in another bowl and whisk until smooth.
5. Top the pancakes with whipped cream on them.

6. Meal Prep Tip: These keto pancakes can also be used as a snack. They taste awesome when serve cold.

Nutrition Calories per serving: 298 Carbohydrates: 4.8g Protein: 12.2g Fat: 26g Sugar: 0.5g Sodium: 326mg

Spinach Quiche

Serves: 2/Prep Time: 15 mins
Ingredients
- 1½ cups Monterey Jack cheese, shredded
- ½ tablespoon butter, melted
- 5-ounce frozen spinach, thawed
- Salt and freshly ground black pepper, to taste
- 2 organic eggs, beaten

Directions
1. Preheat the oven to 350 degrees F and grease a 9-inch pie dish lightly.
2. Heat butter on medium-low heat in a large skillet and add spinach.
3. Cook for about 3 minutes and keep aside.
4. Mix together Monterey Jack cheese, eggs, spinach, salt and black pepper in a bowl.
5. Transfer the mixture into prepared pie dish and place in the oven.
6. Bake for about 30 minutes and dish out to serve by cutting into equal sized wedges.
7. Meal Prep Tip: You can take spinach quiche as your lunch when you are going to work.

Nutrition Calories per serving: 349 Carbohydrates: 3.2g Protein: 23g Fat: 27.8g Sugar: 1.3g Sodium: 532mg

Cream Crepes

Serves: 2/Prep Time: 25 mins
Ingredients
- 1 teaspoon Splenda
- 2 tablespoons coconut flour
- 2 tablespoons coconut oil, melted and divided

- 2 organic eggs
- ½ cup heavy cream

Directions
1. Put 1 tablespoon of coconut oil, eggs, Splenda and salt in a bowl and beat until well combined.
2. Sift in the coconut flour slowly and beat constantly.
3. Stir in the heavy cream and continuously beat until the mixture is well combined.
4. Heat a non-stick pan and pour half of the mixture in it.
5. Cook for about 2 minutes on each side and repeat with the remaining mixture.
6. Dish out to serve and enjoy.
7. For meal prepping, wrap each cream crepe into wax paper pieces and place into a resealable bag. Freeze for up to 3 days and remove from the freezer. Microwave for about 2 minutes to serve.

Nutrition Calories per serving: 298 Carbohydrates: 8g Protein: 7g Fat: 27.1g Sugar: 2.4g Sodium: 70mg

Smoothie Bowl

Serves: 2/Prep Time: 15 mins
Ingredients
- ¼ cup unsweetened almond milk
- 1 cup frozen strawberries
- ½ cup fat-free plain Greek yogurt
- 1 tablespoon walnuts, chopped
- ½ tablespoon unsweetened whey protein powder

Directions
1. Put the strawberries in a blender and pulse until smooth.
2. Add almond milk, Greek yogurt and whey protein powder in the blender and pulse for about 2 minutes.
3. Transfer the mixture evenly into and top with walnuts to serve.
4. You can wrap the bowls with plastic wrap and refrigerate for 2 days for meal prepping. Add 2 tablespoons of unsweetened almond milk and walnuts before serving.

Nutrition Calories per serving: 71 Fat: 19g Carbohydrates: 6.3g Protein: 6.8g Sugar: 0.7g Sodium: 65mg

Pumpkin Pancakes

Serves: 2/Prep Time: 20 mins
Ingredients
- 6 tablespoons pumpkin filling
- ¼ teaspoon cinnamon
- 2 squares puff pastry
- 2 small eggs, beaten

Directions
1. Preheat the Airfryer to 30 degrees F and grease a baking dish.
2. Roll out a square of puff pastry and stuff with pumpkin filling.
3. Leave ¼-inch space around the edges and cut it up into equal sized square pieces.
4. Cover the gaps with beaten egg and place the squares into a baking dish.
5. Cook for about 12 minutes and sprinkle cinnamon to serve.
6. You can wrap these pumpkin pancakes in a plastic sheet and freeze for up to 2 days. Warm for about 1 minute in the microwave before serving.

Nutrition Calories per serving: 51 Carbs: 5g Fats: 2.5g Proteins: 2.4g Sugar: 0.5g Sodium: 48mg

Devilish Pancakes

Serves: 2/Prep Time: 25 mins

Ingredients
- 2-ounce cream cheese, softened
- ½ packet stevia
- 2 organic eggs
- ½ teaspoon ground cinnamon

Directions
1. Blend all ingredients in a blender until smooth and keep aside for about 3 minutes.
2. Heat a skillet over medium heat and half of the mixture, spreading evenly.
3. Cook for about 2 minutes on each side until it becomes golden brown.
4. Repeat with the remaining mixture and dish out to serve.
5. For meal prepping, you can refrigerate these pancakes for about 4 days. Place them in a container and place wax paper between each pancake.

Nutrition Calories per serving: 163 Fat: 14.3g Carbohydrates: 1.6g Protein: 7.7g Sugar: 0.6 g Sodium: 324mg

Cheesy Muffins

Serves: 2/Prep Time: 45 mins

Ingredients
- ¼ cup raw hemp seeds
- ¼ teaspoon baking powder
- 1/8 cup nutritional yeast flakes
- ¼ cup Parmesan cheese, grated finely
- 3 organic eggs, beaten
- ¼ cup almond meal
- 1/8 cup flax seeds meal
- Salt, to taste
- ¼ cup low-fat cottage cheese
- ¼ cup scallion, sliced thinly

Directions
1. Preheat oven to 360 degrees F and grease 2 muffin cups.
2. Combine almond meal, flax seeds, hemp seeds, baking powder and salt in a bowl and mix well.
3. Mix together cottage cheese, parmesan cheese, nutritional yeast flakes and egg in another bowl.
4. Combine the cheese and almond mixture and mix until well combined.
5. Fold in the scallions and pour this mixture into the greased muffin cups.
6. Transfer into the oven and bake for about 30 minutes.
7. Dish out to serve warm immediately or for meal prepping, you can refrigerate muffins in the refrigerator for 3-4 days, by covering them with paper towel and heat again before use.

Nutrition Calories per serving: 179 Fat: 10.9g Carbohydrates: 6.9g Protein: 15.4g Sugar: 2.3g Sodium: 311mg

Scrambled Eggs

Serves: 2/Prep Time: 25 mins

Ingredients
- 1 tablespoon butter
- 4 eggs
- Salt and black pepper, to taste

Directions
1. Combine together eggs, salt and black pepper in a bowl and keep aside.
2. Heat butter in a pan over medium-low heat and slowly add the whisked eggs.
3. Stir the eggs continuously in the pan with the help of a fork for about 4 minutes.
4. Dish out in a plate and serve immediately.
5. You can refrigerate this scramble for about 2 days for meal prepping and reuse by heating it in microwave oven.

Nutrition Calories per serving: 151 Fat: 11.6g Carbohydrates: 0.7g Protein: 11.1g Sodium: 144mg Sugar: 0.7g

Bacon Veggies Combo

Serves: 2/Prep Time: 35 mins
Ingredients
- ½ green bell pepper, seeded and chopped
- 2 bacon slices
- ¼ cup Parmesan Cheese
- ½ tablespoon mayonnaise
- 1 scallion, chopped

Directions
1. Preheat the oven to 375 degrees F and grease a baking dish.
2. Place bacon slices on the baking dish and top with mayonnaise, bell peppers, scallions and Parmesan Cheese.
3. Transfer in the oven and bake for about 25 minutes.
4. Dish out to serve immediately or refrigerate for about 2 days wrapped in a plastic sheet for meal prepping.

Nutrition Calories per serving: 197 Fat: 13.8g Carbohydrates: 4.7g Protein: 14.3g Sugar: 1.9g Sodium: 662mg

Tofu with Mushrooms

Serves: 2/Prep Time: 25 mins
Ingredients
- 1 cup fresh mushrooms, chopped finely
- 1 block tofu, pressed and cubed into 1-inch pieces
- 4 tablespoons butter
- Salt and black pepper, to taste
- 4 tablespoons Parmesan cheese, shredded

Directions
1. Season the tofu with salt and black pepper.
2. Put butter and seasoned tofu in a pan and cook for about 5 minutes.
3. Add mushrooms and Parmesan cheese and cook for another 5 minutes, stirring occasionally.
4. Dish out and serve immediately or refrigerate for about 3 days wrapped in a foil for meal prepping and microwave it to serve again.

Nutrition Calories per serving: 423 Fat: 37g Carbohydrates: 4g Protein: 23.1g Sugar: 0.9g Sodium: 691mg

Ham Spinach Ballet

Serves: 2/Prep Time: 40 mins
Ingredients
- 4 teaspoons cream
- ¾ pound fresh baby spinach
- 7-ounce ham, sliced
- Salt and black pepper, to taste
- 1 tablespoon unsalted butter, melted

Directions
1. Preheat the oven to 360 degrees F. and grease 2 ramekins with butter.
2. Put butter and spinach in a skillet and cook for about 3 minutes.
3. Add cooked spinach in the ramekins and top with ham slices, cream, salt and black pepper.
4. Bake for about 25 minutes and dish out to serve hot.
5. For meal prepping, you can refrigerate this ham spinach ballet for about 3 days wrapped in a foil.

Nutrition Calories per serving: 188 Fat: 12.5g Carbohydrates: 4.9g Protein: 14.6g Sugar: 0.3g Sodium: 1098mg

Creamy Parsley Soufflé

Serves: 2/Prep Time: 25 mins
Ingredients
- 2 fresh red chili peppers, chopped
- Salt, to taste
- 4 eggs
- 4 tablespoons light cream
- 2 tablespoons fresh parsley, chopped

Directions
1. Preheat the oven to 375 degrees F and grease 2 soufflé dishes.
2. Combine all the ingredients in a bowl and mix well.
3. Put the mixture into prepared soufflé dishes and transfer in the oven.
4. Cook for about 6 minutes and dish out to serve immediately.
5. For meal prepping, you can refrigerate this creamy parsley soufflé in the ramekins covered in a foil for about 2-3 days.

Nutrition Calories per serving: 108 Fat: 9g Carbohydrates: 1.1g Protein: 6g Sugar: 0.5g Sodium: 146mg

Vegetarian Three Cheese Quiche Stuffed Peppers

Serves: 2/Prep Time: 50 mins
Ingredients
- 2 large eggs
- ¼ cup mozzarella, shredded
- 1 medium bell peppers, sliced in half and seeds removed
- ¼ cup ricotta cheese
- ¼ cup grated Parmesan cheese
- ½ teaspoon garlic powder
- 1/8 cup baby spinach leaves
- ¼ teaspoon dried parsley
- 1 tablespoon Parmesan cheese, to garnish

Directions
8. Preheat oven to 375 degrees F.
9. Blend all the cheeses, eggs, garlic powder and parsley in a food processor and process until smooth.
10. Pour the cheese mixture into each sliced bell pepper and top with spinach leaves.
11. Stir with a fork, pushing them under the cheese mixture and cover with foil.
12. Bake for about 40 minutes and sprinkle with Parmesan cheese.
13. Broil for about 5 minutes and dish out to serve.

Nutrition Calories: 157 Carbs: 7.3g Fats: 9g Proteins: 12.7g Sodium: 166mg Sugar: 3.7g

Spinach Artichoke Egg Casserole

Serves: 2/Prep Time: 45 mins
Ingredients
- 1/8 cup milk
- 2.5-ounce frozen chopped spinach, thawed and drained well
- 1/8 cup parmesan cheese
- 1/8 cup onions, shaved
- ¼ teaspoon salt
- ¼ teaspoon crushed red pepper
- 4 large eggs
- 3.5-ounce artichoke hearts, drained
- ¼ cup white cheddar, shredded
- 1/8 cup ricotta cheese
- ½ garlic clove, minced
- ¼ teaspoon dried thyme

Directions
1. Preheat the oven to 350 degrees F and grease a baking dish with non-stick cooking spray.
2. Whisk eggs and milk together and add artichoke hearts and spinach.

3. Mix well and stir in rest of the ingredients, withholding the ricotta cheese.
4. Pour the mixture into the baking dish and top evenly with ricotta cheese.
5. Transfer in the oven and bake for about 30 minutes.
6. Dish out and serve warm.

Nutrition Calories: 228 Carbs: 10.1g Fats: 13.3g Proteins: 19.1g Sodium: 571mg Sugar: 2.5g

Avocado Baked Eggs

Serves: 2/Prep Time: 25 mins
Ingredients
- 2 eggs
- 1 medium sized avocado, halved and pit removed
- ¼ cup cheddar cheese, shredded
- Kosher salt and black pepper, to taste

Directions
1. Preheat oven to 425 degrees and grease a muffin pan.
2. Crack open an egg into each half of the avocado and season with salt and black pepper.
3. Top with cheddar cheese and transfer the muffin pan in the oven.
4. Bake for about 15 minutes and dish out to serve.

Nutrition Calories: 210 Carbs: 6.4g Fats: 16.6g Proteins: 10.7g Sodium: 151mg Sugar: 2.2g

Cinnamon Faux-St Crunch Cereal

Serves: 2/Prep Time: 35 mins
Ingredients
- ¼ cup hulled hemp seeds
- ½ tablespoon coconut oil
- ¼ cup milled flax seed
- 1 tablespoon ground cinnamon
- ¼ cup apple juice

Directions
1. Preheat the oven to 300 degrees F and line a cookie sheet with parchment paper.
2. Put hemp seeds, flax seed and ground cinnamon in a food processor.
3. Add coconut oil and apple juice and blend until smooth.
4. Pour the mixture on the cookie sheet and transfer in the oven.
5. Bake for about 15 minutes and lower the temperature of the oven to 250 degrees F.
6. Bake for another 10 minutes and dish out from the oven, turning it off.

7. Cut into small squares and place in the turned off oven.
8.   Place the cereal in the oven for 1 hour until it is crisp.
9. Dish out and serve with unsweetened almond milk.

Nutrition Calories: 225 Carbs: 9.2g Fats: 18.5g Proteins: 9.8g Sodium: 1mg Sugar: 1.6g

Quick Keto McMuffins

Serves: 2/Prep Time: 15 mins
Ingredients
Muffins:
- ¼ cup flaxmeal
- ¼ cup almond flour
- ¼ teaspoon baking soda
- 1 large egg, free-range or organic
- 2 tablespoons water
- 1 pinch salt
- 2 tablespoons heavy whipping cream
- ¼ cup cheddar cheese, grated

Filling:

- 1 tablespoon ghee
- 2 slices cheddar cheese
- Salt and black pepper, to taste
- 2 large eggs
- 1 tablespoon butter
- 1 teaspoon Dijon mustard

Directions

1. **For Muffins:** Mix together all the dry ingredients for muffins in a small bowl and add egg, cream, cheese and water.
2. Combine well and pour in 2 single-serving ramekins.
3. Microwave on high for about 90 seconds.
4. **For Filling:** Fry the eggs on ghee and season with salt and black pepper.
5. Cut the muffins in half and spread butter on the inside of each half.
6. Top each buttered half with cheese slices, eggs and Dijon mustard.
7. Serve immediately.

Nutrition Calories: 299 Carbs: 8.8g Fats: 24.3g Proteins: 13g Sodium: 376mg Sugar: 0.4g

Keto Egg Fast Snickerdoodle Crepes

Serves: 2/Prep Time: 15 mins

Ingredients

For the crepes:
- 5 oz cream cheese, softened
- 6 eggs
- 1 teaspoon cinnamon
- Butter, for frying
- 1 tablespoon Swerve

For the filling:
- 2 tablespoons granulated Swerve
- 8 tablespoons butter, softened
- 1 tablespoon cinnamon

Directions

1. **For the crepes:** Put all the ingredients together in a blender except the butter and process until smooth.
2. Heat butter on medium heat in a non-stick pan and pour some batter in the pan.
3. Cook for about 2 minutes, then flip and cook for 2 more minutes.
4. Repeat with the remaining mixture.

5. Mix Swerve, butter and cinnamon in a small bowl until combined.
6. Spread this mixture onto the centre of the crepe and serve rolled up.

Nutrition Calories: 543 Carbs: 8g Fats: 51.6g Proteins: 15.7g Sodium: 455mg Sugar: 0.9g

Cauliflower Hash Brown Breakfast Bowl

Serves: 2/Prep Time: 30 mins

Ingredients
- 1 tablespoon lemon juice
- 1 egg
- 1 avocado
- 1 teaspoon garlic powder
- 2 tablespoons extra virgin olive oil
- 2 oz mushrooms, sliced
- ½ green onion, chopped
- ¼ cup salsa
- ¾ cup cauliflower rice
- ½ small handful baby spinach
- Salt and black pepper, to taste

Directions

1. Mash together avocado, lemon juice, garlic powder, salt and black pepper in a small bowl.
2. Whisk eggs, salt and black pepper in a bowl and keep aside.
3. Heat half of olive oil over medium heat in a skillet and add mushrooms.

4. Sauté for about 3 minutes and season with garlic powder, salt, and pepper.
5. Sauté for about 2 minutes and dish out in a bowl.
6. Add rest of the olive oil and add cauliflower, garlic powder, salt and pepper.
7. Sauté for about 5 minutes and dish out.
8. Return the mushrooms to the skillet and add green onions and baby spinach.
9. Sauté for about 30 seconds and add whisked eggs.
10. Sauté for about 1 minute and scoop on the sautéed cauliflower hash browns.
11. Top with salsa and mashed avocado and serve.
Nutrition Calories: 400 Carbs: 15.8g Fats: 36.7g Proteins: 8g Sodium: 288mg Sugar: 4.2g

Cheesy Thyme Waffles

Serves: 2/Prep Time: 15 mins
Ingredients
- ½ cup mozzarella cheese, finely shredded
- ¼ cup Parmesan cheese
- ¼ large head cauliflower
- ½ cup collard greens
- 1 large egg
- 1 stalk green onion
- ½ tablespoon olive oil
- ½ teaspoon garlic powder
- ¼ teaspoon salt
- ½ tablespoon sesame seed
- 1 teaspoon fresh thyme, chopped
- ¼ teaspoon ground black pepper

Directions
1. Put cauliflower, collard greens, spring onion and thyme in a food processor and pulse until smooth.
2. Dish out the mixture in a bowl and stir in rest of the ingredients.
3. Heat a waffle iron and transfer the mixture evenly over the griddle.
4. Cook until a waffle is formed and dish out in a serving platter.
Nutrition Calories: 144 Carbs: 8.5g Fats: 9.4g Proteins: 9.3g Sodium: 435mg Sugar: 3g

Baked Eggs and Asparagus with Parmesan

Serves: 2/Prep Time: 30 mins
Ingredients
- 4 eggs
- 8 thick asparagus spears, cut into bite-sized pieces
- 2 teaspoons olive oil
- 2 tablespoons Parmesan cheese
- Salt and black pepper, to taste

Directions
1. Preheat the oven to 400 degrees F and grease two gratin dishes with olive oil.
2. Put half the asparagus into each gratin dish and place in the oven.
3. Roast for about 10 minutes and dish out the gratin dishes.
4. Crack eggs over the asparagus and transfer into the oven.
5. Bake for about 5 minutes and dish out the gratin dishes.
6. Sprinkle with Parmesan cheese and put the dishes back in the oven.
7. Bake for another 3 minutes and dish out to serve hot.
Nutrition Calories: 336 Carbs: 13.7g Fats: 19.4g Proteins: 28.1g Sodium: 2103mg Sugar: 4.7g

Low Carb Green Smoothie

Serves: 2/Prep Time: 15 mins
Ingredients
- 1/3 cup romaine lettuce
- 1/3 tablespoon fresh ginger, peeled and chopped

- 1½ cups filtered water
- 1/8 cup fresh pineapple, chopped
- ¾ tablespoon fresh parsley
- 1/3 cup raw cucumber, peeled and sliced
- ¼ Hass avocado
- ¼ cup kiwi fruit, peeled and chopped
- 1/3 tablespoon Swerve

Directions

1. Put all the ingredients in a blender and blend until smooth.
2. Pour into 2 serving glasses and serve chilled.

Nutrition Calories: 108 Carbs: 7.8g Fats: 8.9g Proteins: 1.6g Sodium: 4mg Sugar: 2.2g

Hard Boiled Eggs

Serves: 16

Ingredients:

- 1 cup water
- 16 large eggs

Directions:

1. Place the metal rack in the Instant Pot and pour in the water.

2. Place the eggs on the rack and fit in as many as you can. Lock the lid and seal the valve. Press the Manual button and cook on high pressure for 4 minutes.

3. When cooking time is up, press Cancel and open the valve to release pressure. Transfer the eggs to a large bowl and add cold water until all is covered. Let rest for about 5 minutes.

4. While still warm, peel the eggs and rinse off any remaining shell pieces. Serve immediately and store the rest in the fridge.

Crispy Potatoes

Serves: 4

Ingredients:

- ½ cup water
- 1 lb. Yukon Gold potatoes, skinned and cut into 1-inch cubes
- 2 tbsp. ghee
- Kosher salt and ground black pepper
- Juice of 1 small lemon
- ¼ cup fresh chives, minced

Directions:

1. Add water into the pot and fit with a steamer insert. Add the potatoes.

2. Lock the lid and set the valve in sealing position. Hit the Manual button and cook on high pressure for 5 minutes.

3. When the timer goes off, turn off the Instant Pot and release pressure naturally for about 10 minutes. Transfer the potatoes to a bowl.

4. In a large nonstick skillet set over medium-high heat, melt and ghee until it begins to sputter. Add the steamed potatoes and season with generous amount of salt and pepper. Allow to cook by itself for 1 minute.

5. After 1 minutes, flip the potatoes to cook the other side for another minute or until slightly browned.

6. Transfer the crispy potatoes to a serving bowl. Pour the lemon juice over and top with minced chives. Serve warm.

Breakfast Casserole

Serves: 6

Ingredients:

- 2 tbsp. coconut oil
- 2 tsp. minced garlic
- 1 cup chopped kale
- 1 1/3 cups sliced leeks
- 8 eggs
- 1 ½ cups breakfast sausage, cooked
- 2/3 cup sweet potato, skinned and grated
- 1 ½ cups water

Directions:

1. Set the pot to Sauté and add coconut oil. Once melted, sauté garlic, kale, and leeks until softened.

2. Transfer sautéed vegetables to a large mixing bowl and combine with eggs, sausage, and sweet potatoes. Clean the Instant Pot.

3. Grease an oven-proof bowl or pan and pour in the mixture.

4. Add water to the pot and place the wire rack inside. Lower the greased pan or bowl onto the rack. Lock the lid and seal the valve. Set timer to 25 minutes and cook on high pressure.

5. Once done, quick-release pressure. Remove casserole from the pot and slice into equal parts. Serve immediately.

Tahini Breakfast Porridge

Serves: 2
Prep Time: 15 mins
Ingredients
- 1 tablespoon tahini
- 2 tablespoons unsweetened coconut, shredded
- 1 tablespoon chia seed
- 1/2 teaspoon cinnamon
- 1 teaspoon ginger, ground
- Pinch of turmeric, ground
- Pinch of sea salt
- 1/2 cup coconut milk
- 1 cup squash, cooked
- Optional hemp protein or collagen
- Pure maple syrup or raw honey

Directions
1. Add 1 tablespoon coconut oil to the insert of the Instant Pot. Select Sauté mode.

2. Stir in squash, cinnamon, and nutmeg and sauté for 5 minutes.
3. Pour 1/3 water to the insert then seal the Instant Pot lid.
4. Select Manual Mode for 6 minutes at High pressure.
5. Once it beeps, release all the steam naturally from the Instant Pot.
6. Remove the Instant Pot lid and drain the cooked squash.
7. Puree this squash using a handheld blender then stir in remaining ingredients.
8. Mix well and garnish as desired.
9. Serve fresh.

Nutrition
Calories per serving: 322 Carbohydrate2: 52.4g Protein: 9.3g Fat: 9.6g Sugar: 20.4g
  Sodium: 42mg

Barley Ham Breakfast

Serves: 4
Prep Time: 15 mins
Ingredients
- 1 tablespoon olive oil
- 1 cup pearl barley
- 1/4 cup red or sweet onion, diced
- 4 cups broth
- 1/2 to 1 teaspoon sea salt
- 4 ounces turkey ham, diced
- 4 ounces baby kale
- 4 eggs, cooked as desired

Directions
1. Add olive oil to the insert of the instant pot and heat it on Sauté mode.
2. Stir in onion and barley, sauté for 2-3 minutes.
3. Pour in salt and liquid then seal the lid.
4. Select Manual mode for 18 minutes with high pressure.
5. Meanwhile, dice the ham and keep it aside.
6. Once the barley is cooked, release the pressure completely.
7. Switch the Instant Pot to Sauté mode and add diced ham to the insert.
8. Sauté the mixture for 1 minute then add kale.
9. Let it sit for 3 minutes then dish out.
10. Garnish as desired and serve warm.

Nutrition
Calories per serving: 284 Carbohydrate: 37.2g Protein: 8.2g Fat: 12.4g Sugar: 10.6g
  Sodium: 55mg

Crustless Lorraine Quiche

Serves: 6
Prep Time: 15 mins
Tip: Enjoy this quiche with warm or toasted bread

Ingredients
- 8 slices bacon, diced
- 1/2 large onion, diced
- 2 cups freshly shredded swiss cheese, separated
- 8 large eggs
- 1 1/2 cups heavy whipping cream
- 1/2 teaspoon salt
- 1/2 teaspoon freshly grated nutmeg
- 1/4 teaspoon cayenne pepper
- 1 cup of water
- Fresh chopped chives for garnish

Directions

1. Grease a 7-inch baking pan with olive oil.
2. Layer the greased baking pan with parchment paper.
3. Set the Instant Pot on Sauté mode and add bacon to its insert.
4. Sauté it until crispy then transfer the bacon to a plate lined with a paper towel.
5. Add onion to the pot and sauté for 3 minutes then transfer it to a bowl.
6. Spread the bacon in the prepared pan then top it with 1.5 cups cheese, and onions.

7. Pour egg over into the pan and let it set.
8. Place trivet in the insert of Instant Pot and pour 1 cup water into it.
9. Place the baking pan over the trivet and cover the pan with aluminum foil.
10. Seal the Instant Pot lid then set the Instant pot on manual mode at high pressure for 25 minutes.
11. Once done, release the pressure completely then remove the lid.
12. Spread the remaining cheese over the egg casserole and broil it for 5 minutes.
13. Garnish with chives and bacon.
14. Serve.

Nutrition

Calories per serving: 247 Carbohydrate: 43.5g Protein: 6.9g Fat: 5.4g Sugar: 23.7g Sodium: 90mg

Apple Cinnamon Oats

Serves: 4
Prep Time: 30 mins
Ingredients

- 2 cups steel cut oats
- 4 1/2 cups water
- 2 medium apples, medium diced
- 2 teaspoons brown sugar
- 2 teaspoons cinnamon
- 2 cinnamon sticks
- 1/4 teaspoon nutmeg

Directions

1. Put all the ingredient into the insert of the Instant Pot.
2. Mix well then seal the Instant Pot lid and turn its valve to sealing position.
3. Select Manual Mode for 4 minutes at high pressure.
4. Once done, release the pressure completely then remove the lid.
5. Add cinnamon and dice apple.
6. Serve with a splash of milk.
7. Enjoy.

Nutrition

Calories per serving: 232 Carbohydrate: 48.2g Protein: 5.5g Fat: 2.7g Sugar: 18.1g Sodium: 19mg

Breakfast Ham Burritos

Serves: 6
Prep Time: 15 mins
Ingredients
egg base

- 8 eggs

- 1/2 cup half and half cream
- 1/2 teaspoon coarse salt
- 1/4 teaspoon pepper
- 1/2 teaspoon garlic powder

Any of these
- 2 tablespoons chives, chopped
- 1/4 cup onion, diced
- 1 cup ham, cooked, cubed
- 3/4 cup cheese, shredded
- 1/2 cup red bell pepper, diced
- 1 cup potato, diced

Directions
1. Add 1.5 cup water to the insert of the Instant Pot.
2. Grease a casserole dish with cooking.
3. Whisk eggs with cream in a bowl then stir in remaining ingredients.
4. Pour this mixture into the prepared pan and cover it with aluminum foil.
5. Set a trivet in the insert of the Instant Pot and place the casserole dish over it.
6. Seal the Instant Pot and select Manual mode for 30 minutes at high pressure.
7. Once done, release the pressure completely then remove the lid.
8. Slice and serve with a warm tortilla.

Nutrition
Calories per serving: 406 Carbohydrate: 23.1g Protein: 27.9g Fat: 19.2g Sugar: 2.9g
 Sodium: 512mg

Spinach Congee

Serves: 4
Prep Time: 25 mins
Ingredients:
- 6 cups chicken broth
- 2 chicken breasts
- 1 cup Jasmine rice, uncooked
- 2 teaspoons ginger, grated
- 1/2 teaspoon fine sea salt
- 4 cups baby spinach
- 2 teaspoons toasted sesame oil
- 2 green onions, chopped

 Toppings
- Boiled or fried eggs
- Sriracha sauce or homemade chili oil
- Chinese pickles or fermented tofu
- Crushed roasted peanuts or roasted sesame seeds
- Chopped cilantro

Directions
1. Rinse and drain the Jasmine rice then transfer them to the insert of the Instant Pot.
2. Add ginger, chicken, and broth to the pot and seal its lid.
3. Select Manual Mode for 15 minutes at high pressure.
4. Once done, release the pressure completely then remove the lid.
5. Remove the chicken from the pot and shred it using forks.
6. Return the chicken shreds to the pot.
7. Select Sauté and add spinach to the pot.
8. Stir cook for 1 minute the dish out.
9. Garnish with green onion and sesame oil.
10. Serve right away.

Nutrition
Calories per serving: 299 Carbohydrate: 59.3g Protein: 8.2g Fat: 4.8g Sugar: 32.9g Sodium: 21mg

Buckwheat Raisins Porridge

Serves: 4
Prep Time: 15 mins
Ingredients
- 1 cup raw buckwheat
- 3 cups of rice milk
- 1 banana sliced
- 1/4 cup raisins
- 1 teaspoon ground cinnamon
- 1/2 teaspoon vanilla
- chopped nuts optional

Directions
1. Rinse and drain the buckwheat and add it to the insert of the Instant Pot.
2. Add vanilla, cinnamon, banana, raisins and rice milk.
3. Seal the Instant Pot lid and set the Instant pot on Manual mode for 6 minutes at high pressure.
4. Once done, release the pressure completely then remove the lid.
5. Garnish with rice milk and chopped nuts.
6. Enjoy.

Nutrition
Calories per serving: 400 Carbohydrate: 24.8g Protein:30.1g Fat: 20.7g Sugar: 3g Sodium: 533mg

Tempeh Kale Bowl

Serves: 4
Prep Time: 20 mins
Ingredients
Potato Layer
- 1 28-oz bag new or baby potatoes, cut into quarters

Tempeh layer
- A ¼ cup of water
- 2 tablespoons maple syrup
- 2 teaspoons soy sauce
- 1 teaspoon sriracha
- 1 8-oz package tempeh, cut into small cubes

Kale layer
- 4 cups chopped kale
- 2 tablespoons nutritional yeast
- 1 tablespoon water
- 1 teaspoon minced garlic

Potato seasoning
- 1 teaspoon smoked paprika
- Salt and pepper, to taste

Directions
Potato Layer
1. Pour 1.5 cup water into the Insert of the Instant Pot.
2. Place a steamer basket above it then spread the potatoes in it.
Tempeh Layer

3. Toss the tempeh ingredients in a Pyrex pan.
4. Cover this pan with aluminum foil and place the pan over the potatoes.
Kale Layer
5. Toss kale with garlic, water and nutritional yeast in a bowl.
6. Spread this mixture in a Pyrex pan and cover it with an aluminum foil.
7. Place this pan over the tempeh layer.
8. Seal the Instant Pot lid and select Manual function for 10 minutes at high pressure.
9. Once done, release the pressure completely then remove the lid.
Potato Seasoning
10. Toss the cooked potatoes with paprika, salt, and pepper.
11. Dish it out then top with cooked tempeh and kale mixture.
12. Serve.

Nutrition
Calories per serving: 614 Carbohydrate: 36.4g Protein: 9.6g Fat: 10.4g Sugar: 5.6g Sodium: 619mg

Maple Quinoa Bowl

Serves: 4
Prep Time: 35 mins
Ingredients
Quinoa:
- 1 1/2 cups quinoa, soaked in water at least 1 hour
- 1 (15 ounces) can coconut milk or milk of choice
- 1 1/2 cups water
- 1 teaspoon ground cinnamon
- 1/4 cup pure maple syrup
- 2 teaspoons vanilla extract
- 1/4 teaspoon salt

Toppings:
- Fresh fruit
- Coconut flakes
- Hemp hearts
- Non-dairy milk

Directions
1. Soak, rinse and drain the soaked quinoa.
2. Add this quinoa along with water, coconut milk, maple syrup, cinnamon, vanilla and salt to the Insert of the Instant Pot.
3. Seal the Instant Pot lid and select Rice mode for cooking.
4. Once done, release the pressure completely then remove the lid.
5. Garnish as desired.
6. Serve.

Nutrition
Calories per serving: 351 Carbohydrate: 45.3g Protein: 6.4g Fat: 16.8g Sugar: 14.5g Sodium: 238mg

Baked Morning Beans

Serves: 4
Prep Time: 30 mins
Ingredients
- 1 1/2 cups dry cannellini beans

- 1 oz. Dried porcini mushrooms
- 1 cup of warm water
- 2 tablespoons olive oil
- 1 medium to the large brown onion, finely diced
- 1/2 long red chili diced or sliced
- 1/4 teaspoon salt
- 2 cloves of garlic, finely diced
- 1 medium carrot, diced into small cubes
- 1 can chopped tomatoes
- 1 tablespoon soy sauce
- 1 tablespoon ketchup
- 2 tablespoons brown sugar
- 1 onion stock cube
- 1 teaspoon smoked paprika
- 1/2 teaspoon regular paprika
- 1/2 teaspoon allspice powder
- 2 bay leaves

Directions
1. Soak beans in a large bowl filled with water and a teaspoon of salt, overnight.
2. Drain and rinse the soaked beans and set them aside.
3. Meanwhile, soak the porcini mushrooms in a bowl filled with warm water for 20 minutes then strain and reserve its liquid aside.
4. Preheat the Instant Pot on sauté mode.
5. Add olive oil, chili, and onions to the insert of the Instant Pot.
6. Sauté for 5 minutes in the pot.
7. Chop the mushrooms then add them to the insert.
8. Add beans and mushroom liquid then seal the lid.
9. Seal and lock the Instant Pot lid then select Manual mode for 12 minutes at high pressure.
10. Once done, release the pressure completely then remove the lid.
11. Serve warm.

Nutrition
Calories per serving: 436 Carbohydrate: 75g Protein: 14.7g Fat: 8g Sugar: 22g Sodium: 360mg

Lunch Recipes

Salmon Stew

Serves: 2/Prep Time: 20 mins
Ingredients
- 1 pound salmon fillet, sliced
- 1 onion, chopped
- Salt, to taste
- 1 tablespoon butter, melted
- 1 cup fish broth
- ½ teaspoon red chili powder

Directions
1. Season the salmon fillets with salt and red chili powder.
2. Put butter and onions in a skillet and sauté for about 3 minutes.
3. Add seasoned salmon and cook for about 2 minutes on each side.
4. Add fish broth and secure the lid.
5. Cook for about 7 minutes on medium heat and open the lid.
6. Dish out and serve immediately.
7. Transfer the stew in a bowl and keep aside to cool for meal prepping. Divide the mixture into 2 containers. Cover the containers and refrigerate for about 2 days. Reheat in the microwave before serving.

Nutrition Calories per serving: 272 Carbohydrates: 4.4g Protein: 32.1g Fat: 14.2g Sugar: 1.9g Sodium: 275mg

Asparagus Salmon Fillets

Serves: 2/Prep Time: 30 mins
Ingredients

- 1 teaspoon olive oil
- 4 asparagus stalks
- 2 salmon fillets
- ¼ cup butter
- ¼ cup champagne
- Salt and freshly ground black pepper, to taste

Directions

1. Preheat the oven to 355 degrees F and grease a baking dish.
2. Put all the ingredients in a bowl and mix well.
3. Put this mixture in the baking dish and transfer it in the oven.
4. Bake for about 20 minutes and dish out.
5. Place the salmon fillets in a dish and keep aside to cool for meal prepping. Divide it into 2 containers and close the lid. Refrigerate for 1 day and reheat in microwave before serving.

Nutrition Calories per serving: 475 Carbohydrates: 1.1g Protein: 35.2g Fat: 36.8g Sugar: 0.5g Sodium: 242mg

Crispy Baked Chicken

Serves: 2/Prep Time: 40 mins
Ingredients

- 2 chicken breasts, skinless and boneless
- 2 tablespoons butter
- ¼ teaspoon turmeric powder
- Salt and black pepper, to taste
- ¼ cup sour cream

Directions

1. Preheat the oven to 360 degrees F and grease a baking dish with butter.
2. Season the chicken with turmeric powder, salt and black pepper in a bowl.
3. Put the chicken on the baking dish and transfer it in the oven.

4. Bake for about 10 minutes and dish out to serve topped with sour cream.
5. Transfer the chicken in a bowl and set aside to cool for meal prepping. Divide it into 2 containers and cover the containers. Refrigerate for up to 2 days and reheat in microwave before serving.

Nutrition Calories per serving: 304 Carbohydrates: 1.4g Protein: 26.1g Fat: 21.6g Sugar: 0.1g Sodium: 137mg

Sour and Sweet Fish

Serves: 2/Prep Time: 25 mins
Ingredients

- 1 tablespoon vinegar
- 2 drops stevia
- 1 pound fish chunks
- ¼ cup butter, melted
- Salt and black pepper, to taste

Directions

1. Put butter and fish chunks in a skillet and cook for about 3 minutes.
2. Add stevia, salt and black pepper and cook for about 10 minutes, stirring continuously.
3. Dish out in a bowl and serve immediately.
4. Place fish in a dish and set aside to cool for meal prepping. Divide it in 2 containers and refrigerate for up to 2 days. Reheat in microwave before serving.

Nutrition Calories per serving: 258 Carbohydrates: 2.8g Protein: 24.5g Fat: 16.7g Sugar: 2.7g Sodium: 649mg

Creamy Chicken

Serves: 2/Prep Time: 25 mins
Ingredients

- ½ small onion, chopped
- ¼ cup sour cream
- Salt and black pepper, to taste
- 1 tablespoon butter
- ¼ cup mushrooms
- ½ pound chicken breasts

Directions

1. Heat butter in a skillet and add onions and mushrooms.
2. Sauté for about 5 minutes and add chicken breasts and salt.
3. Secure the lid and cook for about 5 more minutes.
4. Add sour cream and cook for about 3 minutes.
5. Open the lid and dish out in a bowl to serve immediately.
6. Transfer the creamy chicken breasts in a dish and set aside to cool for meal prepping. Divide them in 2 containers and cover their lid. Refrigerate for 2-3 days and reheat in microwave before serving.

Nutrition Calories per serving: 335 Carbohydrates: 2.9g Protein: 34g Fat: 20.2g Sugar: 0.8g Sodium: 154mg

Paprika Butter Shrimps

Serves: 2/Prep Time: 30 mins
Ingredients

- ¼ tablespoon smoked paprika
- 1/8 cup sour cream
- ½ pound tiger shrimps
- 1/8 cup butter
- Salt and black pepper, to taste

Directions

1. Preheat the oven to 390 degrees F and grease a baking dish.
2. Mix together all the ingredients in a large bowl and transfer into the baking dish.
3. Place in the oven and bake for about 15 minutes.
4. Place paprika shrimp in a dish and set aside to cool for meal prepping. Divide it in 2 containers and cover the lid. Refrigerate for 1-2 days and reheat in microwave before serving.

Nutrition Calories per serving: 330 Carbohydrates: 1.5g Protein: 32.6g Fat: 21.5g Sugar: 0.2g Sodium: 458mg

Bacon Wrapped Asparagus

Serves: 2/Prep Time: 30 mins
Ingredients

- 1/3 cup heavy whipping cream
- 2 bacon slices, precooked
- 4 small spears asparagus
- Salt, to taste
- 1 tablespoon butter

Directions

1. Preheat the oven to 360 degrees F and grease a baking sheet with butter.
2. Meanwhile, mix cream, asparagus and salt in a bowl.
3. Wrap the asparagus in bacon slices and arrange them in the baking dish.
4. Transfer the baking dish in the oven and bake for about 20 minutes.
5. Remove from the oven and serve hot.
6. Place the bacon wrapped asparagus in a dish and set aside to cool for meal prepping. Divide it in 2 containers and cover the lid. Refrigerate for about 2 days and reheat in the microwave before serving.

Nutrition Calories per serving: 204 Carbohydrates: 1.4g Protein: 5.9g Fat: 19.3g Sugar: 0.5g Sodium: 291mg

Spinach Chicken

Serves: 2/Prep Time: 20 mins
Ingredients
- 2 garlic cloves, minced
- 2 tablespoons unsalted butter, divided
- ¼ cup parmesan cheese, shredded
- ¾ pound chicken tenders
- ¼ cup heavy cream
- 10 ounce frozen spinach, chopped
- Salt and black pepper, to taste

Directions
1. Heat 1 tablespoon of butter in a large skillet and add chicken, salt and black pepper.
2. Cook for about 3 minutes on both sides and remove the chicken in a bowl.
3. Melt remaining butter in the skillet and add garlic, cheese, heavy cream and spinach.
4. Cook for about 2 minutes and transfer the chicken in it.
5. Cook for about 5 minutes on low heat and dish out to immediately serve.

6. Place chicken in a dish and set aside to cool for meal prepping. Divide it in 2 containers and cover them. Refrigerate for about 3 days and reheat in microwave before serving.

Nutrition Calories per serving: 288 Carbohydrates: 3.6g Protein: 27.7g Fat: 18.3g Sugar: 0.3g Sodium: 192mg

Chicken with Herbed Butter

Serves: 2/Prep Time: 35 mins
Ingredients
- 1/3 cup baby spinach
- 1 tablespoon lemon juice
- ¾ pound chicken breasts
- 1/3 cup butter
- ¼ cup parsley, chopped
- Salt and black pepper, to taste
- 1/3 teaspoon ginger powder
- 1 garlic clove, minced

Directions
1. Preheat the oven to 450 degrees F and grease a baking dish.
2. Mix together parsley, ginger powder, lemon juice, butter, garlic, salt and black pepper in a bowl.
3. Add chicken breasts in the mixture and marinate well for about 30 minutes.
4. Arrange the marinated chicken in the baking dish and transfer in the oven.
5. Bake for about 25 minutes and dish out to serve immediately.
6. Place chicken in 2 containers and refrigerate for about 3 days for meal prepping. Reheat in microwave before serving.

Nutrition Calories per serving: 568 Carbohydrates: 1.6g Protein: 44.6g Fat: 42.1g Sugar: 0.3g Sodium: 384mg

Lemongrass Prawns

Serves: 2/Prep Time: 25 mins
Ingredients
- ½ red chili pepper, seeded and chopped
- 2 lemongrass stalks
- ½ pound prawns, deveined and peeled
- 6 tablespoons butter
- ¼ teaspoon smoked paprika

Directions
1. Preheat the oven to 390 degrees F and grease a baking dish.
2. Mix together red chili pepper, butter, smoked paprika and prawns in a bowl.

3. Marinate for about 2 hours and then thread the prawns on the lemongrass stalks.
4. Arrange the threaded prawns on the baking dish and transfer it in the oven.
5. Bake for about 15 minutes and dish out to serve immediately.
6. Place the prawns in a dish and set aside to cool for meal prepping. Divide it in 2 containers and close the lid. Refrigerate for about 4 days and reheat in microwave before serving.

Nutrition Calories per serving: 322 Carbohydrates: 3.8g Protein: 34.8g Fat: 18g Sugar: 0.1g Sodium: 478mg

Stuffed Mushrooms

Serves: 2/Prep Time: 45 mins
Ingredients
- 2 ounce bacon, crumbled
- ½ tablespoon butter
- ¼ teaspoon paprika powder
- 2 portobello mushrooms
- 1 ounce cream cheese
- ¾ tablespoon fresh chives, chopped
- Salt and black pepper, to taste

Directions
1. Preheat the oven to 400 degrees F and grease a baking dish.
2. Heat butter in a skillet and add mushrooms.
3. Sauté for about 4 minutes and keep aside.
4. Mix together cream cheese, chives, paprika powder, salt and black pepper in a bowl.
5. Stuff the mushrooms with this mixture and transfer on the baking dish.
6. Place in the oven and bake for about 20 minutes.
7. These mushrooms can be refrigerated for about 3 days for meal prepping and can be served with scrambled eggs.

Nutrition Calories per serving: 570 Carbohydrates: 4.6g Protein: 19.9g Fat: 52.8g Sugar: 0.8g Sodium: 1041mg

Honey Glazed Chicken Drumsticks

Serves: 2/Prep Time: 30 mins
Ingredients
- ½ tablespoon fresh thyme, minced
- 1/8 cup Dijon mustard
- ½ tablespoon fresh rosemary, minced
- ½ tablespoon honey
- 2 chicken drumsticks
- 1 tablespoon olive oil
- Salt and black pepper, to taste

Directions
1. Preheat the oven at 325 degrees F and grease a baking dish.
2. Combine all the ingredients in a bowl except the drumsticks and mix well.
3. Add drumsticks and coat generously with the mixture.
4. Cover and refrigerate to marinate overnight.
5. Place the drumsticks in in the baking dish and transfer it in the oven.
6. Cook for about 20 minutes and dish out to immediately serve.
7. Place chicken drumsticks in a dish and set aside to cool for meal prepping. Divide it in 2 containers and cover them. Refrigerate for about 3 days and reheat in microwave before serving.

Nutrition Calories per serving: 301 Carbs: 6g Fats: 19.7g Proteins: 4.5g Sugar: 4.5g Sodium: 316mg

Keto Zucchini Pizza

Serves: 2/Prep Time: 15 mins
Ingredients
- 1/8 cup spaghetti sauce
- ½ zucchini, cut in circular slices
- ½ cup cream cheese
- Pepperoni slices, for topping
- ½ cup mozzarella cheese, shredded

Directions
1. Preheat the oven to 350 degrees F and grease a baking dish.
2. Arrange the zucchini on the baking dish and layer with spaghetti sauce.
3. Top with pepperoni slices and mozzarella cheese.
4. Transfer the baking dish in the oven and bake for about 15 minutes.
5. Remove from the oven and serve immediately.
6. Meal prep tip: Prevent burning of cheese, otherwise it will taste bitter.

Nutrition Calories per serving: 445 Carbohydrates: 3.6g Protein: 12.8g Fat: 42g Sugar: 0.3g Sodium: 429mg

Omega-3 Salad

Serves: 2/Prep Time: 15 mins
Ingredients
- ½ pound skinless salmon fillet, cut into 4 steaks
- ¼ tablespoon fresh lime juice
- 1 tablespoon olive oil, divided
- 4 tablespoons sour cream
- ¼ zucchini, cut into small cubes
- ¼ teaspoon jalapeño pepper, seeded and chopped finely
- Salt and black pepper, to taste
- ¼ tablespoon fresh dill, chopped

Directions
1. Put olive oil and salmon in a skillet and cook for about 5 minutes on both sides.
2. Season with salt and black pepper, stirring well and dish out.
3. Mix remaining ingredients in a bowl and add cooked salmon to serve.
4. Meal Prep Tip: You can refrigerate it for 1 day and not more than that.

Nutrition Calories per serving: 291 Fat: 21.1g Carbohydrates: 2.5g Protein: 23.1g Sugar: 0.6g Sodium: 112mg

Crab Cakes

Serves: 2/Prep Time: 30 mins
Ingredients
- ½ pound lump crabmeat, drained
- 2 tablespoons coconut flour
- 1 tablespoon mayonnaise
- ¼ teaspoon green Tabasco sauce
- 3 tablespoons butter
- 1 small organic egg, beaten
- ¾ tablespoon fresh parsley, chopped
- ½ teaspoon yellow mustard
- Salt and black pepper, to taste

Directions
1. Mix together all the ingredients in a bowl except butter.
2. Make patties from this mixture and keep aside.
3. Heat butter in a skillet over medium heat and add patties.
4. Cook for about 10 minutes on each side and dish out to serve hot.
5. You can store the raw patties in the freezer for about 3 weeks for meal prepping. Place patties in a container and place parchment paper in between the patties to avoid stickiness.

Nutrition Calories per serving: 153 Fat: 10.8g Carbohydrates: 6.7g Protein: 6.4g Sugar: 2.4g Sodium: 46mg

Salmon Burgers

Serves: 2/Prep Time: 20 mins
Ingredients
- 1 tablespoon sugar-free ranch dressing
- ½-ounce smoked salmon, chopped roughly
- ½ tablespoon fresh parsley, chopped
- ½ tablespoon avocado oil
- 1 small organic egg
- 4-ounce pink salmon, drained and bones removed
- 1/8 cup almond flour
- ¼ teaspoon Cajun seasoning

Directions
1. Mix together all the ingredients in a bowl and stir well.
2. Make patties from this mixture and keep aside.
3. Heat a skillet over medium heat and add patties.
4. Cook for about 3 minutes per side and dish out to serve.
5. You can store the raw patties in the freezer for about 3 weeks for meal prepping. Place patties in a container and place parchment paper in between the patties to avoid stickiness.

Nutrition Calories per serving: 59 Fat: 12.7g Carbohydrates: 2.4g Protein: 6.3g Sugar: 0.7g Sodium: 25mg

Indian Style Butter Chicken

Serves: 2/Prep Time: 25 mins
Ingredients
- ½ medium onion, chopped
- ½ teaspoon fresh ginger, minced
- ½ tablespoon garam masala
- ½ teaspoon fenugreek seeds
- ½ teaspoon ground cumin
- ½ cup heavy cream
- 1 tablespoon unsalted butter
- 1 garlic clove, minced
- 3-ounce sugar-free tomato paste
- ¾ pound grass-fed chicken breasts, cut into ¾-inch chunks
- ½ teaspoon red chili powder
- Salt and black pepper, to taste

Directions
1. Put butter, garlic, ginger and onions in a skillet and sauté for about 4 minutes.
2. Add chicken, tomato paste and spices and cook for about 5 minutes.
3. Stir in heavy cream and allow it to simmer for about 10 minutes.
4. Dish out to serve hot and enjoy.
5. Stir continuously while adding heavy cream in the skillet for meal prepping. You can store in the refrigerator for up to 4 days.

Nutrition Calories per serving: 427 Fat: 24g Carbohydrates: 9g Protein: 42.1g Sugar: 4.4g Sodium: 258mg

Burrito Bowl

Serves: 2/Prep Time: 40 mins
Ingredients
For Chicken:
- 1 tablespoon olive oil
- Salt and black pepper, to taste
- ¼ cup fresh cilantro, chopped
- 1 teaspoon garlic, minced

- ½ pound grass-fed skinless, boneless chicken breasts
- 1/8 cup fresh lime juice

For Cauliflower Rice:
- 1½ cups cauliflower rice
- 1 tablespoon olive oil
- 1 teaspoon garlic powder
- Salt, to taste
- 1/8 cup yellow onion, sliced thinly
- ½ teaspoon ground cumin
- ¼ cup carrot, peeled and shredded

Directions
For Chicken:
1. Put oil, garlic, chicken, salt and black pepper in a large skillet and cook for about 8 minutes each side.
2. Remove it from heat and allow it to cool down, shredding chicken lightly.
3. Mix together rest of the ingredients in a bowl and add chicken, tossing well.

For Cauliflower Rice:
4. Put oil, cumin and onions in a large skillet and sauté for about 3 minutes.
5. Add cauliflower rice, garlic powder and salt and cook for about 5 minutes.
6. Stir in carrots and remove from heat to cool down.
7. Combine chicken and cauliflower rice in a serving bowl and serve.
8. You can store both chicken and cauliflower rice in separate containers up to 5 days for meal prepping. Reheat before serving it.

Nutrition Calories per serving: 303 Fat: 18.3g Carbohydrates: 8.8g Protein: 27.6g
Sugar: 3.4g Sodium: 135mg

Tuna Salad

Serves: 2/Prep Time: 20 mins
Ingredients
- 2/3 cup mayonnaise
- 6 hard-boiled organic eggs, peeled and chopped
- ½ teaspoon seasoned salt
- 1 can water packed tuna, drained
- ½ cup cucumber, chopped

Directions
1. Put all the ingredients in a bowl and mix until well combined.
2. Serve immediately.
3. For meal prepping, place the salad in a container and refrigerate it for 1 day, not more than that.

Nutrition Calories per serving: 615 Fat: 38.9g Carbohydrates: 2.2g Protein: 39.9g
Sugar: 0.4g Sodium: 224mg

Chicken Meal

Serves: 2/Prep Time: 35 mins
Ingredients
- ½ medium zucchini, chopped
- ½ small yellow onion, chopped
- 1 (6-ounce) grass-fed skinless, boneless chicken breasts, cut into ½-inch pieces
- ½ cup fresh broccoli florets
- 1 garlic clove, minced
- ¼ teaspoon paprika
- 1 tablespoon olive oil
- ½ teaspoon Italian seasoning
- Salt and black pepper, to taste

Directions
1. Preheat the oven to 450 degrees F and line a baking dish with foil.
2. Put all the ingredients in a bowl and toss to coat well.
3. Place the chicken mixture in the baking dish and transfer into the oven.
4. Bake for about 20 minutes and dish out to serve hot.

5. For meal prepping, cool the mixture and wrap it with plastic wrap. Refrigerate for about 5 days.

Nutrition Calories per serving: 195 Fat: 10.6g Carbohydrates: 5.6g Protein: 20.5g Sugar: 2.1g Sodium: 134mg

Tangy Chicken

Serves: 2/Prep Time: 25 mins
Ingredients

- ¾ pound grass-fed skinless, boneless chicken thighs
- 1/8 cup onion, chopped finely
- 1 tablespoon unsalted butter, divided
- Freshly ground black pepper, to taste
- ½ cup chicken broth
- ½ tablespoon fresh lemon juice
- 1 tablespoon maple syrup
- 1 tablespoon fresh ginger, minced
- ½ cup fresh cranberries

Directions
1. Put butter, chicken, salt and black pepper in a large skillet and cook for about 5 minutes per side.
2. Dish out the chicken in a bowl and wrap it with foil to keep it warm.
3. Put onions, ginger and lemon juice in the same skillet and sauté for about 4 minutes.
4. Stir in broth and bring it to boil while continuously stirring.
5. Add cranberries and cook for about 5 minutes.
6. Stir in maple syrup and black pepper and cook for about 2 minutes.
7. Unwrap the chicken and pour this mixture over it.
8. Serve hot.
9. For meal prepping, you can store this cranberry mixture for 2 days and reheat in microwave when you want to use it again.

Nutrition Calories per serving: 199 Fat: 8g Carbohydrates: 4.2g Protein: 25.9g Sugar: 1.4g Sodium: 78mg

Mushroom Risotto with Cauliflower Rice

Serves: 2/Prep Time: 50 mins

Ingredients
- ¾ tablespoon olive oil
- 1/3 small onion, diced
- 3 ounces cremini mushrooms, thinly sliced
- ¾ tablespoon butter
- 2 cloves garlic, minced
- ½ small shallot, minced
- ¾ cup vegetable stock, divided
- 1/3 cup heavy cream
- ¾ tablespoon fresh flat-leaf parsley, chopped
- 1½ cups riced cauliflower
- ¼ cup Parmesan cheese, grated
- Sea salt and black pepper, to taste

Directions
1. Heat butter and olive oil in a large sauté pan over medium heat and add garlic, onion and shallot.
2. Sauté for about 4 minutes and add mushrooms and half of vegetable stock.
3. Sauté for about 5 minutes and add cauliflower and remaining vegetable stock.
4. Sauté for about 10 minutes and reduce the heat to low.
5. Stir in the Parmesan cheese, heavy cream, parsley, salt and black pepper.
6. Allow it to simmer for about 15 minutes and dish out.

Nutrition Calories: 207 Carbs: 9.4g Fats: 17.9g Proteins: 4.7g Sodium: 117mg Sugar: 3.7g

Cheesy Zucchini Gratin

Serves: 2/Prep Time: 55 mins
Ingredients
- ¼ small onion, peeled and sliced thinly
- ½ cup pepper jack cheese, shredded
- ¼ teaspoon garlic powder
- 1 cup raw zucchini, sliced
- Salt and black pepper, to taste
- ¾ tablespoon butter
- ¼ cup heavy whipping cream
- 1/8 teaspoon xanthan gum

Directions
1. Preheat the oven to 375 degrees F and grease an oven proof pan.
2. Mix together zucchini, onions, half of pepper jack cheese, salt and black pepper in a bowl.
3. Put the mixture in the pan and top with rest of the cheese.
4. Combine butter, garlic powder, xanthan gum and heavy cream in a microwave safe dish.
5. Microwave for about 1 minute and whisk until smooth.
6. Pour this mixture over the zucchini layers and transfer the pan in the oven.
7. Bake for about 45 minutes and dish out to serve warm.

Nutrition Calories: 136 Carbs: 9.7g Fats: 12.2g Proteins: 3.5g Sodium: 296mg Sugar: 1.5g

Eggplant Gratin with Feta Cheese

Serves: 2/Prep Time: 55 mins
Ingredients
- ¼ cup Crème Fraiche
- 1 oz Feta cheese, crumbled
- 2 basil leaves
- ¼ cup tomato sauce
- ¾ eggplant, sliced ½ inch thick
- ¼ cup half and half
- 1/3 teaspoon thyme leaves, chopped
- ½ tablespoon chives, chopped
- ¼ cup Gruyere cheese, grated
- 1 tablespoon olive oil
- Salt and black pepper, to taste

Directions
1. Preheat the oven to 375 degrees F and line a baking pan with parchment paper.
2. Sprinkle both sides of eggplant slices with salt and black pepper and drizzle with olive oil.
3. Transfer the eggplant slices into the baking pan and bake for about 20 minutes until eggplant is tender.
4. Mix together Crème Fraiche, half and half and Feta cheese in a small saucepan.
5. Bring to a boil and add thyme and chives and keep aside.
6. Spread tomato sauce in the bottom of a gratin dish and place eggplant slices.
7. Layer with tomato sauce and sprinkle half of Gruyere cheese.
8.   Top with basil leaves and continue layering with remaining eggplant, sauce and basil.
9. Top with cream, Feta cheese and the remaining Gruyere cheese.
10.   Bake for about 20 minutes until the top is browned and serve warm.

Nutrition Calories: 244 Carbs: 13.8g Fats: 18.3g Proteins: 9.1g Sodium: 380mg Sugar: 7.1g

Garlic and Chive Cauliflower Mash

Serves: 2/Prep Time: 25 mins
Ingredients
- 1/6 cup avocado mayonnaise
- ½ tablespoon water
- 2 pinches black pepper
- 2 cups cauliflower florets

- ½ clove garlic, peeled
- ¼ teaspoon Kosher salt
- 1/8 teaspoon lemon juice
- ½ tablespoon fresh chives, chopped
- ¼ teaspoon lemon zest

Directions

1. Mix together cauliflower, avocado mayonnaise, water, garlic, salt and black pepper in a large microwave safe bowl.
2. Microwave on high for about 15 minutes and transfer the cooked mixture to a food processor.
3. Puree until smooth and add lemon juice, zest and chives.
4. Pulse until combined and dish out in a platter to serve.

Nutrition Calories: 160 Carbs: 5.7g Fats: 16.1g Proteins: 2.1g Sodium: 474mg Sugar: 2.4g

Stuffed Zucchini with Goat Cheese and Marinara

Serves: 2/Prep Time: 25 mins
Ingredients

- 2½-ounces log goat cheese
- 2 medium-sized zucchinis, cut in half lengthwise
- ¾ cup marinara sauce
- Chopped parsley, for garnish

Directions

1. Preheat the oven to 400 degrees F and grease a baking sheet.
2. Season the zucchini with salt and black pepper and transfer on a baking sheet.
3. Layer with half of goat cheese followed by marinara sauce and top with remaining goat cheese.
4. Bake for about 10 minutes and serve immediately.

Nutrition Calories: 145 Carbs: 9.2g Fats: 10.2g Proteins: 8.1g Sodium: 263mg Sugar: 4.2g

Spinach & Artichoke Dip Cauliflower Casserole

Serves: 2/Prep Time: 45 mins
Ingredients

- 4 tablespoons butter
- 2 oz full fat cream cheese
- 2 pinches ground nutmeg
- 1/8 teaspoon smoked paprika
- ¼ cup frozen artichoke hearts, drained and chopped
- 1 cup raw cauliflower florets, roughly chopped
- 1/8 cup Silk Cashew Milk, unsweetened
- Kosher salt and black pepper, to taste
- 1/8 teaspoon garlic powder
- ¼ cup frozen spinach, chopped
- ½ cup whole milk mozzarella cheese, shredded
- 1/8 cup parmesan cheese, grated

Directions

1. Preheat the oven to 400 degrees F and grease a casserole.
2. Mix together the cauliflower, Silk Cashew Milk, butter, cream cheese, nutmeg, garlic powder, salt, black pepper and paprika in a microwave safe dish.
3. Microwave for 10 minutes on high and add spinach, artichoke hearts, half of the mozzarella cheese and parmesan cheese.
4. Stir well and dish out the mixture in an ovenproof casserole dish.
5. Sprinkle the remaining mozzarella cheese over the top and transfer in the oven.

6. Bake for about 20 minutes at 400 degrees F and dish out to serve hot.

Nutrition Calories: 357 Carbs: 6.8g Fats: 34.2g Proteins: 8.9g Sodium: 697mg Sugar: 2.7g

Parmesan Cauliflower Steak

Serves: 2/Prep Time: 35 mins
Ingredients
- 2 tablespoons butter
- ½ large head cauliflower, sliced lengthwise and core into 1-inch steaks
- 1 tablespoon Urban Accents Manchego and Roasted Garlic seasoning blend
- Salt and black pepper, to taste
- 1/8 cup parmesan cheese

Directions
1. Preheat the oven to 400 degrees F and line a baking sheet with parchment paper.
2. Melt butter in microwave and combine with seasoning blend to make paste.
3. Brush this mixture over cauliflower steaks and season with salt and black pepper.

4. Cook cauliflower steaks in a non-stick pan over medium heat for about 3 minutes on each side until browned lightly.
5. Transfer the cauliflower steaks on baking sheet and place in the oven.
6. Bake for about 20 minutes until golden and sprinkle with parmesan cheese to serve.

Nutrition Calories: 160 Carbs: 11.2g Fats: 12.1g Proteins: 4.9g Sodium: 161mg Sugar: 5.1g

Mediterranean Zucchini Noodle Pasta

Serves: 2/Prep Time: 25 mins
Ingredients
- ½ cup spinach, packed
- 1 tablespoon butter
- Sea salt and black pepper, to taste
- 1 tablespoon capers
- 5 kalamata olives, halved
- 1/8 cup feta cheese, crumbled
- 1 large zucchini, spiral sliced
- 1 tablespoon olive oil
- 3 cloves garlic, minced
- 1/8 cup sun-dried tomatoes
- 1 tablespoon Italian flat leaf parsley, chopped
- 1/8 cup Parmesan cheese, shredded

Directions
1. Put zucchini, spinach, olive oil, butter, garlic, sea salt and black pepper over medium heat in a large sauté pan.
2. Sauté for about 5 minutes and drain excess liquid.
3. Add sun-dried tomatoes, capers, parsley, and kalamata olives in the pan and sauté for about 3 minutes.
4. Remove from heat and top with feta and Parmesan cheeses to serve.

Nutrition Calories: 192 Carbs: 9.1g Fats: 16.7g Proteins: 4.8g Sodium: 410mg Sugar: 3.6g

Vegetarian Red Coconut Curry

Serves: 2/Prep Time: 35 mins
Ingredients
- ¾ cup spinach
- ¼ medium onion, chopped
- 1 teaspoon ginger, minced
- 1 cup broccoli florets
- 4 tablespoons coconut oil
- 1 teaspoon garlic, minced
- 2 teaspoons coconut aminos
- 1 tablespoon red curry paste
- 2 teaspoons soy sauce
- ½ cup coconut cream

Directions
1. Heat 2 tablespoons of coconut oil in a pan and add garlic and onions.
2. Sauté for about 3 minutes and add broccoli.
3. Sauté for about 3 minutes and move vegetables to the side of the pan.
4. Add curry paste and cook for about 1 minute.
5. Mix well and add spinach, cooking for about 3 minutes.
6. Add coconut cream, remaining coconut oil, ginger, soy sauce and coconut aminos.
7. Allow it to simmer for about 10 minutes and dish out to serve.

Nutrition Calories: 439 Carbs: 12g Fats: 44g Proteins: 3.6g Sodium: 728mg Sugar: 3.5g

Zucchini Noodles with Avocado Sauce

Serves: 2/Prep Time: 10 mins
Ingredients
- 1¼ cup basil
- 4 tablespoons pine nuts
- 1 zucchini, spiralized
- 1/3 cup water
- 2 tablespoons lemon juice
- 2 cherry tomatoes, sliced
- 1 avocado

Directions
1. Put all the ingredients except the cherry tomatoes and zucchini in a blender and blend until smooth.
2. Mix together the blended sauce and zucchini noodles and cherry tomatoes in a serving bowl and serve.

Nutrition Calories: 366 Carbs: 19.7g Fats: 32g Proteins: 7.1g Sodium: 27mg Sugar: 6.4g

Zucchini and Sweet Potato Latkes

Serves: 4/Prep Time: 5 mins
Ingredients
- 1 cup shredded zucchini
- 1 cup shredded sweet potato
- 1 egg, beaten
- 1 Tbsp coconut flour
- 1/2 tsp garlic powder
- 1/4 tsp ground cumin
- 1/2 tsp dried parsley
- Salt & pepper to taste
- 1 Tbsp ghee or clarified butter
- 1 Tbsp EV olive oil

Directions
1. Combine the zucchini, sweet potato and egg in a medium bowl.
2. In a small bowl, mix the coconut flour and spices together. Add the dry ingredients to the zucchini mixture and stir until fully combined.
3. Heat the ghee and olive oil in a medium nonstick pan. Divide the mixture into four equal portions and drop into the pan, pressing down with a fork until a 1/2 inch thick cake is formed. Cook on medium heat until golden and crisp, then flip carefully and cook the other side. Remove to a plate lined with paper towels to drain.

4. Season with an additional sprinkle of kosher salt. Serve hot.

Nutrition Calories: 109 Carbs: 6.2g Fats: 9.6g Proteins: 0.9g Sodium: 227mg Sugar: 1.8g

Tomato Basil and Mozzarella Galette

Serves: 2/Prep Time: 35 mins
Ingredients
- 1 large egg
- 1 teaspoon garlic powder
- ¾ cup almond flour
- 2 tablespoons mozzarella liquid
- ¼ cup Parmesan cheese, shredded
- 3 leaves fresh basil
- 2 plum tomatoes
- 1½ tablespoons pesto
- 1/3-ounce Mozzarella cheese

Directions
1. Preheat oven to 365 degrees F and line a cookie sheet with parchment paper.
2. Mix together the garlic powder, almond flour and mozzarella liquid in a bowl.
3. Add Parmesan cheese and egg and mix to form a dough.
4. Form balls out of this dough mixture and transfer on the cookie sheet.
5. Press the dough balls with a fork and spread pesto over the centre of the crust evenly.
6. Layer mozzarella, tomatoes and basil leaves, and fold the edges of the crust up and over the filling.
7. Transfer in the oven and bake for about 20 minutes.
8. Dish out to serve.

Nutrition Calories: 396 Carbs: 17.6g Fats: 29.2g Proteins: 17.5g Sodium: 199mg Sugar: 6.2g

Quick Spiralized Zucchini and Plum Tomatoes

Serves: 2/Prep Time: 30 mins
Ingredients
- 3 garlic cloves, chopped
- 1 pinch red crushed pepper flakes
- 1 large zucchini, spiralized with thicker blade
- 2 tablespoons olive oil
- ½ pound whole plum tomatoes, cut in half
- Kosher salt and black pepper, to taste
- 1 tablespoon fresh basil, chopped

Directions
1. Heat olive oil in a large non-stick pan and add garlic.
2. Sauté for about 30 seconds and add tomatoes, red pepper flakes, salt and black pepper.
3. Reduce the heat to low and simmer for about 15 minutes.
4. Increase heat to medium-high and stir in the basil and zucchini.
5. Season with salt and cook for about 2 minutes and serve.

Nutrition Calories: 174 Carbs: 11.3g Fats: 14.3g Proteins: 3.2g Sodium: 180mg Sugar: 5.5g

Cheesy Spaghetti Squash with Pesto

Serves: 2/Prep Time: 25 mins
Ingredients
- ½ tablespoon olive oil
- ¼ cup whole milk ricotta cheese

- 1/8 cup basil pesto
- 1 cup cooked spaghetti squash, drained
- Salt and black pepper, to taste
- 2 oz fresh mozzarella cheese, cubed

Directions
1. Preheat the oven to 375 degrees F and grease a casserole dish.
2. Mix together squash and olive oil in a medium-sized bowl and season with salt and black pepper.
3. Put the squash in the casserole dish and top with ricotta and mozzarella cheese.
4. Bake for about 10 minutes and remove from the oven.
5. Drizzle the pesto over the top and serve hot.

Nutrition Calories: 169 Carbs: 6.2g Fats: 11.3g Proteins: 11.9g Sodium: 217mg Sugar: 0.1g

Vegan Sesame Tofu and Eggplant

Serves: 2/Prep Time: 30 mins
Ingredients
- ½ cup cilantro, chopped
- 2 tablespoons toasted sesame oil
- ½ teaspoon crushed red pepper flakes
- ½ eggplant, julienned
- ½ pound block firm tofu, pressed
- 1½ tablespoons rice vinegar
- 1 clove garlic, finely minced
- 1 teaspoon Swerve
- ½ tablespoon olive oil
- 1/8 cup sesame seeds
- Salt and black pepper, to taste
- 1/8 cup soy sauce

Directions
1. Preheat the oven to 200 degrees F.
2. Mix together cilantro, eggplant, rice vinegar, half of toasted sesame oil, garlic, red pepper flakes and Swerve in a bowl.
3. Heat olive oil in a skillet and add the marinated eggplant.
4. Sauté for about 4 minutes and transfer the eggplant noodles to an oven safe dish.
5. Cover with a foil and place into the oven to keep warm.
6. Spread the sesame seeds on a plate and press both sides of each piece of tofu into the seeds.
7. Add remaining sesame oil and tofu to the skillet and fry for about 5 minutes.
8. Pour soy sauce into the pan and cook until the tofu slices are browned.
9. Remove the eggplant noodles from the oven and top with tofu to serve.

Nutrition Calories: 333 Carbs: 13.9g Fats: 26.6g Proteins: 13.3g Sodium: 918mg Sugar: 4.5g

Cheesy Spinach Puffs

Serves: 2/Prep Time: 25 mins
Ingredients
- ½ cup almond flour
- 1 large egg
- ¼ cup feta cheese, crumbled
- ½ teaspoon kosher salt
- ½ teaspoon garlic powder
- 1½ tablespoons heavy whipping cream

Directions
1. Preheat the oven to 350 degrees F and grease a cookie sheet.
2. Put all the ingredients in a blender and pulse until smooth.
3. Allow to cool down and form 1-inch balls from this mixture.

4. Arrange on a cookie sheet and transfer into the oven.
5. Bake for about 12 minutes and dish out to serve.

Nutrition Calories: 294 Carbs: 7.8g Fats: 24g Proteins: 12.2g Sodium: 840mg Sugar: 1.1g

Dinner Recipes

Lobster Salad

Serves: 2/Prep Time: 15 mins
Ingredients
- ¼ yellow onion, chopped
- ¼ yellow bell pepper, seeded and chopped
- ¾ pound cooked lobster meat, shredded
- 1 celery stalk, chopped
- Black pepper, to taste
- ¼ cup avocado mayonnaise

Directions
1. Mix together all the ingredients in a bowl and stir until well combined.
2. Refrigerate for about 3 hours and serve chilled.
3. Put the salad into a container for meal prepping and refrigerate for about 2 days.

Nutrition Calories per serving: 336 Carbohydrates: 2g Protein: 27.2g Fat: 25.2g Sugar: 1.2g Sodium: 926mg

Beef Sausage Pancakes

Serves: 2/Prep Time: 30 mins
Ingredients
- 4 gluten-free Italian beef sausages, sliced
- 1 tablespoon olive oil
- 1/3 large red bell peppers, seeded and sliced thinly
- 1/3 cup spinach
- ¾ teaspoon garlic powder
- 1/3 large green bell peppers, seeded and sliced thinly
- ¾ cup heavy whipped cream
- Salt and black pepper, to taste

Directions
1. Mix together all the ingredients in a bowl except whipped cream and keep aside.
2. Put butter and half of the mixture in a skillet and cook for about 6 minutes on both sides.
3. Repeat with the remaining mixture and dish out.
4. Beat whipped cream in another bowl until smooth.
5. Serve the beef sausage pancakes with whipped cream.
6. For meal prepping, it is compulsory to gently slice the sausages before mixing with other ingredients.

Nutrition Calories per serving: 415 Carbohydrates: 7g Protein: 29.5g Fat: 31.6g Sugar: 4.3g Sodium: 1040mg

Holiday Chicken Salad

Serves: 2/Prep Time: 25 mins
Ingredients
- 1 celery stalk, chopped

- 1½ cups cooked grass-fed chicken, chopped
- ¼ cup fresh cranberries
- ¼ cup sour cream
- ½ apple, chopped
- ¼ yellow onion, chopped
- 1/8 cup almonds, toasted and chopped
- 2-ounce feta cheese, crumbled
- ¼ cup avocado mayonnaise
- Salt and black pepper, to taste

Directions
1. Stir together all the ingredients in a bowl except almonds and cheese.
2. Top with almonds and cheese to serve.
3. Meal Prep Tip: Don't add almonds and cheese in the salad if you want to store the salad. Cover with a plastic wrap and refrigerate to serve.

Nutrition Calories per serving: 336 Carbohydrates: 8.8g Protein: 24.5g Fat: 23.2g Sugar: 5.4g Sodium: 383mg

Luncheon Fancy Salad

Serves: 2/Prep Time: 40 mins
Ingredients
- 6-ounce cooked salmon, chopped
- 1 tablespoon fresh dill, chopped
- Salt and black pepper, to taste
- 4 hard-boiled grass-fed eggs, peeled and cubed
- 2 celery stalks, chopped
- ½ yellow onion, chopped
- ¾ cup avocado mayonnaise

Directions
1. Put all the ingredients in a bowl and mix until well combined.
2. Cover with a plastic wrap and refrigerate for about 3 hours to serve.
3. For meal prepping, put the salad in a container and refrigerate for up to 3 days.

Nutrition Calories per serving: 303 Carbohydrates: 1.7g Protein: 10.3g Fat: 30g Sugar: 1g Sodium: 314mg

Italian Platter

Serves: 2/Prep Time: 45 mins
Ingredients
- 1 garlic clove, minced
- 5-ounce fresh button mushrooms, sliced
- 1/8 cup unsalted butter
- ¼ teaspoon dried thyme
- 1/3 cup heavy whipping cream
- Salt and black pepper, to taste
- 2 (6-ounce) grass-fed New York strip steaks

Directions
1. Preheat the grill to medium heat and grease it.
2. Season the steaks with salt and black pepper, and transfer to the grill.
3. Grill steaks for about 10 minutes on each side and dish out in a platter.
4. Put butter, mushrooms, salt and black pepper in a pan and cook for about 10 minutes.
5. Add thyme and garlic and thyme and sauté for about 1 minute.
6. Stir in the cream and let it simmer for about 5 minutes.
7. Top the steaks with mushroom sauce and serve hot immediately.
8. Meal Prep Tip: You can store the mushroom sauce in refrigerator for about 2 days. Season the steaks carefully with salt and black pepper to avoid low or high quantities.

Nutrition Calories per serving: 332 Carbohydrates: 3.2g Protein: 41.8g Fat: 20.5g Sugar: 1.3g Sodium: 181mg

Meat Loaf

Serves: 12/Prep Time: 1 hour 15 mins
Ingredients
- 1 garlic clove, minced
- ½ teaspoon dried thyme, crushed
- ½ pound grass-fed lean ground beef
- 1 organic egg, beaten
- Salt and black pepper, to taste
- ¼ cup onions, chopped
- 1/8 cup sugar-free ketchup
- 2 cups mozzarella cheese, freshly grated
- ¼ cup green bell pepper, seeded and chopped
- ½ cup cheddar cheese, grated
- 1 cup fresh spinach, chopped

Directions
1. Preheat the oven to 350 degrees F and grease a baking dish.
2. Put all the ingredients in a bowl except spinach and cheese and mix well.
3. Arrange the meat over a wax paper and top with spinach and cheese.
4. Roll the paper around the mixture to form a meatloaf.
5. Remove the wax paper and transfer the meat loaf in the baking dish.
6. Put it in the oven and bake for about 1 hour.
7. Dish out and serve hot.
8. Meal Prep Tip: Let the meat loafs cool for about 10 minutes to bring them to room temperature before serving.

Nutrition Calories per serving: 439 Carbohydrates: 8g Protein: 40.8g Fat: 26g Sugar: 1.6g Sodium: 587mg

Grilled Steak

Serves: 2/Prep Time: 15 mins
Ingredients
- ¼ cup unsalted butter
- 2 garlic cloves, minced
- ¾ pound beef top sirloin steaks
- ¾ teaspoon dried rosemary, crushed
- 2 oz. parmesan cheese, shredded
- Salt and black pepper, to taste

Directions
1. Preheat the grill and grease it.
2. Season the sirloin steaks with salt and black pepper.

3. Transfer the steaks on the grill and cook for about 5 minutes on each side.
4. Dish out the steaks in plates and keep aside.
5. Meanwhile, put butter and garlic in a pan and heat until melted.
6. Pour it on the steaks and serve hot.
7. Divide the steaks in 2 containers and refrigerate for about 3 days for meal prepping purpose. Reheat in microwave before serving.

Nutrition Calories per serving: 383 Carbohydrates: 1.5g Protein: 41.4g Fat: 23.6g Sugar: 0g Sodium: 352mg

Cheese Casserole

Serves: 2/Prep Time: 46 mins
Ingredients
- 2½ ounce marinara sauce

- ½ tablespoon olive oil
- 4 ounce parmesan cheese, shredded
- ½ pound sausages, scrambled
- 4 ounce mozzarella cheese, shredded

Directions

1. Preheat the oven to 375 degrees F and grease a baking dish with olive oil.
2. Place half of the sausage scramble in it and top with half of marinara sauce, mozzarella cheese and parmesan cheese.
3. Place the remaining sausage scramble in the baking dish and top again with marinara sauce, mozzarella cheese and parmesan cheese.
4. Transfer in the oven and bake for about 20 minutes.
5. Place the casserole in a dish and set aside to cool for meal prepping. Divide it in 6 containers and refrigerate for 1-2 days. Reheat in microwave before serving.

Nutrition Calories per serving: 353 Carbohydrates: 5.5g Protein: 28.4g Fat: 24.3g Sugar: 5g Sodium: 902mg

Air Fried Simple Steak

Serves: 2/Prep Time: 15 mins

Ingredients
- ½ pound quality cut steaks
- Salt and black pepper, to taste

Directions

1. Preheat the Air fryer to 385 degrees F.
2. Rub the steaks evenly with salt and black pepper.
3. Place the steak in an Air fryer basket and cook for about 15 minutes.
4. Dish out and serve immediately.
5. Divide the steaks in 2 containers and refrigerate for about 3 days for meal prepping purpose. Reheat in microwave before serving.

Nutrition Calories per serving: 301 Carbs: 0g Fats: 25.1g Proteins: 19.1g Sugar: 0g Sodium: 65mg

Almonds Crusted Rack of Lamb

Serves: 2/Prep Time: 50 mins

Ingredients
- ¾ pound rack of lamb
- 2-ounce almonds, finely chopped
- ½ tablespoon fresh rosemary, chopped
- 1 garlic clove, minced
- ½ tablespoon olive oil
- 1 small egg
- 1 tablespoon breadcrumbs
- Salt and black pepper, to taste

Directions

1. Preheat the oven to 350 degrees F and grease a baking tray.
2. Mix together garlic, oil, salt and black pepper in a bowl.
3. Coat the rack of lamb evenly with the garlic rub.
4. Whisk egg in a bowl and keep aside.
5. Mix together breadcrumbs, almonds and rosemary in another dish.
6. Dip the rack of lamb in egg and coat with almond mixture.
7. Place the rack of lamb in the baking tray and transfer in the oven.
8. Bake for about 35 minutes and dish out to serve.
9. Put the rack of lamb in a container and refrigerate for about 3 days for meal prepping purpose. Reheat in microwave before serving.

Nutrition Calories per serving: 471 Carbs: 8.5g Fats: 31.6g Proteins: 39g Sugar: 1.5g Sodium: 145mg

Rib Eye Steak

Serves: 2/Prep Time: 35 mins
Ingredients
- 1 tablespoon steak rub
- ¾ pound rib eye steak
- 1 tablespoon olive oil

Directions
1. Preheat the oven to 400 degrees and grease a baking tray.
2. Drizzle the steak with olive oil and coat with steak rub generously.
3. Place the steak in the baking tray and transfer in the oven.
4. Bake for about 25 minutes and dish out to immediately serve.
5. Put the rib eye steak in a container and refrigerate for about 3 days for meal prepping purpose. Reheat in microwave before serving.

Nutrition Calories per serving: 462 Carbs: 1g Fats: 38.1g Proteins: 26.8g Sugar: 0g Sodium: 307mg

Spicy Skirt Steak

Serves: 2/Prep Time: 40 mins
Ingredients
- 2 tablespoons fresh mint leaves, finely chopped
- 2 tablespoons fresh oregano, finely chopped
- ¾ tablespoon ground cumin
- ¾ cup olive oil
- ¾ teaspoon cayenne pepper
- 2 (8-ounce) skirt steaks
- ¾ cup fresh parsley leaves, finely chopped
- 2 garlic cloves, minced
- 1½ teaspoons smoked paprika
- ¾ teaspoon red pepper flakes, crushed
- 2 tablespoons red wine vinegar
- Salt and black pepper, to taste

Directions
1. Preheat the oven to 390 degrees F and grease a baking tray.
2. Put all the ingredients in a bowl except the steaks and stir well.
3. Add steaks and coat well with the marinade.
4. Put marinated steaks and ¼ cup of the herb mixture in a resealable bag and shake to coat well.
5. Refrigerate for about 1 day and reserve the remaining herb mixture.
6. Remove steaks from the refrigerator and keep at room temperature for about half an hour.
7. Arrange the steaks in the baking tray and transfer in the oven.
8. Bake for about 25 minutes and top with the remaining herb mixture to serve.
9. Put the steaks in a container and refrigerate for about 3 days for meal prepping purpose. Reheat in microwave before serving.

Nutrition Calories per serving: 445 Carbs: 5.8g Fats: 43.1g Proteins: 12.9g Sugar: 0.5g Sodium: 46mg

Leg of Lamb

Serves: 2/Prep Time: 1 hour 30 mins
Ingredients
- ¾ pound leg of lamb

- ¾ tablespoon olive oil
- Salt and black pepper, to taste
- 1 fresh rosemary sprig
- 1 fresh thyme sprig

Directions
1. Preheat the oven to 330 degrees F and grease a baking tray.
2. Season with salt and black pepper and drizzle the leg of lamb with olive oil.
3. Cover the leg of lamb with rosemary and thyme sprigs.
4. Arrange the leg of lamb in the baking tray and transfer in the oven.
5. Bake for about 1 hour 15 minutes and dish out to serve.
6. Put the leg of lamb in a container and refrigerate for about 3 days for meal prepping purpose. Reheat in microwave before serving.

Nutrition Calories per serving: 325 Carbs: 0.7g Fats: 15.9g Proteins: 42.5g Sugar: 0g Sodium: 115mg

Jamaican Jerk Pork

Serves: 2/Prep Time: 35 mins
Ingredients
- ¾ pound pork shoulder
- ¼ cup whipped cream
- ¼ cup butter, melted
- ¼ cup Jamaican jerk spice blend
- ¼ cup beef broth

Directions
1. Marinate the pork with Jamaican jerk spice blend and keep aside.
2. Put butter, cream and marinated pork in an instant pot.
3. Sauté for about 5 minutes and add beef broth.
4. Cover the lid and cook on High Pressure for about 20 minutes.
5. Release the pressure naturally and dish out to serve.
6. Place the pork in a dish and keep aside to cool for meal prepping purpose. Divide it in 2 containers and refrigerate for about 3 days. Reheat in microwave before serving.

Nutrition Calories per serving: 457 Carbohydrates: 0.3g Protein: 27g Fat: 38.2g Sugar: 0.1g Sodium: 209mg

Creamy Turkey Breasts

Serves: 2/Prep Time: 1 hour
Ingredients
- ¼ cup sour cream
- ¼ cup butter
- Salt and black pepper, to taste
- ¾ pound turkey breasts
- ½ cup heavy whipping cream
- 2 garlic cloves, minced

Directions
1. Preheat the oven to 390 degrees F and grease the baking dish with some butter.
2. Marinate the turkey breasts with butter, garlic, salt and black pepper in a bowl.
3. Place the marinated turkey breasts on a baking dish and top with heavy whipping cream and sour cream.
4. Bake for about 45 minutes and dish out in a platter.
5. For meal prepping, place the creamy turkey breasts on a dish and keep aside to cool. Divide it in 2 containers and refrigerate for about 2 days. Reheat in microwave before serving.

Nutrition Calories per serving: 304 Carbohydrates: 4.8g Protein: 20.3g Fat: 23.1g Sugar: 4.1g Sodium: 1246mg

Buttered Scallops

Serves: 2/Prep Time: 15 mins

Ingredients
- ¾ pound sea scallopsSalt and black pepper, to taste
- 1 tablespoon butter, melted
- ½ tablespoon fresh thyme, minced

Directions
1. Preheat the oven to 390 degrees F and grease a baking dish.
2. Put all the ingredients in a large bowl and toss to coat well.
3. Arrange the scallops in the baking dish and transfer in the oven.
4. Bake for about 5 minutes and dish out to serve.
5. You can store the buttered scallops into a container in refrigerator for about 2 days for meal prepping purpose. You can reheat it in the microwave before serving.

Nutrition Calories per serving: 202 Carbs: 4.4g Fats: 7.1g Proteins: 28.7g Sugar: 0g Sodium: 315mg

Ham Wrapped Prawns with Bell Pepper Dip

Serves: 2/Prep Time: 25 mins

Ingredients
- 1 tablespoon olive oil
- 1 garlic clove, minced
- 2 ham slices, halved
- Salt and black pepper, to taste
- ½ tablespoon paprika
- 4 king prawns, peeled, deveined and chopped

Directions
1. Preheat the air fryer to 400 degrees F and place the bell pepper in a fryer basket
2. Cook for about 10 minutes and dish out the bell pepper in a bowl.
3. Cover with a foil paper and keep aside for about 30 minutes.
4. Add the bell pepper along with garlic, paprika and olive oil in a blender.
5. Pulse to form a puree and keep aside.
6. Wrap each prawn with a ham slice and arrange in the fryer basket.
7. Cook for about 4 minutes until golden brown and serve with bell pepper dip.
8. You can store the bell pepper dip into a container in refrigerator for 3 days for meal prepping purpose. Reheat it in the microwave before serving with the ha, wrapped prawns.

Nutrition Calories per serving: 553 Carbs: 2.5g Fats: 33.6g Proteins: 5g Sugar: 7.2g Sodium: 366mg

Chicken Wraps

Serves: 2/Prep Time: 45 mins

Ingredients
- ¼ pound lean ground chicken
- ¼ green bell pepper, seeded and chopped
- 1/8 cup yellow squash, chopped
- ½ tablespoon low-sodium soy sauce
- Freshly ground black pepper, to taste
- ½ cup Parmesan cheese, shredded
- ½ tablespoon unsalted butter
- ¼ onion, chopped
- 1 garlic clove, minced
- ¼ cup carrot, peeled and chopped
- 1/8 cup zucchini, chopped
- ¼ teaspoon curry powder
- 2 large lettuce leaves

Directions
1. Put butter and chicken in a skillet and cook for about 5 minutes.

2. Break the lumps and stir in the vegetables.
3. Cook for about 5 minutes and add curry powder, soy sauce and black pepper.
4. Cook for 5 more minutes and keep aside.
5. Arrange the lettuce leaves in serving plates and place chicken mixture over them.
6. Sprinkle with cheese and serve.
7. You have to place the mixture on the leaves evenly for meal prepping purpose. You can refrigerate it in a container for about 2 days.

Nutrition Calories per serving: 71 Fat: 6.7g Carbohydrates: 4.2g Protein: 4.8g Sugar: 30.5g Sodium: 142mg

Indian Beef

Serves: 2/Prep Time: 35 mins

Ingredients

- ½ tablespoon olive oil
- ¼ yellow onion, chopped
- 1 garlic clove, minced
- ½ jalapeño pepper, chopped
- ½ pound grass-fed ground beef
- ½ cup cherry tomatoes, quartered
- ½ pound fresh collard greens, trimmed and chopped
- ½ teaspoon fresh lemon juice

Spices

- ½ teaspoon ground coriander
- ½ teaspoon ground cumin
- ¼ teaspoon ground fennel seeds
- ¼ teaspoon ground ginger
- ¼ teaspoon ground cinnamon
- ¼ teaspoon ground turmeric
- Salt and black pepper, to taste

Directions

1. Put olive oil and onions in a skillet and sauté for about 5 minutes.
2. Add garlic and jalapeno and sauté for about 1 minute.
3. Add beef and spices and cook for about 10 minutes, continuously stirring.
4. Stir in tomatoes and collard greens and cook for about 4 minutes.
5. Add lemon juice, salt and black pepper and dish out to serve.
6. You can refrigerate it by placing it in containers for meal prepping purpose and refrigerate it up to 4 days. Reheat in microwave when you want to use it again.

Nutrition Calories per serving: 294 Fat: 13.1g Carbohydrates: 10g Protein: 37.7 Sugar: 5.1g Sodium: 463mg

Hearty Meatballs

Serves: 2/Prep Time: 35 mins

Ingredients

For Meatballs:

- ½ tablespoon sugar-free tomato paste
- 1 garlic clove, minced
- Freshly ground black pepper, to taste
- ½ pound grass-fed lean ground lamb
- 1/8 cup fresh coriander leaves, chopped
- ½ small yellow onion, finely chopped
- ¼ teaspoon ground cumin

For Tomato Gravy:

- ½ large yellow onions, finely chopped
- ½ tablespoon fresh ginger, minced
- ½ teaspoon ground cumin
- 1 large tomato, finely chopped
- ¾ cup chicken broth
- 1 tablespoon olive oil, divided
- 1 garlic clove, minced
- ½ teaspoon dried thyme, crushed
- ½ teaspoon cayenne pepper
- Salt and black pepper, to taste

Directions
For Meatballs:
1. Put all the ingredients in a bowl and mix well.
2. Make small balls of equal sizes out of this mixture and keep aside.

For Gravy:
3. Put ½ tablespoon olive oil and meatballs in a pan and cook for about 5 minutes.
4. Dish out the meatballs in a plate and keep aside.
5. Put remaining olive oil and onions in the same pan and sauté for about 3 minutes.
6. Add garlic, ginger, thyme and spices and sauté for about 1 minute.
7. Stir in the tomatoes and cook for about 4 minutes, crushing them with the back of the spoon.
8. Add beef broth and bring it to boil.
9. Stir in the meatballs in it and cook for about 5 minutes without stirring.
10. Reduce the heat to low and allow it to simmer for about 15 minutes.
11. Dish out to serve hot and enjoy.
12. You can freeze the raw meatballs for over a month covered in a plastic wrap in the freezer for meal prepping purpose.

Nutrition Calories per serving: 250 Fat: 13.3g Carbohydrates: 9.1g Protein: 24g Sugar: 6.3g Sodium: 414mg

Creamy Steak

Serves: 2/Prep Time: 20 mins
Ingredients
- 1½ tablespoons Parmesan cheese, shredded
- 1/8 teaspoon ground nutmeg
- 1/8 teaspoon garlic powder
- 2 (8-ounce) beef tenderloin steaks
- 2 cups heavy cream
- 1½-ounce gorgonzola cheese, crumbled
- Salt and black pepper, to taste
- 1/8 teaspoon onion powder
- 1/8 teaspoon lemon pepper

Directions
1. Preheat the outdoor grill of the oven to medium high and grease it.
2. Boil the heavy cream in a pan and allow to simmer on low heat for about 30 minutes, stirring continuously.
3. Remove from heat and add gorgonzola cheese, Parmesan cheese, nutmeg, salt, pepper, both cheeses and mix well.
4. Meanwhile, mix together garlic powder, onion powder, lemon pepper, salt and black pepper in a bowl.
5. Sprinkle the steaks with the seasoning mixture and transfer to the grill.
6. Grill for about 5 minutes on each side and dish out on the serving plates.
7. Top with creamy sauce and serve immediately.
8. While sprinkling the seasoning on the steaks, sprinkle it evenly for meal prepping purpose. You can refrigerate it in the refrigerator for about 2 days.

Nutrition Calories per serving: 915 Fat: 64.9g Carbohydrates: 4.9g Protein: 76.4g Sugar: 1.2g Sodium: 680mg

Tofu in Purgatory

Serves: 2/Prep Time: 25 mins
Ingredients
- 4 large garlic cloves
- Salt and black pepper, to taste
- 1 tablespoon olive oil
- 1 can diced tomatoes

- 2 teaspoons dried herbs
- 1 block medium tofu, not pressed and cut into rounds
- ½ teaspoon dried chili flakes

Directions
1. Heat olive oil in a skillet over medium heat and add garlic.
2. Sauté for about 1 minute and add tomatoes, chili flakes, herbs, salt and black pepper.
3. Simmer for about 5 minutes over a medium heat and add the tofu.
4. Reduce the heat to medium-low and simmer for about 15 minutes.
5. Dish out and serve with a baguette.

Nutrition Calories: 123 Carbs: 8.3g Fats: 8.9g Proteins: 4.8g Sodium: 10mg Sugar: 1.3g

Caprese Style Portobellos

Serves: 2/Prep Time: 25 mins
Ingredients
- 4 plum tomatoes, halved
- 2 large portobello mushroom caps, gills removed
- ¼ cup Mozzarella cheese, shredded
- 4 tablespoons olive oil
- ¼ cup fresh basil

Directions
1. Preheat the oven to 400 degrees F and line a baking sheet with foil.
2. Brush the mushrooms with olive oil.
3. Place cherry tomatoes in a bowl and add remaining olive oil, basil, salt and black pepper.
4. Put Mozzarella cheese on the bottom of the mushroom cap and add tomato basil mixture.
5. Bake for about 15 minutes and dish out to serve.

Nutrition Calories: 315 Carbs: 14.2g Fats: 29.2g Proteins: 4.7g Sodium: 55mg Sugar: 10.4g

Four Cheese Pesto Zoodles

Serves: 2/Prep Time: 20 mins
Ingredients
- 1/8 cup parmesan cheese, grated
- ¼ teaspoon kosher salt
- 2 pinches ground nutmeg
- ½ cup mozzarella cheese, grated
- 4 ounces Mascarpone cheese
- 1/8 cup Romano cheese, grated
- ½ teaspoon ground black pepper
- 1/8 cup basil pesto
- 4 cups raw zucchini noodles

Directions
1. Preheat the oven to 400 degrees F and grease a casserole dish.
2. Microwave the zucchini noodles for 3 minutes on high and keep aside.
3. Mix together the parmesan cheese, mascarpone cheese, Romano cheese, nutmeg, salt and black pepper in a large microwave safe bowl.
4. Microwave for 1 minute on high and whisk together until smooth.
5. Fold in the basil pesto, mozzarella cheese and cooked zoodles.
6. Transfer to a casserole dish and place in the oven.
7. Bake for about 10 minutes and serve immediately.

Nutrition Calories: 139 Carbs: 3.3g Fats: 9.7g Proteins: 10.2g Sodium: 419mg Sugar: 0.2g

Roasted Baby Eggplant with Ricotta

Serves: 2/Prep Time: 45 mins
Ingredients
- ¼ tablespoon olive oil
- 1 eggplant, halved
- ¼ teaspoon Wild Fennel Pollen

To serve:
- 1/8 cup ricotta cheese
- Sea salt and black pepper, to taste

- ¼ teaspoon black pepper
- ¼ teaspoon sea salt

- ¼ tablespoon extra-virgin olive oil

Directions
1. Preheat the oven to 350 degrees F and grease a cookie sheet.
2. Place the eggplant halves on a cookie sheet, cut side up and top with olive oil, fennel pollen, salt and black pepper.
3. Transfer in the oven and bake for about 45 minutes, until lightly browned.
4. Remove from the oven and allow to cool slightly.
5. Serve warm topped with ricotta cheese, olive oil, salt and black pepper.

Nutrition Calories: 69 Carbs: 3.4g Fats: 5.5g Proteins: 2.4g Sodium: 247mg Sugar: 1.6g

Moroccan Roasted Green Beans

Serves: 2/Prep Time: 45 mins
Ingredients
- 1/3 teaspoon kosher salt
- 2 cups raw green beans, trimmed
- ¼ teaspoon ground black pepper

- 2 tablespoons olive oil
- 1/3 tablespoon Ras el Hanout seasoning

Directions
1. Preheat the oven to 400 degrees F and grease a roasting pan.
2. Mix together green beans, olive oil and seasonings in a bowl and transfer into the roasting pan.
3. Roast for about 20 minutes and remove from the oven.
4. Return to the oven and roast for another 10 minutes.
5. Dish out and serve warm.

Nutrition Calories: 160 Carbs: 8.5g Fats: 14.1g Proteins: 2g Sodium: 437mg Sugar: 1.5g

Spinach Artichoke Stuffed Portobello

Serves: 8/Prep Time: 30 mins
Ingredients
- 1 medium portobello mushrooms, stems and gills removed
- ¼ can artichoke hearts drained and chopped, 14 ounce can
- ½ tablespoon sour cream
- 1 clove garlic, chopped
- ½ tablespoon olive oil

- ¼ package (10 ounces) frozen spinach, chopped, cooked and drained
- 1-ounce cream cheese
- ¼ cup Parmesan cheese, grated
- Salt and black pepper, to taste
- ¾-ounce mozzarella cheese, shredded

Directions
1. Preheat the oven to 375 degrees F and line a baking pan with foil.
2. Brush the mushrooms with olive oil and transfer on baking pan.
3. Broil for about 5 minutes each side and dish out.

4. Mix together the spinach, cream cheese, artichoke, sour cream, garlic, Parmesan cheese, salt and black pepper until well combined.
5. Stuff each mushroom cap with the spinach mixture and sprinkle with mozzarella cheese.
6. Transfer into the oven and bake for about 12 minutes.
7. Dish out and serve warm.

Nutrition Calories: 143 Carbs: 4g Fats: 11.9g Proteins: 6.8g Sodium: 218mg Sugar: 0.5g

Grilled Halloumi Bruschetta

Serves: 2/Prep Time: 20 mins
Ingredients
- 2 tablespoons fresh basil, chopped
- ½ tablespoon olive oil
- 1/3 medium tomatoes, chopped
- ½ clove garlic, minced
- Salt and black pepper, to taste
- 1½-ounce package Halloumi cheese, sliced

Directions
1. Mix together tomatoes, basil, garlic, olive oil, salt and black pepper in a bowl.
2. Refrigerate for about 1 hour.
3. Grill the Halloumi cheese for about 2 minutes on each side and transfer to a serving platter.
4. Top with tomato basil mixture and serve chilled.

Nutrition Calories: 84 Carbs: 1.6g Fats: 7.2g Proteins: 3.8g Sodium: 1mg Sugar: 1g

Roasted Mushroom and Walnut Cauliflower Grits

Serves: 2/Prep Time: 25 mins
Ingredients
- 1½ cloves garlic, minced
- ¼ cup walnuts, chopped
- 1 tablespoon olive oil
- ¼ cup water
- ½ cup cheddar cheese, shredded
- Salt, to taste
- 3 ounces portobello mushrooms, sliced
- ½ tablespoon rosemary
- ½ tablespoon smoked paprika
- ½ medium cauliflower
- ½ cup half and half
- 1 tablespoon butter

Directions
1. Preheat oven to 400 degrees F and line a cookie sheet with foil.
2. Mix together mushrooms, garlic, rosemary, walnuts, olive oil, smoked paprika and salt in a small dish.
3. Arrange the mixture evenly on the cookie sheet and transfer in the oven.
4. Roast for about 15 minutes and dish out to keep aside.
5. Pulse cauliflower florets in a food processor and steam for 5 minutes with water.
6. Stir in half and half into the cauliflower and simmer for about 3 minutes on medium-low heat.
7. Add sharp cheddar and butter and reduce heat to low.
8. Season with salt and top with the mushroom mixture to serve.

Nutrition Calories: 456 Carbs: 15.8g Fats: 38.9g Proteins: 17.3g Sodium: 367mg Sugar: 4.8g

Cheesy Ranch Roasted Broccoli

Serves: 2/Prep Time: 45 mins
Ingredients
- 1/8 cup ranch dressing
- 1½ cups broccoli florets
- ¼ cup sharp cheddar cheese, shredded
- Kosher salt and black pepper, to taste
- 1/8 cup heavy whipping cream

Directions
1. Preheat the oven to 375 degrees F and grease oven proof casserole dish.
2. Mix together all the ingredients in a medium-sized bowl and transfer to the casserole dish.
3. Place in the oven and bake for about 30 minutes.
4. Dish out in a platter and serve hot.

Nutrition Calories: 111 Carbs: 5.7g Fats: 7.7g Proteins: 5.8g Sodium: 198mg Sugar: 1.6g

Easy Low-Carb Cauliflower Fried Rice

Serves: 2/Prep Time: 15 mins
Ingredients
- 6 ounces cauliflower fresh or frozen, riced
- 1 large green onion, sliced with white and green parts separated
- 1 tablespoon butter
- 1/8 cup carrots, finely diced
- 1 clove garlic, crushed
- 1 tablespoon gluten-free soy sauce
- 1 small egg, beaten
- ½ teaspoon toasted sesame oil

Directions
1. Melt butter in a large heavy skillet over medium-high heat and add carrots and riced cauliflower.
2. Cook for about 5 minutes and stir in garlic and white part of the green onions.
3. Cook for about 3 minutes and whisk in the egg.
4. Cook for about 2 minutes and stir in the soy sauce, green part of green onions, and the sesame oil.
5. Dish out and serve hot.

Nutrition Calories: 123 Carbs: 7.3g Fats: 8.9g Proteins: 5g Sodium: 484mg Sugar: 2.8g

Creamy Avocado Pasta with Shirataki

Serves: 2/Prep Time: 5 mins
Ingredients
- ½ avocado
- ½ teaspoon dried basil
- ½ packet shirataki noodles
- 1/8 cup heavy cream
- ½ teaspoon black pepper
- ½ teaspoon salt

Directions
1. Boil some water and cook the shirataki for about 2 minutes.
2. Mash avocado in a bowl and add cream, basil, salt and black pepper.
3. Transfer into a blender and blend until smooth.
4. Put shirataki noodles in the frying pan and add blended mixture.
5. Cook for about 2 minutes and dish out to serve hot.

Nutrition Calories: 131 Carbs: 4.9g Fats: 12.6g Proteins: 1.2g Sodium: 588mg Sugar: 0.3g

Spicy Crockpot Cauliflower Mac & Cheese

Serves: 2/Prep Time: 2 hours 15 mins

Ingredients

- ¼ stick butter
- 4 ounces sharp cheddar cheese shredded
- ¼ teaspoon garlic powder
- ½ large head cauliflower, boiled
- 2 ounces cream cheese
- 1/8 cup pickled jalapenos, diced
- ¼ teaspoon onion powder
- 1/3 cup half and half cream
- ¼ teaspoon dry mustard
- 1/8 teaspoon paprika

Directions

1. Put all the ingredients in a crockpot and stir well.
2. Cover the lid and cook for about 2 hours on high heat.
3. Dish out in large serving bowl and let it cool for about 10 minutes before serving

Nutrition Calories: 540 Carbs: 15.4g Fats: 45.2g Proteins: 22g Sodium: 597mg Sugar: 5.9g

Cheesy Broccoli & Cauliflower Rice

Serves: 2/Prep Time: 15 mins

Ingredients

- ½ cup broccoli, riced
- ¼ teaspoon kosher salt
- 1½ cups cauliflower, riced
- ½ tablespoon butter
- ¼ teaspoon ground black pepper
- Pinch of ground nutmeg
- 1/8 cup mascarpone cheese
- ¼ teaspoon garlic powder
- ¼ cup sharp cheddar cheese, shredded

Directions

1. Mix together cauliflower, butter, broccoli, garlic powder, nutmeg, salt and black pepper in a medium sized microwave safe bowl.
2. Microwave for about 5 minutes on high and add the cheddar cheese.
3. Microwave for 2 more minutes and stir in the mascarpone cheese until creamy.
4. Dish out and serve hot.

Nutrition Calories: 138 Carbs: 6.6g Fats: 9.8g Proteins: 7.5g Sodium: 442mg Sugar: 2.4g

Zucchini Noodle Alfredo

Serves: 2/Prep Time: 25 mins

Ingredients

- ½ tablespoon olive oil
- ½ pound zucchini, spiralized into noodles
- ¾ ounces cream cheese
- ¼ cup Parmesan cheese, grated
- ½ tablespoon sour cream

Directions

1. Heat olive oil in a large pan over medium heat and add zucchini noodles.
2. Sauté for about 5 minutes and add cream cheese, sour cream and Parmesan cheese.
3. Stir well and pour this mixture over noodles.
4. Dish out and serve hot.

Nutrition Calories: 103 Carbs: 4.3g Fats: 8.8g Proteins: 3.4g Sodium: 77mg Sugar: 2g

Creamy Mushroom and Cauliflower Risotto

Serves: 2/Prep Time: 5 mins
Ingredients
- 1 garlic clove, sliced
- ½ cup cream
- ½ cup cauliflower, riced
- ½ cup mushrooms, sliced
- Coconut oil, for frying
- Parmesan cheese, for topping

Directions
1. Heat coconut oil over medium-high heat in a frying pan and add garlic and mushrooms.
2. Sauté for about 4 minutes and add cauliflower and cream.
3. Simmer for about 12 minutes and dish out in a bowl.
4. Top with Parmesan cheese and serve.

Nutrition Calories: 179 Carbs: 4.4g Fats: 17.8g Proteins: 2.8g Sodium: 61mg Sugar: 2.1g

Hearty Soups and Salads Recipes

Spinach and Bacon Salad

Serves: 4
Prep Time: 15 mins
Ingredients
- 2 eggs, boiled, halved, and sliced
- 10 oz. organic baby spinach, rinsed, and dried
- 8 pieces thick bacon, cooked and sliced
- ½ cup plain mayonnaise
- ½ medium red onion, thinly sliced

Directions
1. Mix together the mayonnaise and spinach in a large bowl.
2. Stir in the rest of the ingredients and combine well.
3. Dish out in a glass bowl and serve well.

Nutrition
Calories: 373 Carbs: 4g Fats: 34.5g Proteins: 11g Sodium: 707mg Sugar: 1.1g

Sausage Kale Soup with Mushrooms

Serves: 6
Prep Time: 1 hour 10 mins
Ingredients
- 2 cups fresh kale, cut into bite sized pieces
- 6.5 ounces mushrooms, sliced
- 6 cups chicken bone broth
- 1 pound sausage, cooked and sliced
- Salt and black pepper, to taste

Directions
1. Heat chicken broth with two cans of water in a large pot and bring to a boil.
2. Stir in the rest of the ingredients and allow the soup to simmer on low heat for about 1 hour.
3. Dish out and serve hot.

Nutrition
Calories: 259 Carbs: 4g Fats: 20g Proteins: 14g Sodium: 995mg Sugar: 0.6g

Cheesy Broccoli Soup

Serves: 4
Prep Time: 30 mins
Ingredients

- ½ cup heavy whipping cream
- 1 cup broccoli
- 1 cup cheddar cheese
- Salt, to taste
- 1½ cups chicken broth

Directions

1. Heat chicken broth in a large pot and add broccoli.
2. Bring to a boil and stir in the rest of the ingredients.
3. Allow the soup to simmer on low heat for about 20 minutes.
4. Ladle out into a bowl and serve hot.

Nutrition
Calories: 188 Carbs: 2.6g Fats: 15.5g Proteins: 9.8g Sodium: 514mg Sugar: 0.8g

Creamy Keto Cucumber Salad

Serves: 2
Prep Time: 5 mins
Ingredients

- 2 tablespoons mayonnaise
- Salt and black pepper, to taste
- 1 cucumber, sliced and quartered
- 2 tablespoons lemon juice

Directions

1. Mix together the mayonnaise, cucumber slices, and lemon juice in a large bowl.
2. Season with salt and black pepper and combine well.
3. Dish out in a glass bowl and serve while it is cold.

Nutrition
Calories: 84 Carbs: 9.3g Fats: 5.2g Proteins: 1.2g Sodium: 111mg Sugar: 3.8g

Egg, Avocado and Tomato Salad

Serves: 4
Prep Time: 40 mins
Ingredients

- 2 boiled eggs, chopped into chunks
- 1 ripe avocado, chopped into chunks
- 1 medium-sized tomato, chopped into chunks
- Salt and black pepper, to taste
- 1 lemon wedge, juiced

Directions

1. Mix together all the ingredients in a large bowl until well combined.
2. Dish out in a glass bowl and serve immediately.

Nutrition
Calories: 140 Carbs: 5.9g Fats: 12.1g Proteins: 4g Sodium: 35mg Sugar: 1.3g

Creamy Low Carb Butternut Squash Soup

Serves: 8
Prep Time: 1 hour 10 mins
Ingredients

- 2 tablespoons avocado oil, divided
- 2 pounds butternut squash, cut in half length-wise and seeds removed
- Sea salt and black pepper, to taste
- 1 (13.5-oz) can coconut milk
- 4 cups chicken bone broth

Directions
1. Preheat the oven to 400 degrees F and grease a baking sheet.
2. Arrange the butternut squash halves with open side up on the baking sheet.
3. Drizzle with half of the avocado oil and season with sea salt and black pepper.
4. Flip over and transfer into the oven.
5. Roast the butternut squash for about 55 minutes.
6. Heat the remaining avocado oil over medium heat in a large pot and add the broth and coconut milk.
7. Let it simmer for about 20 minutes and scoop the squash out of the shells to transfer into the soup.
8. Puree this mixture in an immersion blender until smooth and serve immediately.

Nutrition
Calories: 185 Carbs: 12.6g Fats: 12.6g Proteins: 4.7g Sodium: 393mg Sugar: 4.5g

Turkey Arugula Salad

Serves: 2
Prep Time: 5 mins
Ingredients
- 4 oz turkey breast meat, diced into small pieces
- 3.5 oz arugula leaves
- 10 raspberries
- Juice from ½ a lime
- 2 tablespoons extra virgin olive oil

Directions
1. Mix together the turkey with the rest of the ingredients in a large bowl until well combined.
2. Dish out in a glass bowl and serve immediately.

Nutrition
Calories: 246 Carbs: 15.4g Fats: 15.9g Proteins: 12.2g Sodium: 590mg Sugar: 7.6g

Mint Avocado Chilled Soup

Serves: 2
Prep Time: 5 mins
Ingredients
- 1 cup coconut milk, chilled
- 1 medium ripe avocado
- 1 tablespoon lime juice
- Salt, to taste
- 20 fresh mint leaves

Directions
1. Put all the ingredients into an immersion blender and blend until a thick mixture is formed.
2. Allow to cool in the fridge for about 10 minutes and serve chilled.

Nutrition
Calories: 286 Carbs: 12.6g Fats: 26.9g Proteins: 4.2g Sodium: 70mg Sugar: 4.6g

Kombu Seaweed Salad

Serves: 6
Prep Time: 40 mins
Ingredients
- 4 garlic cloves, crushed
- 1 pound fresh kombu seaweed, boiled and cut into strips
- 2 tablespoons apple cider vinegar
- Salt, to taste
- 2 tablespoons coconut aminos

Directions
1. Mix together the kombu, garlic, apple cider vinegar, and coconut aminos in a large bowl.
2. Season with salt and combine well.
3. Dish out in a glass bowl and serve immediately.

Nutrition
Calories: 257 Carbs: 16.9g Fats: 19.4g Proteins: 6.5g Sodium: 294mg Sugar: 2.7g

Rich Potato Soup

Serves: 4
Prep Time: 30 mins
Ingredients
- 1 tablespoon butter
- 1 medium onion, diced
- 3 cloves garlic, minced
- 3 cups chicken broth
- 1 can/box cream of chicken soup
- 7-8 medium-sized russet potatoes, peeled and chopped
- 1 1/2 teaspoons salt
- Black pepper to taste
- 1 cup milk
- 1 tablespoon flour
- 2 cups shredded cheddar cheese

Garnish:
- 5-6 slices bacon, chopped
- Sliced green onions
- Shredded cheddar cheese

Directions
1. Heat butter in the insert of the Instant Pot on sauté mode.
2. Add onions and sauté for 4 minutes until soft.
3. Stir in garlic and sauté it for 1 minute.
4. Add potatoes, cream of chicken, broth, salt, and pepper to the insert.
5. Mix well then seal and lock the lid.
6. Cook this mixture for 10 minutes at Manual Mode with high pressure.
7. Meanwhile, mix flour with milk in a bowl and set it aside.
8. Once the instant pot beeps, release the pressure completely.
9. Remove the Instant Pot lid and switch the instant pot to Sauté mode.
10. Pour in flour slurry and stir cook the mixture for 5 minutes until it thickens.
11. Add 2 cups of cheddar cheese and let it melt.
12. Garnish it as desired.
13. Serve.

Nutrition
Calories per serving: 784 Carbohydrate: 54.8g Protein: 34g Fat: 46.5g Sugar: 7.5g Sodium: 849mg

Split Pea Soup

Serves: 6
Prep Time: 30 mins
Ingredients

- 3 tablespoons butter
- 1 onion diced
- 2 ribs celery diced
- 2 carrots diced
- 6 oz. diced ham
- 1 lb. dry split peas sorted and rinsed
- 6 cups chicken stock
- 2 bay leaves
- kosher salt and black pepper

Directions

1. Set your Instant Pot on Sauté mode and melt butter in it.
2. Stir in celery, onion, carrots, salt, and pepper.
3. Sauté them for 5 minutes then stir in split peas, ham bone, chicken stock, and bay leaves.
4. Seal and lock the Instant Pot lid then select Manual mode for 15 minutes at high pressure.
5. Once done, release the pressure completely then remove the lid.
6. Remove the ham bone and separate meat from the bone.
7. Shred or dice the meat and return it to the soup.
8. Adjust seasoning as needed then serve warm.
9. Enjoy.

Nutrition Calories per serving: 190 Carbohydrate: 30.5g Protein: 10.8g Fat: 3.5g Sugar: 4.2g Sodium: 461mg

Mexican Tortilla Soup

Serves: 4
Prep Time: 40 mins
Ingredients

- 1-pound chicken breasts, boneless and skinless
- 1 can (15 ounces) whole peeled tomatoes
- 1 can (10 ounces) red enchilada sauce
- 1 and 1/2 teaspoons minced garlic
- 1 yellow onion, diced
- 1 can (4 ounces) fire-roasted diced green chile
- 1 can (15 ounces) black beans, drained and rinsed
- 1 can (15 ounces) fire-roasted corn, undrained
- 1 container (32 ounces) chicken stock or broth
- 1 teaspoon ground cumin
- 2 teaspoons chili powder
- 3/4 teaspoons paprika
- 1 bay leaf
- Salt and freshly cracked pepper, to taste
- 1 tablespoon chopped cilantro
- Tortilla strips, Freshly squeezed lime juice, freshly grated cheddar cheese,

Directions

1. Set your Instant Pot on Sauté mode.
2. Toss olive oil, onion and garlic into the insert of the Instant Pot.
3. Sauté for 4 minutes then add chicken and remaining ingredients.
4. Mix well gently then seal and lock the lid.
5. Select Manual mode for 7 minutes at high pressure.
6. Once done, release the pressure completely then remove the lid.
7. Adjust seasoning as needed.
8. Garnish with desired toppings.
9. Enjoy.

Nutrition Calories per serving: 390 Carbohydrate: 5.6g Protein: 29.5g Fat: 26.5g Sugar: 2.1g Sodium: 620mg

Mediterranean Lentil Soup

Serves: 4
Prep Time: 20 mins
Ingredients

- 1 tablespoon olive oil
- 1/2 cup red lentils
- 1 medium yellow or red onion
- 2 garlic cloves, chopped
- 1/2 teaspoon ground cumin
- 1/2 teaspoon ground coriander
- 1/2 teaspoon ground sumac
- 1/2 teaspoon red chili flakes
- 1/2 teaspoon dried parsley
- 3/4 teaspoons dried mint flakes
- pinch of sugar
- 2.5 cups water
- salt, to taste
- black pepper, to taste
- juice of 1/2 lime
- parsley or cilantro, to garnish

Directions

1. Preheat oil in the insert of your Instant Pot on Sauté mode.
2. Add onion and sauté until it turns golden brown.
3. Toss in the garlic, parsley sugar, mint flakes, red chili flakes, sumac, coriander, and cumin.
4. Stir cook this mixture for 2 minutes.
5. Add water, lentils, salt, and pepper. Stir gently.
6. Seal and lock the Instant Pot lid and select Manual mode for 8 minutes at high pressure.
7. Once done, release the pressure completely then remove the lid.
8. Stir well then add lime juice.
9. Serve warm.

Nutrition Calories per serving: 525 Carbohydrate: 59.8g Protein: 30.1g Fat: 19.3g Sugar: 17.3g Sodium: 897mg

Chicken Noodle Soup

Serves: 6
Prep Time: 35 mins
Ingredients

- 1 tablespoon olive oil
- 1 1/2 cups peeled and diced carrots
- 1 1/2 cup diced celery
- 1 cup chopped yellow onion
- 3 tablespoons minced garlic
- 8 cups low-sodium chicken broth
- 2 teaspoons minced fresh thyme
- 2 teaspoons minced fresh rosemary
- 1 bay leaf
- salt and freshly ground black pepper
- 2 1/2 lbs. bone-in, skin-on chicken thighs, skinned
- 3 cups wide egg noodles, such as American beauty
- 1 tablespoon fresh lemon juice
- 1/4 cup chopped fresh parsley

Directions

1. Preheat olive oil in the insert of the Instant Pot on Sauté mode.
2. Add onion, celery, and carrots and sauté them for 2 minutes.
3. Stir in garlic and sauté for 1 minute.
4. Add bay leaf, thyme, broth, rosemary, salt, and pepper.
5. Seal and secure the Instant Pot lid and select Manual mode for 10 minutes at high pressure.
6. Once done, release the pressure completely then remove the lid.
7. Add noodles to the insert and switch the Instant Pot to sauté mode.
8. Cook the soup for 6 minutes until noodles are all done.

9. Remove the chicken and shred it using a fork.
10. Return the chicken to the soup then add lemon juice and parsley.
11. Enjoy.

Nutrition Calories per serving: 333 Carbohydrate: 3.3g Protein: 44.7g Fat: 13.7g Sugar: 1.1g Sodium: 509mg

Butternut Squash Soup

Serves: 4
Prep Time: 40 mins
Ingredients
- 1 tablespoon olive oil
- 1 medium yellow onion chopped
- 1 large carrot chopped
- 1 celery rib chopped
- 3 cloves of garlic minced
- 2 lbs. butternut squash, peeled chopped
- 2 cups vegetable broth
- 1 green apple peeled, cored, and chopped
- 1/4 teaspoon ground cinnamon
- 1 sprig fresh thyme
- 1 sprig fresh rosemary
- 1 teaspoon kosher salt
- 1/2 teaspoon black pepper
- Pinch of nutmeg optional

Directions
1. Preheat olive oil in the insert of the Instant Pot on Sauté mode.
2. Add celery, carrots, and garlic, sauté for 5 minutes.
3. Stir in squash, broth, cinnamon, apple nutmeg, rosemary, thyme, salt, and pepper.
4. Mix well gently then seal and secure the lid.
5. Select Manual mode to cook for 10 minutes at high pressure.
6. Once done, release the pressure completely then remove the lid.
7. Puree the soup using an immersion blender.
8. Serve warm.

Nutrition Calories per serving: 282 Carbohydrate: 50g Protein: 13g Fat: 4.7g Sugar: 12.8g Sodium: 213mg

Minestrone Soup

Serves: 6
Prep Time: 25 mins
Ingredients
- 2 tablespoons olive oil
- 3 cloves garlic, minced
- 1 onion, diced
- 2 carrots, peeled and diced
- 2 stalks celery, diced
- 1 1/2 teaspoons dried basil
- 1 teaspoon dried oregano
- 1/2 teaspoon fennel seed
- 6 cups low sodium chicken broth
- 1 (28-ounce) can diced tomatoes
- 1 (16-ounce) can kidney beans, drained and rinsed
- 1 zucchini, chopped
- 1 (3-inch) Parmesan rind
- 1 bay leaf
- 1 bunch kale leaves, chopped
- 2 teaspoons red wine vinegar
- Kosher salt and black pepper, to taste
- 1/3 cup freshly grated Parmesan
- 2 tablespoons chopped fresh parsley leaves

Directions
1. Preheat olive oil in the insert of the Instant Pot on Sauté mode.
2. Add carrots, celery, and onion, sauté for 3 minutes.

3. Stir in fennel seeds, oregano, and basil. Stir cook for 1 minute.
4. Add stock, beans, tomatoes, parmesan, bay leaf, and zucchini.
5. Secure and seal the Instant Pot lid then select Manual mode to cook for 5 minutes at high pressure.
6. Once done, release the pressure completely then remove the lid.
7. Add kale and let it sit for 2 minutes in the hot soup.
8. Stir in red wine, vinegar, pepper, and salt.
9. Garnish with parsley and parmesan.
10. Enjoy.

Nutrition Calories per serving: 805 Carbohydrate: 2.5g Protein: 124.1g Fat: 34g Sugar: 1.4g Sodium: 634mg

Beef Stroganoff Soup

Serves: 6
Prep Time: 35 mins
Ingredients
- 1.5 pounds stew meat
- 6 cups beef broth
- 4 tablespoons Worcestershire sauce
- 1/2 teaspoon Italian seasoning blend
- 1 1/2 teaspoons onion powder
- 2 teaspoons garlic powder
- salt and pepper to taste
- 1/2 cup sour cream
- 8 ounces mushrooms, sliced
- 8 ounces short noodles, cooked
- 1/3 cup cold water
- 1/4 cup corn starch

Directions
1. Add meat, 5 cups broth, Italian seasoning, Worcestershire sauce, garlic powder, salt, pepper, and onion powder to the insert of the Instant Pot.
2. Secure and seal the Instant Pot lid then select Manual mode for 1 hour at high pressure.
3. Once done, release the pressure completely then remove the lid.
4. Set the Instant pot on Soup mode and add sour cream along with 1 cup broth.
5. Mix well then add mushrooms and mix well.
6. Whisk corn-starch with water and pour this mixture into the pot.
7. Cook this mixture until it thickens then add noodles, salt, and pepper.
8. Garnish with cheese parsley, black pepper.
9. Enjoy.

Nutrition Calories per serving: 320 Carbohydrate: 21.6g Protein: 26.9g Fat: 13.7g Sugar: 7.1g Sodium: 285mg

French Onion Soup

Serves: 4
Prep Time: 20 mins
Ingredients
- 3 onions sliced
- 3 tablespoons butter
- 3/4 teaspoons salt
- 2 tablespoons Worcestershire sauce
- 3/4 teaspoons thyme
- 32 oz beef broth
- 3/4 cup mozzarella cheese shredded
- 1 loaf French bread day old, sliced
- 1/4 cup green onions diced, optional

Directions
1. Preheat butter in the insert of the Instant Pot on Sauté mode.

2. Stir in onions and sauté until it is caramelized.
3. Add salt, beef broth, thyme and Worcestershire sauce.
4. Seal and secure the Instant Pot lid and select Manual mode for 3 minutes at high pressure.
5. Once done, release the pressure completely then remove the lid.
6. Garnish with bread and cheese.
7. Serve.

Nutrition Calories per serving: 423 Carbohydrate: 7.8g Protein: 57.6g Fat: 16.7g Sugar: 3.7g Sodium: 202mg

Turkey Meatball and Ditalini Soup

Serves: 4
Prep Time: 40 mins
Ingredients
meatballs:
- 1 pound 93% lean ground turkey
- 1/3 cup seasoned breadcrumbs
- 3 tablespoons grated Pecorino Romano cheese
- 1 large egg, beaten
- 1 clove crushed garlic
- 1 tablespoon fresh minced parsley
- 1/2 teaspoon kosher salt

Soup:
- cooking spray
- 1 teaspoon olive oil
- 1/2 cup chopped onion
- 1/2 cup chopped celery
- 1/2 cup chopped carrot
- 3 cloves minced garlic
- 1 can (28 ounces) diced San Marzano tomatoes
- 4 cups reduced sodium chicken broth
- 4 torn basil leaves
- 2 bay leaves
- 1 cup ditalini pasta
- 1 cup zucchini, diced small
- Parmesan rind, optional
- Grated parmesan cheese, optional for serving

Directions
1. Thoroughly combine turkey with egg, garlic, parsley, salt, pecorino and breadcrumbs in a bowl.
2. Make 30 equal sized meatballs out of this mixture.
3. Preheat olive oil in the insert of the Instant Pot on Sauté mode.
4. Sear the meatballs in the heated oil in batches, until brown.
5. Set the meatballs aside in a plate.
6. Add more oil to the insert of the Instant Pot.
7. Stir in carrots, garlic, celery, and onion. Sauté for 4 minutes.
8. Add basil, bay leaves, tomatoes, and Parmesan rind.
9. Return the seared meatballs to the pot along with the broth.
10. Secure and sear the Instant Pot lid and select Manual mode for 15 minutes at high pressure.
11. Once done, release the pressure completely then remove the lid.
12. Add zucchini and pasta, cook it for 4 minutes on Sauté mode.
13. Garnish with cheese and basil.
14. Serve.
Nutrition Calories per serving: 261 Carbohydrate: 11.2g Protein: 36.6g Fat: 7g Sugar: 3g Sodium: 198g

Side Dishes and Snacks Recipes

Keto Gin Cocktail

Serves: 1
Prep Time: 10 mins
Ingredients
- 4 blueberries
- 2 ounces dry gin
- 1 teaspoon erythritol, powdered
- 1 can club soda
- ½ ounce fresh lime juice

Directions
1. Put the blueberries and mint into a cocktail shaker.
2. Shake well and add the gin, lime juice, erythritol and ice.
3. Shake again and strain into a cocktail glass.
4. Top with club soda and serve chilled.

Nutrition
Calories: 161 Carbs: 7.3g Fats: 0.1g Proteins: 0.2g Sodium: 76mg Sugar: 1.7g

Parmesan and Garlic Keto Crackers

Serves: 4
Prep Time: 40 mins
Ingredients
- 1 cup Parmesan cheese, finely grated
- 1 cup almond flour, blanched
- ½ teaspoon garlic powder
- 1 large egg, whisked
- 1 tablespoon butter, melted

Directions
1. Preheat the oven to 350 degrees F and grease 2 large baking sheets.
2. Mix together the parmesan cheese, almond flour, chives and garlic powder in a large bowl until well incorporated.
3. Whisk together the eggs and butter in a separate bowl.
4. Mix together the dry and wet ingredients until a dough is formed.
5. Divide the dough into two halves and press until ¼ inch thick.
6. Cut each sheet of dough with a pastry cutter into 25 crackers of equal size.
7. Arrange the crackers on the baking sheets and transfer into the oven.
8. Bake for about 15 minutes and allow them to stay in the off oven.
9. Remove from the oven and serve.

Nutrition
Calories: 304 Carbs: 7.4g Fats: 23.5g Proteins: 16.8g Sodium: 311mg Sugar: 0.2g

Low Carb Dried Cranberries

Serves: 4
Prep Time: 4 hours 15 mins
Ingredients
- 1 cup granular erythritol
- ½ teaspoon pure orange extract
- 2 (12 ounce) bags fresh cranberries, rinsed and dried
- 4 tablespoons avocado oil

Directions
1. Preheat the oven to 200 degrees F and grease a large baking sheet.
2. Slice the dried cranberries in half and put into a bowl along with the remaining ingredients.
3. Toss to coat well and arrange the berries in the baking sheet.
4. Bake for about 4 hours and dish out to serve.

Nutrition
Calories: 111 Carbs: 16.3g Fats: 1.8g Proteins: 0.2g Sodium: 1mg Sugar: 6.2g

Keto Sausage Balls

Serves: 6
Prep Time: 30 mins
Ingredients
- 1 cup almond flour, blanched
- 1 pound bulk Italian sausage
- 1¼ cups sharp cheddar cheese, shredded
- 2 teaspoons baking powder
- 1 large egg

Directions
1. Preheat the oven to 360 degrees F and grease a baking sheet.
2. Mix together all the ingredients in a large bowl until well incorporated.
3. Make equal sized balls from this mixture and arrange on the baking sheet.
4. Transfer in the oven and bake for about 20 minutes until golden brown.

Nutrition
Calories: 477 Carbs: 5.1g Fats: 39g Proteins: 25.6g Sodium: 732mg Sugar: 0.2g

Keto Pistachio Truffles

Serves: 5
Prep Time: 10 mins
Ingredients
- ¼ teaspoon pure vanilla extract
- ¼ cup pistachios, chopped
- 1 cup mascarpone cheese, softened
- 3 tablespoons erythritol

Directions
1. Mix together mascarpone cheese, vanilla, and erythritol in a small bowl.
2. Mix thoroughly until smooth and form small balls out of this mixture.
3. Roll the truffles in a plate full of chopped pistachios and refrigerate for 30 minutes before serving.

Nutrition
Calories: 103 Carbs: 11.3g Fats: 7.8g Proteins: 6.2g Sodium: 58mg Sugar: 9.4g

Creamy Basil Baked Sausage

Serves: 12
Prep Time: 45 mins
Ingredients
- 8 oz cream cheese
- 3 pounds Italian chicken sausages

- ¼ cup basil pesto
- 8 oz mozzarella cheese
- ¼ cup heavy cream

Directions
1. Preheat the oven to 400 degrees F and grease a large casserole dish.
2. Put the sausages in the casserole dish and transfer into the oven.
3. Bake for about 30 minutes and dish out.
4. Mix together the pesto, cream cheese and heavy cream in a bowl.
5. Top the sausage with the pesto mixture, followed by mozzarella cheese.
6. Bake for 10 more minutes and remove from the oven to serve.

Nutrition
Calories: 342 Carbs: 8.9g Fats: 23.3g Proteins: 21.6g Sodium: 624mg Sugar: 0.5g

Low Carb Tortilla Chips

Serves: 4
Prep Time: 25 mins
Ingredients
- 2 tablespoons olive oil
- 3 tablespoons lime juice
- 1 tablespoon taco seasoning
- 6 tortillas, low carb

Directions
1. Preheat the oven to 350 degrees F and grease a cookie sheet.
2. Cut each tortilla into small wedges and arrange on a cookie sheet.
3. Mix together the olive oil and lime juice and spray each tortilla wedge.
4. Sprinkle with the taco seasoning and transfer into the oven.
5. Bake for about 8 minutes and rotate the pan.
6. Bake for another 8 minutes and dish out to serve.

Nutrition
Calories: 147 Carbs: 17.8g Fats: 8g Proteins: 2.1g Sodium: 174mg Sugar: 0.7g

Salmon Mousse Cucumber Rolls

Serves: 2
Prep Time: 30 mins
Ingredients
- 2 cucumbers, thinly sliced lengthwise
- 4 oz smoked salmon
- 1 tablespoon dill, fresh
- 8 oz cream cheese
- ½ lemon

Directions
1. Mix together the salmon, dill, cream cheese, and lemon in a bowl and mash thoroughly.
2. Apply this mixture to the cucumber slices and roll gently to serve.

Nutrition
Calories: 515 Carbs: 16.2g Fats: 42.4g Proteins: 21.4g Sodium: 1479mg Sugar: 5.6g

Italian keto plate

Serves: 3

Prep Time: 10 mins
Ingredients

- 7 oz. prosciutto, sliced
- 1/3 cup olive oil
- Salt and black pepper, to taste
- 7 oz. fresh mozzarella cheese
- 10 green olives

Directions

1. Place the prosciutto, mozzarella cheese, and olives in a serving plate.
2. Drizzle with olive oil and season with salt and black pepper to serve.

Nutrition
Calories: 505 Carbs: 3.3g Fats: 40.2g Proteins: 32.5g Sodium: 1572mg Sugar: 0g

Broccoli Cheese Soup

Serves: 6
Prep Time: 5 hours 10 mins
Ingredients

- 1 cup heavy whipping cream
- 2 cups chicken broth
- 2 cups broccoli
- Salt, to taste
- 2 cups cheddar cheese

Directions

1) Place the cheddar cheese, broccoli, chicken broth, heavy whipping cream and salt in a crock pot.
2) Set the crock pot on LOW and cook for about 5 hours.
3) Ladle out in a bowl and serve hot.

Nutrition
Calories: 244 Carbs: 3.4g Fats: 20.4g Proteins: 12.3g Sodium: 506mg Sugar: 1g

Mediterranean Spinach with Cheese

Serves: 6
Prep Time: 25 mins
Ingredients

- 2 pounds spinach, chopped
- ½ cup black olives, halved and pitted
- Salt and black pepper, to taste
- 4 tablespoons butter
- 1½ cups feta cheese, grated
- 4 teaspoons fresh lemon zest, grated

Directions

1) Preheat the Air fryer to 400 degrees F and grease an Air fryer basket.
2) Cook spinach for about 4 minutes in a pan of boiling water. Drain well.
3) Mix together butter, spinach, salt, and black pepper in a bowl.
4) Transfer the spinach mixture into an air fryer basket.
5) Cook for about 15 minutes, tossing once in the middle way.
6) Dish into a bowl and stir in the olives, cheese, and lemon zest to serve.

Nutrition
Calories: 215 Carbs: 8g Fats: 17.5g Proteins: 9.9g Sodium: 690mg Sugar: 2.3g

Cheesy Cauliflower

Serves: 6
Prep Time: 30 mins
Ingredients

- 2 tablespoons mustard
- ½ cup butter, cut into small pieces
- 2 cauliflower heads, chopped
- 1 cup Parmesan cheese, grated
- 2 teaspoons avocado mayonnaise

Directions
1) Preheat the oven to 400 degrees F and grease a baking dish.
2) Mix together mustard and avocado mayonnaise in a bowl.
3) Coat the cauliflower with the mustard mixture and transfer into a baking dish.
4) Top with Parmesan cheese and butter and bake for about 25 minutes.
5) Pull from the oven and serve hot.

Nutrition
Calories: 201 Carbs: 6.2g Fats: 18.9g Proteins: 4.3g Sodium: 192mg Sugar: 2.4g

Parmesan Roasted Bamboo Sprouts

Serves: 6
Prep Time: 25 mins
Ingredients

- 2 cups Parmesan cheese, grated
- 2 pounds bamboo sprouts
- 4 tablespoons butter
- ½ teaspoon paprika
- Salt and black pepper, to taste

Directions
1) Preheat the oven to 365 degrees F and grease a baking dish.
2) Marinate the bamboo sprouts with paprika, butter, salt, and black pepper, and keep aside.
3) Transfer the seasoned bamboo sprouts in the baking dish and place in the oven.
4) Bake for about 15 minutes and dish to serve.

Nutrition
Calories: 162 Carbs: 4.7g Fats: 11.7g Proteins: 7.5g Sodium: 248mg Sugar: 1.4g

Mexican Cheesy Veggies

Serves: 4
Prep Time: 40 mins
Ingredients

- 1 onion, thinly sliced
- 1 tomato, thinly sliced
- 1 zucchini, sliced
- 1 teaspoon mixed dried herbs
- Salt and black pepper, to taste
- 1 teaspoon olive oil
- 1 cup Mexican cheese, grated

Directions
1) Preheat the oven to 370 degrees F and grease a baking dish.
2) Layer the vegetables in the baking dish and drizzle with olive oil.
3) Top evenly with cheese and sprinkle with herbs, salt, and black pepper.
4) Bake for about 30 minutes and dish to serve hot.

Nutrition

Calories: 305 Carbs: 8.3g Fats: 22.3g Proteins: 15.2g Sodium: 370mg Sugar: 4.2g

Green Beans with Mushrooms and Bacons

Serves: 4
Prep Time: 25 mins
Ingredients

- 4 tablespoons onion, minced
- 4 tablespoons butter
- 1 teaspoon garlic, minced
- 4 cooked bacon slices, crumbled
- 2 cups frozen green beans
- 2 (8-ounce) package white mushrooms, sliced
- ¼ teaspoon salt

Directions

1) Put the butter, onions and garlic in the Instant Pot and select "Sauté."
2) Sauté for about 2 minutes and add in bacon and salt.
3) Close the lid and cook at "High" and "Manual" pressure for about 10 minutes.
4) Select "Cancel" and carefully do a natural release.
5) Remove the lid and stir in beans and mushrooms.
6) Lock the lid again and cook at "High" and "Manual" pressure for about 7 minutes.
7) Transfer to a bowl and serve hot.

Nutrition

Calories: 220 Carbs: 11.6g Fats: 17g Proteins: 10g Sodium: 488mg Sugar: 3.2g

Cauliflower Mash

Serves: 4
Prep Time: 20 mins
Ingredients

- 1 tablespoon full-fat coconut milk
- 3 garlic cloves, minced
- 1 teaspoon green chilies, chopped
- 3 tablespoons butter
- ½ cup feta cheese
- 1 head cauliflower stems, completely removed
- Salt and black pepper, to taste

Directions

1) Preheat the oven to 360 degrees F and grease a baking dish.
2) Place cauliflower pieces in the baking dish and transfer into the oven.
3) Bake for about 10 minutes and dish out the cauliflower pieces.
4) Mix with the remaining ingredients and blend with an immersion hand blender to achieve the desired texture.

Nutrition

Calories: 154 Carbs: 5.3g Fats: 13.5g Proteins: 4.3g Sodium: 292mg Sugar: 2.5g

Bacon Wrapped Asparagus

Serves: 3
Prep Time: 30 mins
Ingredients

- 6 small asparagus spears
- 3 bacon slices
- 2 tablespoons butter
- ¼ cup heavy whipping cream
- Salt and black pepper, to taste

Directions
1) Preheat the oven to 370 degrees F and grease the baking dish with butter.
2) Sprinkle the asparagus spears with salt and black pepper.
3) Add heavy whipping cream to the asparagus and wrap with bacon slices.
4) Place the wrapped asparagus in the baking dish and transfer into the oven.
5) Bake for about 20 minutes and dish out to serve hot.

Nutrition
Calories: 176 Carbs: 1.2g Fats: 13.4g Proteins: 0.8g Sodium: 321mg Sugar: 0.5g

Cheesy Brussels Sprout

Serves: 5
Prep Time: 35 mins
Ingredients
- 1 pound Brussels sprouts
- 3 tablespoons olive oil
- ½ cup cream
- Salt and black pepper, to taste
- 2 tablespoons butter
- ½ cup parmesan cheese, grated

Directions
1) Preheat the oven to 360 degrees F and grease a baking dish.
2) Mix together Brussels sprouts, olive oil, parmesan cheese, salt, and black pepper in a bowl.
3) Transfer the Brussels sprouts in the baking dish and drizzle with butter.
4) Transfer it into the oven and bake for about 25 minutes.
5) Dish to serve hot.
Nutrition
Calories: 190 Carbs: 8.5g Fats: 16.8g Proteins: 5g Sodium: 124mg Sugar: 2g

Tomato Soup

Serves: 4
Prep Time: 30 mins
Ingredients
- 2 cups low-sodium vegetable broth
- ¼ cup fresh basil, chopped
- 1 garlic clove, minced
- 1 teaspoon dried parsley, crushed
- Freshly ground black pepper, to taste
- 1 teaspoon dried basil, crushed
- 2 tablespoons Erthyritol
- ½ tablespoon balsamic vinegar
- ½ tablespoon olive oil
- 1 pound fresh tomatoes, chopped
- 1 cup cheddar cheese

Directions
1) Put the oil in a pot and add tomatoes, garlic, herbs, black pepper, and broth.
2) Cover the lid and cook for about 18-20 minutes on medium-low heat.
3) Stir in sugar and vinegar and place the mixture in an immersion blender.
4) Blend until smooth and ladle into a bowl.
5) Garnish with basil and serve immediately.
Nutrition
Calories: 194 Carbs: 5.6g Fats: 15.4g Proteins: 9.2g Sodium: 257mg Sugar: 3.2g

Spinach Quiche

Serves: 6

Prep Time: 45 mins
Ingredients
- 1 tablespoon butter, melted
- Salt and black pepper, to taste
- 1 (10-ounce) package frozen spinach, thawed
- 5 organic eggs, beaten
- 3 cups Monterey Jack cheese, shredded

Directions
1) Preheat the oven to 360 degrees F and grease a 9-inch pie dish lightly.
2) Put butter and spinach in a large skillet on medium-low heat.
3) Cook for about 3 minutes and set aside.
4) Mix together Monterey Jack cheese, spinach, eggs, salt, and black pepper in a bowl.
5) Put the mixture into prepared pie dish and transfer into the oven.
6) Bake for about 30 minutes and remove from the oven.
7) Cut into equal sized wedges and serve hot.
Nutrition
Calories: 349 Carbs: 3.2g Fats: 27.8g Proteins: 23g Sodium: 532mg Sugar: 1.3g

Cheese Casserole

Serves: 6
Prep Time: 40 mins
Ingredients
- 10 ounce parmesan, shredded
- 16 ounce marinara sauce
- 2 tablespoons olive oil
- 2 pounds sausage scramble
- 16 ounce mozzarella cheese, shredded

Directions
1) Preheat the oven to 395 degrees F and grease olive oil on the baking dish.
2) Arrange half of the sausage scramble in the baking dish and layer with half of the marinara sauce.
3) Top with half of the mozzarella and Parmesan cheese.
4) Layer with the remaining half of the sausage scramble and spread the remaining half of Parmesan and mozzarella cheese.
5) Top with rest of the marinara sauce and bake in the oven for about 25 minutes.
6) Dish onto a casserole and serve hot.
Nutrition
Calories: 521 Carbs: 6g Fats: 38.8g Proteins: 35.4g Sodium: 201mg Sugar: 5.4g

Mixed Nuts

Serves: 16
Prep Time: 25 mins
Ingredients
- 1 cup raw peanuts
- Salt, to taste
- 1 cup raw almonds
- 1 tablespoon butter, melted
- ½ cup raw cashew nuts

Directions
1) Preheat the oven at 330 degrees F and grease a baking dish.
2) Put the peanuts, almonds and cashew nuts in a baking dish and transfer into the oven.
3) Bake for about 12 minutes, tossing twice in between.
4) Dish out the nuts from the oven into a bowl and add salt and melted butter.

5) Toss to coat well and return the nuts mixture to the oven.
6) Bake for about 5 more minutes and dish out to serve.

Nutrition

Calories: 189 Carbs: 6.6g Fats: 16.5g Proteins: 6.8g Sodium: 19mg Sugar: 1.3g

Broccoli Pops

Serves: 6
Prep Time: 20 mins
Ingredients

- 1/3 cup Parmesan cheese, grated
- 2 cups cheddar cheese, grated
- Salt and black pepper, to taste
- 3 eggs, beaten
- 3 cups broccoli florets
- 1 tablespoon olive oil

Directions

1) Preheat the oven to 360 degrees F and grease a baking dish with olive oil.
2) Pulse the broccoli in a food processor until finely crumbed.
3) Add broccoli and stir in rest of the ingredients in a large bowl.
4) Make small equal-sized balls from the mixture.
5) Put the balls in a baking sheet and refrigerate for at least 30 minutes.
6) Place balls in the baking dish and transfer the dish into the oven.
7) Bake for about 13 minutes and dish out to serve.

Nutrition

Calories: 162 Carbs: 1.9g Fats: 12.4g Proteins: 11.2g Sodium: 263mg Sugar: 0.5g

Keto Onion Rings

Serves: 4
Prep Time: 20 mins
Ingredients

- 2 large onions, cut into ¼ inch slices
- 2 teaspoons baking powder
- Salt, to taste
- 2 cups cream cheese
- 2 eggs

Directions

1) Preheat the oven to 375 degrees F and separate the onion slices into rings.
2) Mix together salt and baking powder in a bowl.
3) Whisk together cream cheese and eggs in another dish.
4) Dredge the onion rings into baking powder mixture and dip into cream cheese mixture.
5) Place the onion rings in the oven and bake for about 10 minutes.
6) Dish out to serve hot.

Nutrition

Calories: 266 Carbs: 9.9g Fats: 22.5g Proteins: 8g Sodium: 285mg Sugar: 3.5g

Mexican Inspired Beef Soup

Serves: 12
Prep Time: 20 mins
Ingredients

- 1 pound grass-fed lean ground beef
- 2 cups homemade beef broth
- 1 tablespoon chili powder
- ¼ cup cheddar cheese, shredded

- 10-ounce canned sugar-free diced tomatoes with green chiles
- 2 garlic cloves, minced
- 4-ounce cream cheese
- Salt and black pepper, to taste
- ½ teaspoon olive oil
- ¼ cup heavy cream
- 1 teaspoon ground cumin

Directions
1) Place the oil and beef in the pressure cooker and sauté for about 8 minutes.
2) Stir in the remaining ingredients, except cheddar cheese, and cover the lid.
3) Cook at high pressure for about 10 minutes and do the natural pressure release.
4) Top with cheddar cheese and serve hot.

Nutrition
Calories: 405 Carbs: 6.7g Fats: 26.7g Proteins: 31.1g Sodium: 815mg Sugar: 3.5g

Zucchini Cream Cheese Fries

Serves: 4
Prep Time: 20 mins
Ingredients
- 1 cup cream cheese
- 1 pound zucchini, sliced into 2 ½-inch sticks
- 2 tablespoons olive oil
- Salt, to taste

Directions
1) Preheat the oven to 380 degrees F and grease a baking dish with olive oil.
2) Season the zucchini with salt and coat with cream cheese.
3) Place zucchini in the baking dish and transfer into the oven.
4) Bake for about 10 minutes and dish out to serve.
Nutrition
Calories: 374 Carbs: 7.1g Fats: 36.6g Proteins: 7.7g Sodium: 294mg Sugar: 2.8g

Asparagus Bites

Serves: 6
Prep Time: 20 mins
Ingredients
- 1 cup desiccated coconut
- 2 cups asparagus
- 1 cup feta cheese

Directions
1) Preheat the oven to 400 degrees F and grease a baking dish with cooking spray.
2) Place the desiccated coconut in a shallow dish and coat asparagus evenly with coconut.
3) Arrange the coated asparagus in the baking dish and top with cheese.
4) Transfer into the oven and bake for about 10 minutes to serve.
Nutrition
Calories: 135 Carbs: 5g Fats: 10.3g Proteins: 7g Sodium: 421mg Sugar: 3.1g

Scallion Cake

Serves: 4
Prep Time: 30 mins

Ingredients

- ¼ cup flax seeds meal
- ½ cup Parmesan cheese, grated finely
- ½ teaspoon baking powder
- ½ cup low-fat cottage cheese
- 1/3 cup scallion, sliced thinly
- ½ cup almond meal
- ¼ cup nutritional yeast flakes
- 6 organic eggs, beaten
- ½ cup raw hemp seeds
- Salt, to taste

Directions

1) Preheat the oven to 390 degrees F and grease 4 ramekins with oil.
2) Mix together salt, baking powder, almond meal, hemp seeds and flax seeds meal in a large bowl.
3) Mix cottage cheese and eggs in another bowl and transfer this mixture into almond meal mixture.
4) Mix until well combined and gently add scallions.
5) Transfer the mixture evenly into ramekins and bake for about 20 minutes.
6) Remove from the oven and serve warm.

Nutrition

Calories: 306 Carbs: 10.7g Fats: 19.7g Proteins: 23.5g Sodium: 398mg Sugar: 1.3g

Avocado Chips

Serves: 2
Prep Time: 20 mins
Ingredients

- 2 raw avocados, peeled and sliced in chips form
- 2 tablespoons butter
- Salt and freshly ground pepper, to taste

Directions

1) Preheat the oven to 365 degrees F and grease a baking dish.
2) Top with butter and avocado slices and transfer into the oven.
3) Bake for about 10 minutes and season with salt and black pepper to serve.

Nutrition

Calories: 391 Carbs: 15g Fats: 38.2g Proteins: 3.5g Sodium: 96mg Sugar: 0.5g

Fish and Seafood Recipes

Creamy Shrimp and Bacon

Serves: 3
Prep Time: 20 mins
Ingredients

- 1 tablespoon olive oil
- 1 pound raw shrimp
- 2 bacon slices
- Salt and black pepper, to taste
- ¼ cup coconut cream

Directions

1. Season the shrimp with salt and black pepper.
2. Put the olive oil and seasoned shrimp in a non-stick pan.
3. Sauté for about 5 minutes and add bacon and coconut cream.
4. Cook for about 8 minutes and dish out to serve.

Nutrition

Calories: 334 Carbs: 3.6g Fats: 17.3g Proteins: 39.6g Sodium: 665mg Sugar: 0.7g

Lemon Garlic Shrimp

Serves: 3
Prep Time: 25 mins
Ingredients

- 3 tablespoons butter
- 1 pound large raw shrimp
- 2 lemons, sliced
- 1 teaspoon paprika
- 4 garlic cloves

Directions
1. Heat the butter in a skillet and add garlic.
2. Sauté for about 1 minute and add shrimp, paprika, and lemon slices.
3. Cook for about 10 minutes on medium low heat and dish out to serve hot.

Nutrition

Calories: 271 Carbs: 5.3g Fats: 13.4g Proteins: 32.5g Sodium: 422mg Sugar: 1.1g

Cheesy and Creamy Tilapia

Serves: 4
Prep Time: 40 mins
Ingredients

- 1 cup Parmesan cheese, grated
- 4 tilapia fillets
- ¼ cup mayonnaise
- Salt and black pepper, to taste
- ¼ cup fresh lemon juice

Directions
1. Preheat the oven to 350 degrees F and grease 2 baking dishes.
2. Marinate tilapia fillets with mayonnaise, fresh lemon juice, salt and black pepper.
3. Put the marinated fillets in the baking dishes and top with cheese.
4. Transfer into the oven and bake for about 30 minutes.
5. Remove from the oven and serve hot.

Nutrition

Calories: 245 Carbs: 4.9g Fats: 12.1g Proteins: 30.4g Sodium: 411mg Sugar: 1.3g

Roasted Mahi-Mahi Fish

Serves: 3
Prep Time: 45 mins
Ingredients

- ½ cup fresh lemon juice
- 1 pound mahi-mahi fillets
- 4 tablespoons butter
- Salt and black pepper, to taste
- 1 teaspoon dried rosemary, crushed

Directions
1. Preheat the oven to 350 degrees F and grease 2 baking dishes.
2. Season the mahi-mahi fish fillets with salt and black pepper.
3. Put the seasoned fillets in the baking dishes and top with dried oregano, dried rosemary, and fresh lemon juice.
4. Bake for about 30 minutes and remove from the oven to serve hot.

Nutrition
Calories: 267 Carbs: 1.1g Fats: 15.7g Proteins: 28.6g Sodium: 245mg Sugar: 0.9g

Salmon Stew

Serves: 9
Prep Time: 5 hours 10 mins
Ingredients
- 3 tablespoons butter
- 3 pounds salmon fillet, cubed
- 3 medium onions, chopped
- Salt and black pepper, to taste
- 3 cups homemade fish broth

Directions
1. Put all the ingredients in a slow cooker and mix gently.
2. Set the slow cooker on LOW and cook for about 5 hours.
3. Dish out and serve hot.

Nutrition
Calories: 272 Carbs: 4.4g Fats: 14.2g Proteins: 32.1g Sodium: 275mg Sugar: 1.9g

Ketogenic Butter Fish

Serves: 6
Prep Time: 40 mins
Ingredients
- 6 green chilies, chopped
- 2 pounds salmon fillets
- 2 cups butter
- Salt and black pepper, to taste
- 12 garlic cloves, finely chopped

Directions
1. Preheat the oven to 360 degrees F and grease 2 baking dishes.
2. Season the salmon fillets with garlic, salt and black pepper.
3. Top with butter and transfer into the oven.
4. Bake for about 30 minutes and remove from the oven to serve hot.

Nutrition
Calories: 565 Carbs: 1.8g Fats: 53.1g Proteins: 22.8g Sodium: 378mg Sugar: 0.2g

Sweet and Sour Fish

Serves: 6
Prep Time: 25 mins
Ingredients
- ¼ cup butter
- 2 pounds fish chunks
- 2 tablespoons vinegar
- Salt and black pepper, to taste
- 4 drops liquid stevia

Directions
1. Put the butter and fish in a skillet and sauté for about 4 minutes.
2. Pour in the stevia, vinegar, salt and black pepper.
3. Cook for about 10 minutes on medium low heat and dish out to serve hot.

Nutrition
Calories: 190 Carbs: 2.8g Fats: 9g Proteins: 27.1g Sodium: 595mg Sugar: 2.7g

Prawns in Gravy

Serves: 6
Prep Time: 20 mins
Ingredients

- 4 tablespoons butter
- 2 pounds fresh prawns, cubed
- 1 large onion, sliced
- Salt and black pepper, to taste
- 1 cup homemade tomato puree

Directions

1. Put the butter and onions in a large skillet and sauté for about 3 minutes.
2. Add prawns, tomato puree, salt and black pepper and cook for about 12 minutes.
3. Dish out and serve hot.

Nutrition
Calories: 268 Carbs: 6.7g Fats: 10.3g Proteins: 35.1g Sodium: 431mg Sugar: 2.4g

Buffalo Fish

Serves: 4
Prep Time: 20 mins
Ingredients

- ½ cup Franks red hot sauce
- 4 fish fillets
- 1 teaspoon garlic powder
- Salt and black pepper, to taste
- 4 tablespoons butter

Directions

1. Marinate the fish fillets with red hot sauce, garlic powder, salt and black pepper.
2. Refrigerate the marinade for an hour.
3. Put the butter and marinated fish in the slow cooker.
4. Set the slow cooker on LOW and cook for about 6 hours.
5. Dish out and serve hot.

Nutrition
Calories: 317 Carbs: 16.2g Fats: 22.7g Proteins: 13.6g Sodium: 671mg Sugar: 0.2g

Mahi Mahi Cakes

Serves: 4
Prep Time: 30 mins
Ingredients

- 2 teaspoons primal palate seafood seasoning
- 12 oz.mahi mahi, canned
- ¼ cup onions,minced
- 3 tablespoons organic palm oil
- 2 teaspoons parsley,garnish
- 3pasture egg yolks
- 1 teaspoon chives,garnish
- 4 lemon wedges, for garnish

Directions

1) Preheat the oven at 360 degrees F and grease a baking tray.
2) Mix together seafood seasoning, salmon, onions, and egg yolks in a bowl.
3) Make small patties out of this mixture and arrange them on the baking tray.
4) Transfer it in the oven and bake for about 15 minutes.
5) Dish out the patties and keep aside.
6) Put palm oil in a skillet on a medium-high heat and add patties.
7) Flip the sides of the patties and dish onto a plate.

8) Garnish with parsley, lemon wedges, and chives to serve.

Nutrition
Calories: 248 Carbs: 1.8g Fats: 18.9g Proteins: 18.7g Sodium: 464mg Sugar: 0.6g

Salmon Stew

Serves: 3
Prep Time: 20 mins
Ingredients
- 1 cup homemade fish broth
- 1 medium onion, chopped
- 1 pound salmon fillet, cubed
- Salt and black pepper, to taste
- 1 tablespoon butter

Directions
1) Season the salmon fillets with salt and black pepper.
2) Put butter and onions in a skillet and sauté for about 3 minutes.
3) Add salmon and cook for about 2 minutes on each side.
4) Stir in the fish broth and cover the lid.
5) Cook for about 7 minutes and dish out to serve hot.

Nutrition
Calories: 272 Carbs: 4.4g Fats: 14.2g Proteins: 32.1g Sodium: 275mg Sugar: 1.9g

Paprika Shrimp

Serves: 6
Prep Time: 25 mins
Ingredients
- 6 tablespoons butter
- 1 teaspoon smoked paprika
- 2 pounds tiger shrimps
- Salt, to taste

Directions
1) Preheat the oven to 395 degrees F and grease a baking dish with butter.
2) Season the shrimps with smoked paprika and salt.
3) Arrange the seasoned shrimp in the baking dish and transfer the baking dish in oven.
4) Bake for about 15 minutes and dish out to serve.

Nutrition
Calories: 173 Carbs: 0.1g Fats: 8.3g Proteins: 23.8g Sodium: 332mg Sugar: 0g

Ketogenic Butter Fish

Serves: 3
Prep Time: 40 mins
Ingredients
- 2 tablespoons ginger-garlic paste
- 3 green chilies, chopped
- 1 pound salmon fillets
- Salt and black pepper, to taste
- ¾ cup butter

Directions
1) Season the salmon fillets with salt, black pepper, and ginger-garlic paste.
2) Place the salmon fillets in the pot and top with green chilies and butter.

3) Cover the lid and cook on LOW heat for about 30 minutes.
4) Dish out to serve hot.

Nutrition
Calories: 507 Carbs: 2.4g Fats: 45.9g Proteins: 22.8g Sodium: 296mg Sugar: 0.2g

Shrimp Magic

Serves: 3
Prep Time: 25 mins
Ingredients
- 2 tablespoons butter
- ½ teaspoon smoked paprika
- 1 pound shrimps, peeled and deveined
- Lemongrass stalks
- 1 red chili pepper, seeded and chopped

Directions
1) Place all the ingredients in a bowl, except lemongrass, and mix well to marinate for about 2 hours.
2) Preheat the oven to 400 degrees F and thread the shrimps onto lemongrass stalks.
3) Bake for about 15 minutes and serve immediately.
Nutrition
Calories: 251 Carbs: 3g Fats: 10.3g Proteins: 34.6g Sodium: 424mg Sugar: 0.1g

Omega-Rich Dinner

Serves: 8
Prep Time: 40 mins
Ingredients
- 4 garlic cloves, minced
- Salt and black pepper, to taste
- 8 (6-ounce) skinless, boneless salmon fillets
- 2 tablespoons fresh lemon zest, grated finely
- 4 tablespoons olive oil
- 4 tablespoons fresh lemon juice

Directions
1) Preheat the grill to medium-high heat and grease the grill grate.
2) Put all the ingredients in a large bowl, except salmon fillets, and mix well.
3) Coat with garlic mixture generously and grill for about 7 minutes on each side.
4) Dish out to serve hot.

Nutrition
Calories: 278 Carbs: 1g Fats: 13.2g Proteins: 38.2g Sodium: 63mg Sugar: 0.3g

Sweet and Sour Fish

Serves: 3
Prep Time: 25 mins
Ingredients
- ¼ cup butter
- 2 drops liquid stevia
- 1 pound fish chunks
- Salt and black pepper, to taste
- 1 tablespoon vinegar

Directions
1) Heat butter in a large skillet and add fish chunks.

2) Cook for about 3 minutes and add liquid stevia and vinegar.
3) Cook for about 1 minute and add salt and black pepper.
4) Stir continuously at medium-low heat for about 10 minutes.
5) Place onto a serving bowl and serve hot.

Nutrition
Calories: 274 Carbs: 2.8g Fats: 15.4g Proteins: 33.2g Sodium: 604mg Sugar: 0g

Buttered Scallops

Serves: 6
Prep Time: 25 mins
Ingredients
- 4 tablespoons fresh rosemary, chopped
- 4 garlic cloves, minced
- 2 pounds sea scallops
- Salt and black pepper, to taste
- ½ cup butter

Directions
1) Put butter, rosemary and garlic on medium-high heat and sauté for about 1 minute.
2) Stir in the sea scallops, salt, and black pepper and cook for about 2 minutes per side.
3) Add garlic and rosemary and sauté for about 3 minutes.
4) Dish out in a bowl and serve hot.

Nutrition
Calories: 279 Carbs: 5.7g Fats: 16.8g Proteins: 25.8g Sodium: 354mg Sugar: 0g

Buffalo Fish

Serves: 8
Prep Time: 20 mins
Ingredients
- Salt and black pepper, to taste
- 1 teaspoon garlic powder
- 3 tablespoons butter
- 1/3 cup Franks red hot sauce
- 3 salmon fillets

Directions
1) Put butter and fish fillets in a large skillet on medium heat.
2) Cook for about 2 minutes per side and add salt, garlic powder, and black pepper.
3) Cook for about 1 minute and add Franks red hot sauce.
4) Cover the lid and cook for about 7 minutes on low heat.
5) Dish out in a serving platter and serve hot.

Nutrition
Calories: 317 Carbs: 16.4g Fats: 22.7g Proteins: 13.6g Sodium: 659mg Sugar: 0.2g

BBQ Trout

Serves: 4
Prep Time: 20 mins
Ingredients
- 2 garlic cloves, crushed
- Salt and black pepper, to taste
- 4 rainbow trout fillets
- 1 small onion, sliced thinly

- 2 small lemons, seeded, sliced thinly and divided
- 1½ tablespoons olive oil

Directions
1) Preheat the grill to medium-high heat and grease the grill grate.
2) Rub the trout slices with garlic and arrange each trout slice over a piece of foil.
3) Arrange lemon and onion slices evenly over fillets and sprinkle with salt and black pepper.
4) Drizzle with olive oil and fold the foil pieces in order to seal the trout slices.
5) Grill the trout for about 6 minutes and serve hot.

Nutrition
Calories: 190 Carbs: 7g Fats: 13.4g Proteins: 13.5g Sodium: 361mg Sugar: 2.3g

Seafood Jambalaya

Serves: 4
Prep Time: 60 mins
Ingredients
- 4 oz. Catfish, cut into 1-inch cubes
- 4 oz. Shrimp, peeled and deveined
- 1 tablespoon olive oil
- 2 bacon slices, chopped
- 1 1/5 cups vegetable broth
- ¾ cup sliced celery stalk
- 1/4 teaspoon minced garlic
- 1/2 cup chopped onion
- 1 cup canned diced tomatoes
- 1 cup uncooked long-grain white rice
- 1/2 tablespoon Cajun seasoning
- 1/4 teaspoon dried thyme
- 1/4 teaspoon cayenne pepper
- 1/2 teaspoon dried oregano
- Salt and black pepper, to taste

Directions:
1. Select "Sauté" function on your Instant Pot and add oil into it.
2. Add onion, garlic, celery, and bacon to the pot and cook for 10 minutes.
3. Toos in all the remaining ingredients to the pot except seafood.
4. Stir well then secure the cooker lid.
5. Select the "slow cook" function on a medium mode.
6. Keep the pressure release handle on "venting" position. Cook for 4 hours.
7. After it is done, remove the Instant Pot lid and add seafood to the gravy.
8. Secure the Instant Pot lid again; keep the pressure handle in the venting position.
9. Cook for another 45 minutes then serve.

Nutrition Calories per serving: 505 Carbohydrate: 58.6g Protein: 27.4g Fat: 16.8g Sugar: 3.1g Sodium: 848mg

Shrimp Creole

Serves: 2
Prep Time: 1hr. 40 mins
Ingredients
- 1 lb. shrimps (peeled and deveined)
- 1 tablespoon olive oil
- 1 (28 oz.) can crush whole tomatoes
- 1 cup celery stalk (sliced)
- ¾ cup chopped white onion
- 1/2 cup green bell pepper (chopped)
- 1 (8oz.) can tomato sauce
- 1/2 teaspoon minced garlic
- ¼ teaspoon ground black pepper
- 1 tablespoon Worcestershire sauce
- 4 drops hot pepper sauce
- salt, to taste

Directions
1. Add oil to the Instant Pot along with all the ingredients except shrimps.
2. Secure the cooker lid and keep the pressure handle valve to the venting position.
3. Select the "Slow Cook" function on your cooker and set it on medium heat.
4. Let the mixture cook for 6 hours.
5. Remove the Instant Pot lid afterward and add shrimps to the pot.
6. Stir and let the shrimps cook for another 1 hour on "Slow Cook" function.
7. Keep the Instant Pot lid-covered with pressure release handle in the venting position.
8. To serve, pour the juicy shrimp creole over steaming white rice.

Nutrition Calories per serving: 320 Carbohydrate: 39.9g Protein: 26.3g Fat: 7g Sugar: 3.4g Sodium: 331mg

Creamy Chipotle Shrimp Soup

Serves: 4
Prep Time: 30 mins
Ingredients
- 3 slices bacon chopped
- 1 cup onion diced
- 3/4 cup celery chopped
- 1 teaspoon garlic
- 1 tablespoon flour
- 1/4 cup dry white wine
- 1 1/2 cups chicken or vegetable broth
- 1/2 cup whole milk
- 1 1/2 cups potatoes cut into small (1/3-inch) cubes
- 1 cup frozen corn kernels
- 2 teaspoons diced canned chipotle peppers in adobo sauce
- 3/4 teaspoons salt or to taste
- 1/2 teaspoon ground black pepper
- 1/2 teaspoon dried thyme
- 1/2 lb. shrimp peeled and deveined
- 1/4 cup heavy cream

Directions
1. Preheat the insert of the Instant Pot on sauté mode.
2. Add bacon to the insert and sauté for 3 minutes.
3. Stir in garlic, celery, and onions, stir cook for 3 minutes.
4. Add flour and cook for 1 minute.
5. Stir in wine and mix well. Add broth, milk, corn, potatoes, salt, pepper, chipotle and thyme.
6. Seal the Instant Pot lid and turn the pressure valve to sealing position.
7. Select Manual mode for 1 minute at high pressure
8. Once done, release the pressure completely then remove the lid.
9. Add cream and shrimp to the pot and cover the lid.
10. Let it cook in the existing heat for 10 minutes.
11. Garnish with parsley.
12. Serve warm.

Nutrition Calories per serving: 458 Carbohydrate: 27.3g Protein: 29.8g Fat: 54.1g Sugar: 8.2g Sodium: 940mg

Salmon with Orange Ginger Sauce

Serves: 2
Prep Time: 20 mins
Ingredients

- 1-pound salmon
- 1 tablespoon dark soy sauce
- 2 teaspoons minced ginger
- 1 teaspoon minced garlic
- .5-1 teaspoon salt
- 1-1.5 teaspoon ground pepper
- 2 tablespoons low sugar marmalade.

Directions
1. Place salmon in a 6-inch pan.
2. Toss all the ingredients for the sauce then pour it over the salmon.
3. Let it marinate for 30 minutes at room temperature.
4. Pour about 2 cups of water into the insert of the Instant Pot.
5. Place the trivet over the water and place the marinated salmon over it.
6. Pour the marinade over it liberally
7. Seal the Instant Pot lid and turn the pressure valve to sealing position.
8. Select Manual mode for 3 minutes at high pressure
9. Once done, release the pressure completely then remove the lid.
10. Serve warm.

Nutrition Calories per serving: 236 Carbohydrate: 3.2g Protein: 22.2g Fat: 10.6g Sugar: 1.4g Sodium: 53mg

Shrimp with Tomatoes and Feta

Serves: 4
Prep Time: 20 mins
Ingredients
- 2 tablespoons butter
- 1 tablespoon garlic
- 1/2 teaspoon red pepper flakes
- 1.5 cups chopped onion
- 1 14.5-oz can tomato
- 1 teaspoon oregano
- 1 teaspoons salt
- 1-pound frozen shrimp 21-25 count shelled

add after cooking
- 1 cup crumbled feta cheese
- 1/2 cup sliced black olives
- 1/4 cup parsley

Directions
1. Melt butter in the insert of the Instant Pot on sauté mode.
2. Add red pepper flakes and garlic, sauté for 30 seconds.
3. Stir in tomatoes, oregano, onions, salt, and shrimp.
4. Seal the Instant Pot lid and turn the pressure valve to sealing position.
5. Select Manual mode for 1 minute at low pressure
6. Once done, release the pressure completely then remove the lid.
7. Mix well gently then add feta cheese, parsley, and olives.
8. Enjoy.

Nutrition Calories per serving: 313 Carbohydrate: 20.5 g Protein: 23.6g Fat: 15.2g Sugar: 0g Sodium: 1128mg

Lemon Pepper Salmon

Serves: 2
Prep Time: 20 mins
Ingredients

- A ¾ cup of water
- a few sprigs of parsley dill, tarragon, basil or a combo
- 1-pound salmon filet skin on
- 3 teaspoons ghee or other healthy fat divided
- ¼ teaspoon salt or to taste
- ½ teaspoon pepper or to taste
- 1/2 lemon thinly sliced
- 1 zucchini julienned
- 1 red bell pepper julienned
- 1 carrot julienned

Directions
1. Add water and herbs to the insert of the Instant Pot.
2. Place the steamer rack over the water and place salmon over it.
3. Drizzle salt, pepper, and ghee over the fish.
4. Place lemon slices over the fish.
5. Seal the Instant Pot lid and turn the pressure valve to sealing position.
6. Select the Steam mode for 3 minutes at high pressure
7. Once done, release the pressure completely then remove the lid.
8. Remove the fish and trivet from the insert.
9. Discard the herbs and add veggies to the pot.
10. Cover the pot and cook them for 2 minutes on Sauté mode.
11. Serve the salmon with cooked veggies.
12. Enjoy.

Nutrition Calories per serving: 249 Carbohydrate: 11.7g Protein: 28.6g Fat: 9g Sugar: 1.5g Sodium: 881mg

Coconut Fish Curry

Serves: 2
Prep Time: 30 mins
Ingredients
- 1-1.5 lb. fish steaks, rinsed and cut into bite-size pieces
- 1 tomato, chopped
- 2 green chile, sliced into strips
- 2 medium onions, sliced into strips
- 2 garlic cloves, squeezed
- 1 tablespoon freshly grated ginger,
- 6 curry leaves, or bay leaves
- 1 tablespoon ground coriander
- 2 teaspoons ground cumin
- ½ teaspoon ground turmeric
- 1 teaspoon chili powder,
- ½ teaspoon ground fenugreek
- 2 cups unsweetened coconut milk
- salt to taste
- lemon juice to taste

Directions
1. Preheat oil in the insert of the Instant Pot.
2. Add curry leaves and sauté for 1 minute.
3. Toss in ginger, onion, and ginger, sauté until soft.
4. Add all the spices including fenugreek, chili powder, cumin, coriander, and turmeric.
5. Sauté for 2 minutes then add coconut milk and deglaze the pot.
6. Stir in fish pieces, tomatoes, and green chile.
7. Seal the Instant Pot lid and turn the pressure valve to sealing position.
8. Select Manual mode for 5 minutes at low pressure
9. Once done, release the pressure completely then remove the lid.
10. Adjust seasoning with lemon juice and salt.
11. Enjoy.

Nutrition Calories per serving: 270 Carbohydrate: 1.1g Protein: 22.5g Fat: 20.3g Sugar: 0.3g Sodium: 117mg

Salmon with Chili-Lime Sauce

Serves: 4
Prep Time: 20 mins
Ingredients
For steaming salmon:
- 2 salmon fillets 5 ounces each
- 1 cup of water
- Sea salt to taste
- Freshly ground black pepper to taste

For the chili-lime sauce:
- 1 jalapeno, seeds removed and diced
- 1 lime juiced
- 2 cloves garlic minced
- 1 tablespoon honey
- 1 tablespoon olive oil
- 1 tablespoon hot water
- 1 tablespoon chopped fresh parsley
- 1/2 teaspoon paprika
- 1/2 teaspoon cumin

Directions
1. Mix all the ingredients for the sauce in a bowl and keep it aside.
2. Add water to the insert of the Instant Pot and place the trivet over it.
3. Place the salmon fillets over the trivet and drizzle salt and pepper over the salmon.
4. Seal the Instant Pot lid and turn the pressure valve to sealing position.
5. Select Manual mode for 5 minutes at high pressure
6. Once done, release the pressure completely then remove the lid.
7. Serve warm with chili lime sauce on top.
8. Enjoy.

Nutrition Calories per serving: 359 Carbohydrate: 12.2g Protein: 36.9g Fat: 43.2g Sugar: 6.5g Sodium: 106mg

Sweet and Spicy Pineapple Shrimp

Serves: 4

Prep Time: 15 mins
Ingredients
- 1 large red bell pepper cleaned and sliced
- 12 ounces Calrose rice or quinoa
- 3/4 cup unsweetened pineapple juice
- 1/4 cup dry white wine
- 1/4 cup fresh water
- 2 tablespoons soy sauce
- 2 tablespoons Thai sweet chili sauce
- 1 tablespoon sambal Oelek ground chili paste
- 1-pound large shrimp frozen
- 4 scallions chopped, white and greens separated
- 1.5 cups pineapple chunks drained

Directions
1. Separate pineapple chunks from its juice.
2. Add ¾ cup pineapple juice, red bell pepper, water, wine, soy sauce, rice, scallions, chili sauce and sambal oelek to the insert of the Instant Pot.
3. Place the shrimp over this mixture.
4. Seal the Instant Pot lid and turn the pressure valve to sealing position.
5. Select Manual mode for 2 minutes at high pressure

6. Once done, release the pressure completely then remove the lid.
7. Add scallion greens and pineapple chunks.
8. Serve warm.

Nutrition Calories per serving: 284 Carbohydrate: 41.3g Protein: 132.8g Fat: 16.4g Sugar: 23.8g Sodium: 508mg

Coconut Red Curry Shrimp

Serves: 4
Prep Time: 30 mins
Ingredients
Marinade:
- 1/4 cup coconut milk canned
- 1 teaspoon cumin
- 1 teaspoon paprika
- 2 teaspoons curry spice
- 3 tablespoons fresh lime juice

- 1/2 teaspoon sea salt
- 1 teaspoon freshly grated ginger
- 1 clove garlic minced
- 2 lbs. large shrimp peeled and deveined

sauce:
- 2 tablespoons coconut oil or olive oil
- 1 small white onion diced
- 2 teaspoons freshly grated ginger
- 2 cloves garlic minced
- 1 28 oz can have diced tomatoes

- 3 tablespoons red Thai curry paste
- 1 14 oz coconut milk
- 1 teaspoon of sea salt
- 1/3 cup freshly chopped cilantro to garnish

Directions
1. Mix coconut milk, with lime juice, ginger, spices, salt, garlic and ginger in a large bowl.
2. Place shrimp in this marinade and mix well to coat.
3. Preheat oil in the insert of the Instant Pot on sauté mode.
4. Add garlic, ginger, and onion, sauté for 3-4 minutes until soft.
5. Stir in tomatoes, coconut milk, salt and curry paste.
6. Seal the Instant Pot lid and turn the pressure valve to sealing position.
7. Select Manual mode for 7 minutes at high pressure
8. Once done, release the pressure completely then remove the lid.
9. Switch the Instant pot to sauté mode then stir in leftover marinade.
10. Cook for 2 minutes then garnish with cilantro.
11. Serve warm.

Nutrition Calories per serving: 236 Carbohydrate: 24.6g Protein: 25.5g Fat: 7.1g Sugar: 19.6g Sodium: 720mg

Poultry Recipes

Stuffed Chicken with Asparagus and Bacon

Serves: 4
Prep Time: 50 mins
Ingredients
- ½ teaspoon salt
- 1 pound chicken tenders
- ¼ teaspoon black pepper

- 8 bacon slices
- 12 asparagus spears

Directions

1. Preheat the oven to 400 degrees F and grease a baking sheet.
2. Lay bacon slices on a baking sheet and top with chicken tenders.
3. Season with salt and black pepper and add asparagus spears.
4. Wrap the bacon around the chicken and asparagus.
5. Bake for about 40 minutes and dish out to serve hot.

Nutrition

Calories: 377 Carbs: 3g Fats: 25g Proteins: 32g Sodium: 798mg Sugar: 1g

Creamy Turkey Breasts

Serves: 6
Prep Time: 15 mins
Ingredients

- 1 large onion
- 2 pounds chicken breasts
- 1 cup sour cream
- Salt, to taste
- 4 garlic cloves

Directions

1. Season the turkey breasts with salt and add to a non-stick skillet.
2. Cook for about 3 minutes on medium-low heat and stir in the onions, garlic, and sour cream.
3. Cook for about 25 minutes and dish out to serve hot.

Nutrition

Calories: 382 Carbs: 4.6g Fats: 19.3g Proteins: 45.4g Sodium: 179mg Sugar: 1.1g

Mozzarella and Pesto Chicken Casserole

Serves: 8
Prep Time: 40 mins
Ingredients

- 8 oz cream cheese, softened
- ¼ cup pesto
- ½ cup heavy cream
- 8 oz mozzarella cheese, shredded
- 2 pounds chicken, cubed

Directions

1. Preheat the oven to 400 degrees F and grease a large casserole dish.
2. Mix together the cream cheese, pesto, and heavy cream in a bowl.
3. Add chicken to marinate well and place in the casserole dish.
4. Top with mozzarella cheese and transfer into the oven.
5. Bake for about 30 minutes and remove from the oven to serve hot.

Nutrition

Calories: 451 Carbs: 3g Fats: 30g Proteins: 38g Sodium: 653mg Sugar: 1g

Turkey Meatballs

Serves: 3
Prep Time: 40 mins
Ingredients

- 1 teaspoon garlic, minced
- 1 pound ground turkey

- 1 tablespoon butter
- Salt and black pepper, to taste
- 12-ounce tomatoes, peeled and crushed

Directions
1. Put all the ingredients in a bowl except tomatoes and mix until well combined.
2. Make small-sized balls from this mixture and keep aside.
3. Put tomatoes in a non-stick skillet and add the meat balls.
4. Cook for about 30 minutes on low heat and dish out to serve warm.

Nutrition Calories: 351 Carbs: 4.7g Fats: 20.7g Proteins: 42.5g Sodium: 195mg Sugar: 3g

Cheesy Chicken

Serves: 6
Prep Time: 45 mins
Ingredients
- 1 teaspoon garlic salt
- 2 pounds chicken breasts
- 1 cup cream cheese
- 1 cup mozzarella cheese, shredded
- 1 cup sugar-free tomato sauce

Directions
1. Preheat the oven to 360 degrees F and grease a baking sheet.
2. Season the chicken breasts with garlic salt and transfer onto the baking sheet.
3. Layer with cream cheese, followed by tomato sauce and finally topped with cheese.
4. Transfer into the oven and bake for about 25 minutes.
5. Dish out and serve hot.

Nutrition
Calories: 439 Carbs: 1.5g Fats: 25.5g Proteins: 48.2g Sodium: 275mg Sugar: 0.2g

Crock-Pot Whole Roasted Turkey

Serves: 6
Prep Time: 40 mins
Ingredients
- 1 cup mozzarella cheese, shredded
- 1 (2-pound) whole chicken, cleaned, pat dried
- 2 tablespoons fresh lemon juice
- Salt and black pepper, to taste
- 4 whole garlic cloves, peeled

Directions
1. Stuff the turkey cavity with garlic cloves and season with salt and black pepper.
2. Place the turkey into a non-stick skillet and squeeze the lemon juice onto it.
3. Cook for about 30 minutes and dish out to serve hot.

Nutrition
Calories: 310 Carbs: 0.5g Fats: 12.8g Proteins: 45.3g Sodium: 230mg Sugar: 0.1g

Coconut Chicken Curry

Serves: 3
Prep Time: 7 hours 15 mins
Ingredients

- 1 onion, finely sliced
- 1 pound chicken, cubed
- 2 tablespoons curry paste
- Cashews, to garnish
- ¾ cup coconut cream

Directions
1. Place all the ingredients in a slow cooker, except the cashews.
2. Set the slow cooker on LOW and cook, covered for about 7 hours.
3. Dish out and top with cashews to serve hot.

Nutrition
Calories: 475 Carbs: 11.1g Fats: 26.9g Proteins: 46.8g Sodium: 107mg Sugar: 3.8g

Ketogenic Italian Turkey

Serves: 5
Prep Time: 35 mins
Ingredients
- ¾ cup cream cheese
- ¾ cup parmesan cheese, grated
- 1½ pounds turkey breasts, sliced
- 1 teaspoon butter
- 1 teaspoon Italian seasoning

Directions
1. Mix the cream cheese, parmesan cheese and Italian seasoning.
2. Put the butter and turkey breasts in a non-stick skillet.
3. Cook for about 5 minutes on medium heat and add the cheese mixture.
4. Cook for about 25 minutes and dish out to serve hot.

Nutrition
Calories: 336 Carbs: 7.5g Fats: 19.7g Proteins: 32.3g Sodium: 1674mg Sugar: 4.9g

Mushroom Garlic Chicken

Serves: 6
Prep Time: 40 mins
Ingredients
- 2 tablespoons butter
- 2 pounds chicken thighs
- 1 cup mushrooms, sliced
- Salt and black pepper, to taste
- 3 garlic cloves

Directions
1. Season the chicken thighs with salt and black pepper.
2. Put the butter in a skillet and add seasoned chicken.
3. Sauté for about 2 minutes and stir in garlic and mushrooms.
4. Sauté for about 30 minutes on medium-low heat and dish out to serve hot.

Nutrition
Calories: 326 Carbs: 0.9g Fats: 15.1g Proteins: 44.3g Sodium: 158mg Sugar: 0.2g

Creamy Chicken Thighs

Serves: 4
Prep Time: 30 mins
Ingredients
- 1 small onion

- 2 tablespoons butter
- 1 pound chicken thighs
- ½ cup sour cream
- Salt, to taste

Directions
1) Season the chicken thighs generously with salt and keep aside.
2) Put butter and onions in a skillet on medium-low heat and sauté for about 3 minutes.
3) Add chicken thighs and cover the lid.
4) Cook for about 10 minutes and stir in the sour cream.
5) Cook for about 5 minutes and dish out to serve hot.

Nutrition
Calories: 447 Carbs: 3.8g Fats: 26.9g Proteins: 45.3g Sodium: 206mg Sugar: 1.1g

Ham Stuffed Turkey Rolls

Serves: 4
Prep Time: 30 mins
Ingredients
- 2 tablespoons fresh sage leaves
- Salt and black pepper, to taste
- 4 ham slices
- 4 (6-ounce) turkey cutlets
- 1 tablespoon butter, melted

Directions
1) Season the turkey cutlets with salt and black pepper.
2) Roll the turkey cutlets and wrap ham slices tightly around each cutlet.
3) Coat each roll with butter and place the sage leaves evenly.
4) Heat a non-stick pan and cook ham stuffed turkey rolls for about 10 minutes on each side.
5) Dish out and serve immediately.

Nutrition
Calories: 467 Carbs: 1.7g Fats: 24.8g Proteins: 56g Sodium: 534mg Sugar: 0g

Cheesy Chicken Tenders

Serves: 6
Prep Time: 25 mins
Ingredients
- 1 cup cream
- 1 cup feta cheese
- 4 tablespoons butter
- 2 pounds chicken tenders
- Salt and black pepper, to taste

Directions
1) Preheat the oven to 360 degrees F and grease a baking dish.
2) Season chicken tenders with salt and black pepper and keep aside.
3) Heat butter in a non-stick pan and add chicken tenders.
4) Cook for about 5 minutes on each side and transfer to the baking dish.
5) Top with cream and feta cheese and bake for about 15 minutes.
6) Place onto a platter and serve hot.

Nutrition
Calories: 447 Carbs: 2.3g Fats: 26.4g Proteins: 47.7g Sodium: 477mg Sugar: 1.8g

Chili Lime Turkey

Serves: 6
Prep Time: 20 mins
Ingredients

- ¼ cup cooking wine
- ½ teaspoon paprika
- 5 garlic cloves, minced
- 1 tablespoon lime juice
- ¼ cup butter
- 1 onion, diced
- 1 teaspoon sea salt
- ½ cup organic chicken broth
- 2 pounds turkey thighs
- 1 teaspoon dried parsley
- 3 green chilies, chopped

Directions

1) Put butter, onions, and garlic in a large skillet and sauté for about 3 minutes.
2) Add rest of the ingredients and cook for about 20 minutes.
3) Dish out in a platter and serve hot.

Nutrition

Calories: 282 Carbs: 6.3g Fats: 15.2g Proteins: 27.4g Sodium: 2117mg Sugar: 3.3g

Stuffed Whole Chicken

Serves: 6
Prep Time: 8 hours 10 mins
Ingredients

- 1 cup Monterey Jack cheese
- 4 whole garlic cloves, peeled
- 1 (2-pound) whole chicken, cleaned, pat dried
- Salt and black pepper, to taste
- 2 tablespoons fresh lemon juice

Directions

1) Stuff the chicken cavity with Monterey Jack cheese and garlic cloves.
2) Season the chicken with salt and black pepper.
3) Transfer the chicken into the slow cooker and drizzle with lemon juice.
4) Set the slow cooker on LOW and cook for about 8 hours.
5) Dish out and serve hot.

Nutrition

Calories: 309 Carbs: 1.6g Fats: 12.1g Proteins: 45.8g Sodium: 201mg Sugar: 0.7g

Mediterranean Turkey Cutlets

Serves: 4

Prep Time: 25 mins
Ingredients

- 2 tablespoons olive oil
- 1 pound turkey cutlets
- ½ cup almond flour
- 1 teaspoon turmeric powder
- 1 teaspoon Greek seasoning

Directions

1) Mix together Greek seasoning, almond flour, and turmeric powder in a bowl and coat turkey cutlets with this mixture.

2) Heat oil in a skillet and add the turkey cutlets.
3) Cover the lid and cook for about 20 minutes on medium-low heat.
4) Dish out in a serving platter and serve.

Nutrition
Calories: 340 Carbs: 3.7g Fats: 19.4g Proteins: 36.3g Sodium: 124mg Sugar: 0g

Caprese Hasselback Chicken

Serves: 4
Prep Time: 25 mins
Ingredients
- 4 large chicken breasts
- 2 tablespoons butter
- 1 cup fresh mozzarella cheese, thinly sliced
- 2 large roma tomatoes, thinly sliced
- Salt and freshly ground black pepper, to taste

Directions
1) Make slits in the chicken breasts and season with salt and black pepper.
2) Stuff the mozzarella cheese slices and tomatoes in the chicken slits.
3) Preheat the oven to 365 degrees F and grease the baking dish with butter.
4) Arrange the stuffed chicken breasts in the baking dish and transfer into the oven.
5) Bake for about 1 hour and dish to serve.

Nutrition
Calories: 287 Carbs: 3.8g Fats: 15g Proteins: 33.2g Sodium: 178mg Sugar: 2.4g

Keto Garlic Turkey Breasts

Serves: 4
Prep Time: 25 mins
Ingredients
- 4 tablespoons butter
- ½ teaspoon garlic powder
- ¼ teaspoon dried oregano
- ½ teaspoon salt
- 1 pound turkey breasts, boneless
- ¼ teaspoon dried basil
- 1 teaspoon black pepper

Directions
1) Preheat the oven to 420 degrees F and grease a baking tray.
2) Season the turkey with garlic powder, dried oregano, salt, dried basil, and black pepper.
3) Put butter and seasoned turkey in a skillet and cook for about 4 minutes on each side.
4) Transfer the turkey in the oven and bake for about 15 minutes.
5) Dish out in a platter and serve hot.

Nutrition
Calories: 223 Carbs: 5.4g Fats: 13.4g Proteins: 19.6g Sodium: 1524mg Sugar: 4.1g

Air Fried Chicken

Serves: 4
Prep Time: 20 mins
Ingredients
- 2 tablespoons olive oil

- 8 skinless, boneless chicken tenderloins
- 2 eggs
- Salt and black pepper, to taste
- 1 teaspoon turmeric powder

Directions
1) Preheat the air fryer to 360 degrees F and coat the basket with olive oil.
2) Whisk together eggs in a bowl and dip the tenderloins in it.
3) Mix together turmeric powder, salt, and black pepper in a bowl and dredge the chicken tenderloins in it.
4) Transfer the tenderloins in the fryer basket and cook for about 10 minutes.
5) Dish out and serve with tomato ketchup or any dip of your choice.

Nutrition
Calories: 342 Carbs: 0.4g Fats: 14.9g Proteins: 50g Sodium: 80mg Sugar: 0g

Creamy Turkey Breast

Serves: 6
Prep Time: 2 hours 10 mins
Ingredients
- 2 tablespoons butter
- ½ cup sour cream
- 1½ cups Italian dressing
- 1 (2-pound) bone-in turkey breast
- 2 garlic cloves, minced
- Salt and black pepper, to taste

Directions
1) Preheat the oven to 360 degrees F and grease a baking dish with butter.
2) Mix together garlic cloves, salt, and black pepper. Then rub the turkey breast with this mixture.
3) Transfer the turkey breast in the baking dish and top with sour cream and Italian dressing.
4) Bake for about 2 hours, coating with pan juices intermittently.
5) Dish out and serve immediately.

Nutrition
Calories: 369 Carbs: 6.5g Fats: 23.2g Proteins: 35.4g Sodium: 990mg Sugar: 4.9g

Honey Garlic Chicken Breasts

Serves: 2
Prep Time: 40 mins
Ingredients
- 1/3 cup water
- ¼ cup low sodium soy sauce
- ¼ cup honey
- 2 cloves garlic minced
- ¼ teaspoon black pepper
- 1 1/2 pounds chicken breasts, boneless and skinless
- 2 teaspoons cornstarch

Directions
1. Mix broth or water with soy sauce, garlic, honey and pepper in the insert of the Instant Pot.
2. Place the chicken breasts in the pot and secure the lid.
3. Turn the pressure valve to the sealing position.
4. Select manual mode at high pressure with 8 minutes of cooking time.
5. Once done, release the pressure completely then remove the lid.
6. Remove the chicken from the Instant Pot and place it on a cutting board.

7. Mix corn-starch with water in a bowl and pour this mixture into the pot.
8. Turn the Instant Pot to sauté mode and cook the mixture for 3 minutes until it thickens.
9. Slice the cooked chicken and return it to the thickened sauce.
10. Enjoy warm.

Nutrition Calories per serving: 355 Carbohydrate: 11.5g Protein: 36.5g Fat: 18.3g Sugar: 5.6g Sodium: 624mg

Butter Chicken

Serves: 6
Prep Time: 25 mins
Ingredients
- 6 chicken thighs boneless, skinless, cut into cubes
- 1 1/2 cup heavy cream
- 1 1/2 cup tomato sauce
- 1/2 onion
- 5 tablespoon butter
- 1 tablespoon garlic minced
- 1 tablespoon ginger chopped
- 1 1/2 teaspoon chili powder
- 1 1/2 teaspoon cumin
- 3 teaspoons garam masala
- 2 tablespoons corn starch

Directions
1. Melt butter in your Instant Pot on Sauté mode.
2. Add onion and chicken cubes.
3. Stir cook them until chicken turns golden.
4. Toss in the remaining ingredients and secure the lid.
5. Select Manual function on your Instant Pot with low pressure and 5 minutes cooking time.
6. Once it is done, release the pressure completely then remove the lid.
7. Mix corn-starch with water and pour this slurry into the pot.
8. Cook this mixture on Sauté mode until it thickens.
9. Serve warm.

Nutrition Calories per serving: 360 Carbohydrate: 3g Protein: 49g Fat: 16g Sugar: 0.9g Sodium: 869mg

Chicken Pho

Serves: 6
Prep Time: 45 mins
Ingredients
- 14 oz of rice noodles
- 1 tablespoon olive oil extra virgin
- 1 large yellow onion halved
- 1 2-inch piece ginger cut into 1/4-inch slices
- 3 cardamom pods lightly smashed
- 1 cinnamon stick
- 1 tablespoon coriander seeds
- 1 fuji apple peeled, cored and diced
- 1/2 cup coarsely chopped cilantro leaves
- 6 chicken thighs bone-in, skin-on
- 3 tablespoons fish sauce
- 3-star anise pods
- 1 tablespoon sugar
- 5 cloves
- 8 cups of water
- 1 1/2 teaspoon salt

Garnish
- 1 lime cut into wedges
- 2 jalapenos thinly sliced
- 1/2 red onion thinly sliced
- Fresh herbs (mint, cilantro, basil)
- Bean sprouts
- Sriracha sauce
- Daikon radish sprouts (optional)

Directions
1. Soak noodles in a large bowl filled with hot water for 45 minutes.
2. Heat oil in the insert of the Instant Pot on Sauté mode.
3. Add onion and ginger. Sauté them for 4 minutes.
4. Stir in cinnamon, cardamom, star anise cloves, and coriander.
5. Cook for 1 minute then adds water, cilantro, apple, fish sauce, sugar, and chicken.
6. Seal and secure the Instant Pot lid of the Instant Pot.
7. Press the Manual button with high pressure and 15 minutes of cooking time.
8. Once done, release the pressure completely then remove the lid.
9. Remove the chicken from the Instant Pot and keep it aside.
10. Strain the remaining broth and mix it with salt and pepper.
11. Shred the chicken using a fork and discard all the bones.
12. Divide the chicken shreds in the serving bowls.
13. Strain the cooked noodles then add them to the serving bowls.
14. Pour in the broth and garnish as desired.
15. Serve warm.

Nutrition Calories per serving: 220 Carbohydrate: 12.9g Protein: 12.3g Fat: 13.4g Sugar: 6.1g Sodium: 804mg

Cajun Chicken and Rice

Serves: 4
Prep Time: 20 mins
Ingredients
- 1 lb. Chicken breast
- 1 tablespoon Cajun seasoning divided
- 1 tablespoon oil olive or avocado
- 1 small onion diced
- 3 garlic cloves minced
- 1.5 cups white rice, rinsed
- 1 bell pepper, diced
- 1 tablespoon tomato paste
- 1.75 cups chicken or vegetable broth

Directions
1. Rinse the rice thoroughly and set them aside.
2. Slice the chicken into half cross-sectionally. And season liberally with 2 teaspoons Cajun seasoning.
3. Preheat cooking oil in an Instant Pot on sauté mode.
4. Add onion and garlic, sauté for 3 minutes just until soft.
5. Stir in 2 tablespoons water to deglaze the pot.
6. Stir in tomato paste, bell peppers, and 1 teaspoon Cajun seasoning.
7. Add broth and mix well. Place the chicken breasts over it.
8. Spread the rinsed rice over the chicken then seal the lid.
9. Select Manual mode for 8 minutes at high pressure.
10. Once done, release the pressure completely then remove the lid.
11. Remove the chicken and shred it using a fork.
12. Return the chicken to the rice.
13. Adjust seasoning with salt and pepper.
14. Garnish with cilantro.
15. Serve warm.

Nutrition Calories per serving: 407 Carbohydrate: 11g Protein: 32g Fat: 25g Sugar: 9g Sodium: 262mg

Faux-Tisserie Chicken

Serves: 8
Prep Time: 35 mins
Ingredients

- 3-pound whole chicken
- 2 tablespoons olive oil
- Sea salt & black pepper, to taste
- 1/2 medium onion, cut into quarters

- 5 large cloves fresh garlic, peeled
- 2 tablespoons southwest seasoning mix
- 1 cup chicken stock/broth

Southwest seasoning

- 1 teaspoon garlic powder
- 1 teaspoon onion powder
- 1 teaspoon chili powder

- 1/2 teaspoon cumin
- 1/2 teaspoon basil

Directions

1. Season the chicken with olive oil, salt, and pepper.
2. Stuff the chicken with garlic cloves and onion wedges.
3. Tie both the legs of the chicken using butcher's wine.
4. Select Sauté mode on your Instant Pot.
5. Add remaining oil to the insert of the Instant pot and add chicken.
6. Sear the chicken for 4 minutes per side.
7. Transfer the chicken to plate then place a trivet in the pot.
8. Pour in chicken stock then place the chicken over the trivet.
9. Drizzle seasoning mix over the chicken then secures the lid.
10. Select Manual mode at high pressure with 25 minutes of cooking time.
11. Once done, allow the cooker's pressure to release naturally.
12. Remove the Instant Pot lid and serve warm.

Nutrition Calories per serving: 697 Carbohydrate: 2.9g Protein: 127.3g Fat: 15.1g Sugar: 0.7 Sodium: 401mg

Orange Chicken

Serves: 4
Prep Time: 25 mins
Ingredients

- 2 lbs. Chicken breast cut into 1-2-inch pieces
- 2 tablespoons vegetable oil
- Sauce:
- 1 cup orange juice no sugar added
- 1 tablespoon ginger grated
- 6 cloves garlic minced

- 1 tablespoon rice wine
- 1/2 cup tomato sauce optional
- ¼ cup granulated sugar
- ¼ cup brown sugar
- ¼ cup lite soy sauce
- 1 tablespoon sriracha
- zest from 1 orange

Cornstarch slurry:

- 2 tablespoons cornstarch

- 2 tablespoons orange juice

Garnish:

- 4 green onions sliced

- extra orange zest

Directions

1. Select Sauté on your Instant pot and add oil to its insert.
2. Add chicken and sauté for 3 minutes until golden brown.

3. Pour in ¼ cup orange juice and deglaze the pot.
4. Start adding the remaining sauce ingredients to the pot.
5. Secure and seal the Instant Pot lid then select Manual mode for 5 minutes at high pressure.
6. Once done, release the pressure completely then remove the lid.
7. Switch the Instant Pot to Sauté mode.
8. Mix corn-starch with orange juice and pour this mixture into the pot.
9. Stir cook this mixture for 2 minutes until it thickens.
10. Garnish with green onion and orange zest.
11. Serve warm.

Nutrition Calories per serving: 640 Carbohydrate: 26.3g Protein: 69.9g Fat: 27.6g Sugar: 13.7g Sodium: 854mg

Chicken Paprikash

Serves: 4
Prep Time: 25 mins
Ingredients
- 1 large onion, diced
- 2 garlic cloves, minced
- 3 tablespoons olive oil
- 2 lb. skinless chicken thighs, bone in
- 1 teaspoon salt
- ¼ teaspoon black pepper
- 2 tablespoons sweet paprika
- 1 bay leaf
- 1½ cup chicken stock
- 1 cup heavy cream
- 2 tablespoons sour cream
- 5 tablespoon corn starch
- ½ lemon or more to taste

Directions
1. Select Sauté mode on your Instant Pot.
2. Add 3 tablespoons to the Instant Pot and preheat it.
3. Stir in garlic and onion, sauté for 3 minutes until soft.
4. Toss in chicken thighs and cook them for 3 minutes per side.
5. Add sweet paprika, pepper, and salt. Mix well.
6. Pour in chicken stock and add the bay leaf.
7. Seal and secure the Instant Pot lid then select the Manual mode for 5 minutes at high pressure.
8. Once done, release the pressure completely then remove the lid.
9. Switch your Instant pot to Sauté mode.
10. Mix corn-starch with 1 tablespoon water and pour this mixture into the pot.
11. Stir in sour cream and heavy cream.
12. Cook until the sauce thickens then add juice from the ½ lemon.
13. Adjust seasoning as desired.
14. Serve warm.

Nutrition Calories per serving: 270 Carbohydrate: 6.6g Protein: 17.9g Fat: 20.1g Sugar: 2.8g Sodium: 50mg

Chicken Parmesan

Serves: 4
Prep Time: 20 mins
Ingredients
- 1 teaspoon extra virgin olive oil
- 2 garlic cloves, thinly sliced
- 1-1/2 cups prepared marinara sauce
- 3 tablespoons grated parmesan cheese

- freshly ground black pepper
- 4 thin chicken cutlets
- ½ teaspoon kosher salt, or more to taste
- ½ teaspoon dried oregano
- 4 ounces fresh mozzarella cheese, grated
- chopped basil, for garnish (optional)

Directions
1. Preheat oil in the insert of the Instant Pot on Sauté mode.
2. Add garlic and sauté for 2 minutes then stir in marinara sauce, ¼ teaspoon pepper, and 2 tablespoons parmesan.
3. Rub the chicken cutlets with salt, pepper, and oregano.
4. Place the chicken in the Instant pot then secure the lid.
5. Select Manual mode for 3 minutes on low pressure.
6. Once done, release the pressure completely then remove the lid.
7. Add 1 tablespoon Parmesan and mozzarella.
8. Simply cover the Instant Pot lid and let it sit for 5 minutes to melt the cheese.
9. Serve warm.

Nutrition Calories per serving: 447 Carbohydrate: 15.2g Protein: 66.2g Fat: 11.7g Sugar: 3.9g Sodium: 188mg

Creamy Italian Chicken Breasts

Serves: 4
Prep Time: 30 mins
Ingredients
- 4 chicken breasts, boneless and skinless
- 1 cup low sodium chicken broth
- 1 teaspoon minced garlic
- 1 teaspoon Italian seasoning
- 1/4 teaspoon salt
- 1/4 teaspoon black pepper
- 1/3 cup heavy cream
- 1/3 cup roasted red peppers
- 1 1/2 tablespoons corn starch
- 1 tablespoon basil pesto

Directions
1. Add chicken to the insert of the Instant Pot.
2. Stir in broth, Italian seasoning, salt, pepper, and garlic.
3. Seal and secure the Instant Pot lid then select the manual mode for 8 minutes at high pressure.
4. Once done, release the pressure completely then remove the lid.
5. Transfer the chicken to the cutting board.
6. Switch the Instant pot to Sauté mode.
7. Mix cream with corn starch, pesto, and red pepper in a small bowl.
8. Pour this mixture into the Instant pot and cook the sauce until it thickens.
9. Return the chicken to the sauce.
10. Serve warm.

Nutrition Calories per serving: 524 Carbohydrate: 29.3g Protein: 68.5g Fat: 10.3g Sugar: 1.2g Sodium: 310mg

Chicken Carnitas

Serves: 4
Prep Time: 20 mins
Ingredients
- 1 tablespoon cumin
- 1 tablespoon oregano
- 1 teaspoon salt
- 1 teaspoon black pepper

- 1 teaspoon chili powder
- 1 tablespoon olive oil
- 1 medium onion, chopped
- 4 cloves garlic, minced
- 1/4 cup pineapple juice
- 1/4 cup lime juice
- 1/4 cup chicken stock
- 1-pound boneless, skinless chicken breasts
- fresh cilantro for topping

Directions
1. Thoroughly mix oregano, cumin, chili powder, salt and pepper in a small bowl.
2. Preheat olive oil in the insert of the Instant Pot on Sauté mode.
3. Add onion to the oil and sauté for 3 minutes until soft.
4. Stir in garlic and stir cook for 1 minute.
5. Add lime juice, pineapple juice, spice mixture, and chicken stock.
6. Mix well then place the chicken in it.
7. Seal and secure the Instant Pot lid then select Manual mode for 8 minutes at high pressure.
8. Once done, release the pressure completely then remove the lid.
9. Shred the chicken using a fork.
10. Mix gently then serve warm.
11. Devour.

Nutrition Calories per serving: 204 Carbohydrate: 7.6g Protein: 32.9g Fat: 4.2g Sugar: 2.2g Sodium: 735mg

Vegetable Recipes

Zucchini Noodles

Serves: 4
Prep Time: 25 mins
Ingredients
- ¼ cup butter
- 1 pound zucchini, spiralized
- ½ cup cream cheese
- ¼ cup Parmesan cheese, grated
- 1 tablespoon sour cream

Directions
1. Mix together cream cheese, sour cream and Parmesan cheese in a bowl.
2. Put the butter in the skillet and add zucchini noodles.
3. Cook for about 5 minutes and stir in the cheese mixture.
4. Cook for 8 minutes and dish out to serve hot.

Nutrition
Calories: 250 Carbs: 5g Fats: 24g Proteins: 6.1g Sodium: 246mg Sugar: 2g

Bacon Wrapped Asparagus

Serves: 6
Prep Time: 35 mins
Ingredients
- 6 bacon slices
- 24 small spears asparagus
- 4 tablespoons butter
- Salt and black pepper, to taste
- 1 cup heavy whipping cream

Directions
1. Season the asparagus spears with salt and black pepper.
2. Add heavy whipping cream to the asparagus.
3. Wrap the asparagus in the bacon slices.
4. Put the butter and wrapped asparagus in the skillet.
5. Cook for about 20 minutes on medium-low heat, rotating every 5 minutes.
6. Dish out and serve hot.

Nutrition
Calories: 249 Carbs: 2.7g Fats: 23.1g Proteins: 8.6g Sodium: 502mg Sugar: 0.9g

Roasted Cauliflower and Broccoli

Serves: 3
Prep Time: 22 mins
Ingredients
- 1 cup broccoli floret
- ¼ cup butter
- Salt and black pepper, to taste
- 1 cup cauliflower floret
- ½ cup Parmesan cheese, grated

Directions
1. Preheat the oven to 360 degrees F and grease a baking tray.
2. Mix together broccoli florets, cauliflower florets, butter, salt and black pepper in a bowl.
3. Put the veggie mixture on the baking tray and top with Parmesan cheese.
4. Bake for about 20 minutes and remove from the oven to serve hot.

Nutrition
Calories: 215 Carbs: 4.5g Fats: 19.5g Proteins: 7.7g Sodium: 305mg Sugar: 1.3g

Mushroom Bacon Skewers

Serves: 4
Prep Time: 20 mins
Ingredients
- 1 pound mushrooms
- 6 bacon strips
- 2 cups cheddar cheese, shredded
- Skewers
- 2 tablespoons mesquite seasoning

Directions
1. Preheat the oven to 395 degrees F and grease a baking tray.
2. Season the mushrooms with mesquite seasoning.
3. Pierce one end of the bacon strip in the skewer, followed by the mushroom.
4. Spear the other end of the bacon strip above the mushroom on the skewer.
5. Put the skewers on the baking tray and top with cheddar cheese.
6. Bake for about 15 minutes and remove from oven to serve.

Nutrition
Calories: 409 Carbs: 5.6g Fats: 32.7g Proteins: 23.9g Sodium: 1482mg Sugar: 2.2g

Roasted Brussels Sprouts

Serves: 3
Prep Time: 35 mins

Ingredients

- ½ cup butter
- ¾ pound brussels sprouts
- ½ teaspoon ginger-garlic paste
- Salt and black pepper, to taste
- ½ tablespoon Dijon mustard

Directions

1. Preheat the oven to 395 degrees F and grease a baking tray.
2. Marinate the brussels sprouts with Dijon mustard, ginger-garlic paste, butter, salt and black pepper.
3. Arrange the marinated brussels sprouts on the baking tray and transfer in the oven.
4. Roast for about 20 minutes and dish out to serve hot.

Nutrition

Calories: 328 Carbs: 10.7g Fats: 31.7g Proteins: 4.3g Sodium: 276mg Sugar: 2.5g

Creamed Peas

Serves: 3
Prep Time: 15 mins
Ingredients

- 1 cup water
- 1 cup fresh green peas
- 3 tablespoons butter
- Salt, to taste
- 1 cup heavy cream

Directions

1. Heat the butter in the skillet and add fresh peas.
2. Sauté for about 3 minutes and add salt, water, and heavy cream.
3. Cook for about 5 minutes on medium-low heat and dish out to serve hot.

Nutrition

Calories: 279 Carbs: 8.1g Fats: 26.5g Proteins: 3.6g Sodium: 152mg Sugar: 2.8g

Parmesan Roasted Bamboo Sprouts

Serves: 2
Prep Time: 20 mins
Ingredients

- ¼ teaspoon paprika
- 1 pound bamboo sprouts
- 1 cup Parmesan cheese, grated
- Salt and black pepper, to taste
- 2 tablespoons butter

Directions

1. Preheat the oven to 360 degrees F and lightly grease a baking dish.
2. Mix together the butter, bamboo sprouts, salt, black pepper, and paprika.
3. Arrange this bamboo sprouts mixture on the baking dish and transfer it into the oven.
4. Sprinkle the Parmesan cheese on the top of the bamboo sprouts.
5. Bake for about 20 minutes and dish out to serve hot.

Nutrition

Calories: 397 Carbs: 19.7g Fats: 26.2g Proteins: 25.9g Sodium: 683mg Sugar: 7.5g

Spinach Balls

Serves: 6
Prep Time: 40 mins
Ingredients
- 1 cup cheddar cheese, grated
- 6 cup fresh spinach leaves, trimmed
- ½ cup butter
- ½ teaspoon garlic salt
- ¼ cup fresh parsley, finely chopped

Directions
1. Preheat the oven to 400 degrees F and lightly grease a baking tray.
2. Put the butter, garlic salt, cheddar cheese, fresh spinach leaves. and fresh parsley in a skillet.
3. Cook for about 20 minutes on medium-low heat and dish out.
4. Mold the spinach mixture into small-sized balls and arrange on the baking tray.
5. Transfer in the oven and bake for about 10 minutes.
6. Dish out and serve warm.

Nutrition
Calories: 220 Carbs: 1.7g Fats: 21.7g Proteins: 5.8g Sodium: 251mg Sugar: 0.3g

Cheesy Cauliflowers

Serves: 4
Prep Time: 35 mins
Ingredients
- ¾ cup sour cream
- 1 pound cauliflower florets
- ¾ cup cheddar cheese, grated
- Salt and black pepper, to taste
- 3 tablespoons butter

Directions
1. Preheat the oven to 400 degrees F and lightly grease a baking dish.
2. Put the sour cream, cauliflower, salt and black pepper in a food processor.
3. Process until coarse and transfer to the baking dish.
4. Top with cheddar cheese and melted butter.
5. Bake for about 20 minutes and remove from oven to serve.

Nutrition
Calories: 282 Carbs: 8.2g Fats: 24.8g Proteins: 9g Sodium: 250mg Sugar: 2.9g

Tofu with Mushrooms

Serves: 6
Prep Time: 30 mins
Ingredients
- 2 cups fresh mushrooms, chopped finely
- 8 tablespoons Parmesan cheese, shredded
- 2 blocks tofu, pressed and cubed into 1-inch pieces
- 8 tablespoons butter
- Salt and freshly ground black pepper, to taste

Directions
1) Mix together tofu, salt and black pepper in a bowl.
2) Put butter and seasoned tofu in a pan over medium-low heat.

3) Cook for about 5 minutes and stir in the mushrooms and Parmesan cheese.
4) Cook for about 4 minutes, occasionally stirring and dish onto a serving plate.

Nutrition
Calories: 211 Carbs: 2g Fats: 18.5g Proteins: 11.5g Sodium: 346mg Sugar: 0.5g

Bacon Veggies Combo

Serves: 4
Prep Time: 35 mins
Ingredients
- 1 green bell pepper, seeded and chopped
- 2 scallions, chopped
- 4 bacon slices
- 3 garlic cloves, minced
- ½ cup Parmesan Cheese
- 1 tablespoon avocado mayonnaise

Directions
1) Preheat the oven to 380 degrees F and grease a baking dish.
2) Arrange the bacon slices in the baking dish and top with scallions, bell peppers, avocado mayonnaise, and Parmesan Cheese.
3) Bake for about 25 minutes and serve immediately.

Nutrition
Calories: 197 Carbs: 4.7g Fats: 13.8g Proteins: 14.3g Sodium: 662mg Sugar: 1.9g

Onion Tofu Scramble

Serves: 4
Prep Time: 20 mins
Ingredients
- 4 tablespoons butter
- 2 blocks tofu, pressed and cubed into 1 inch pieces
- 1 cup cheddar cheese, grated
- Salt and black pepper, to taste
- 2 medium onions, sliced

Directions
1) Season tofu with salt and black pepper in a bowl.
2) Put butter and onions in a pan over medium-low heat.
3) Cook for about 3 minutes and add tofu mixture.
4) Cook for about 2 minutes and add cheddar cheese.
5) Cover with lid and cook for about 5 minutes on low heat.
6) Dish in a bowl to serve for breakfast.

Nutrition
Calories: 184 Carbs: 6.3g Fats: 7.3g Proteins: 12.2g Sodium: 222mg Sugar: 2.7g

Ham Spinach Blast

Serves: 4
Prep Time: 40 mins
Ingredients
- ¼ cup cream
- Salt and black pepper, to taste
- 1½ pounds fresh baby spinach
- 14-ounce ham, sliced
- 2 tablespoons butter, melted

Directions

1) Preheat the oven to 375 degrees F and grease 4 ramekins with butter.
2) Put butter and spinach in a pan over medium-low heat.
3) Cook for about 3 minutes and drain the liquid from the spinach completely.
4) Return spinach in the pan and top with ham slices, cream, salt, and black pepper.
5) Bake for about 25 minutes and dish into a large serving bowl to serve hot.

Nutrition

Calories: 188 Carbs: 4.9g Fats: 12.5g Proteins: 14.6g Sodium: 1098mg Sugar: 0.3g

Bacon Bok Choy Samba

Serves: 6
Prep Time: 25 mins
Ingredients

- 2 tablespoons olive oil
- 4 bacon slices
- 8 tablespoons cream
- 8 bok choy, sliced
- Salt and black pepper, to taste
- 1 cup Parmesan cheese, grated

Directions

1) Season bok choy with salt and black pepper.
2) Put olive oil and bacon slices in a skillet on medium-high heat.
3) Sauté for about 5 minutes and stir in cream and bok choy.
4) Sauté for about 6 minutes and sprinkle with Parmesan cheese.
5) Cook for about 4 minutes on low heat and dish out in a serving platter.

Nutrition

Calories: 112 Carbs: 1.9g Fats: 4.9g Proteins: 3g Sodium: 355mg Sugar: 0.8g

Garlic Parmesan Fried Eggplant

Serves: 12
Prep Time: 30 mins
Ingredients

- 1 teaspoon salt
- 2 medium eggplants, cut into 1/3 inch thick slices
- 2 large eggs
- 2 cups almond flour
- 4 teaspoons garlic powder
- 1 teaspoon black pepper
- 2 cups Parmesan cheese grated
- 1 teaspoon salt
- ½ cup butter

Directions

1) Arrange the eggplants in a single layer in a dish and season with salt.
2) Whisk together eggs in a shallow bowl.
3) Mix together Parmesan, almond flour, garlic powder, salt, and black pepper in another bowl.
4) Heat butter in a large skillet over medium heat.
5) Dip each slice of eggplant in egg and then coat with almond flour mixture.
6) Drop the eggplant slices in a skillet in batches and fry until browned.
7) Dish out and serve with your favorite dip.

Nutrition

Calories: 271 Carbs: 10g Fats: 22g Proteins: 12g Sodium: 696mg Sugar: 2.6g

Roasted Broccoli and Cauliflower

Serves: 6
Prep Time: 25 mins
Ingredients

- 1 cup Parmesan cheese, grated
- 2 cups broccoli florets
- 2 cups cauliflower florets
- Salt and black pepper, to taste
- ½ cup butter

Directions

1) Preheat the oven to 395 degrees F and grease a baking dish.
2) Mix the butter, cauliflower florets, broccoli florets, salt, and black pepper in a bowl.
3) Transfer to baking dish and top with Parmesan cheese.
4) Place the baking dish in the oven and bake for about 15 minutes.
5) Remove from the oven to serve hot.

Nutrition

Calories: 169 Carbs: 4g Fats: 16.5g Proteins: 3.2g Sodium: 172mg Sugar: 1.3g

Creamed Peas

Serves: 3
Prep Time: 25 mins
Ingredients

- 1 cup frozen green peas, thawed
- 1 cup water
- Salt, to taste
- 1 cup heavy cream
- 3 tablespoons butter

Directions

1) Put the butter and frozen peas in the pot and sauté for about 2 minutes.
2) Add salt, heavy cream, and water and cover the lid.
3) Cook for about 10 minutes on medium-low heat and dish out to serve hot.

Nutrition

Calories: 279 Carbs: 8.1g Fats: 26.5g Proteins: 3.6g Sodium: 152mg Sugar: 2.8g

Whole Garlic Roast

Serves: 4
Prep Time: 25 mins
Ingredients

- 4 tablespoons herbed butter
- 1 cup water
- Salt and black pepper, to taste
- 4 large garlic bulbs

Directions

1) Preheat the oven to 395 degrees F and grease a baking dish.
2) Season the garlic bulbs with salt and pepper.
3) Transfer in the baking dish and top with herbed butter.
4) Place the baking dish in the oven and bake for about 15 minutes.
5) Remove from the oven and serve hot.

Nutrition

Calories: 117 Carbs: 3g Fats: 11.5g Proteins: 0.1g Sodium: 84mg Sugar: 0g

Grilled Halloumi Salad

Serves: 6
Prep Time: 15 mins
Ingredients

- 3 cucumbers, sliced
- 1½ oz walnuts, chopped
- 9 oz halloumi cheese, cut into 1/3 inch slices
- 3 handful baby arugula
- Olive oil
- Salt, to taste
- Balsamic vinegar

Directions

1) Grill the halloumi cheese for about 5 minutes per side to achieve grill marks on both sides.
2) Put cucumbers, walnuts and arugula in a bowl and place halloumi cheese on the top.
3) Sprinkle some salt and top with balsamic vinegar and olive oil to serve.

Nutrition
Calories: 259 Carbs: 9.8g Fats: 19.9g Proteins: 13.4g Sodium: 269mg Sugar: 3.7g

Vegan

Vegan Potato Curry

Serves: 6
Prep Time: 40 mins
Ingredients

- 1 medium yellow onion, chopped
- 4 large cloves of garlic, chopped finely
- 5 heaping cups baby potatoes,
- 2 tablespoons curry powder or curry paste
- 2 cups of water
- 2 heaping cups fresh green beans, chopped
- 1 can coconut milk, full fat or light
- 1 tablespoon sugar
- salt & pepper to taste
- 1 teaspoon chili pepper flakes
- 3 tablespoons arrowroot powder

Directions

1. Preheat the insert of the Instant Pot with few drops of water, on sauté mode.
2. Add onions and sauté until soft.
3. Stir in garlic then stir cook for 1 minute.
4. Add rest of the ingredients except arrowroot powder and green beans.
5. Seal the Instant Pot lid and turn the pressure valve to sealing position.
6. Select Manual mode for 20 minutes at high pressure
7. Once done, release the pressure completely then remove the lid.
8. Add green beans, salt, pepper to the pot.
9. Switch the Instant pot to sauté mode.
10. Mix arrowroot with 1 tablespoon water and pour this mixture into the pot.
11. Stir cook for 5 minutes until it thickens.
12. Serve warm.

Nutrition Calories per serving: 211 Carbohydrate: 26.2g Protein: 7.8g Fat: 9.4g Sugar: 4.8g Sodium: 65mg

Vegan Lentil Chili

Serves: 4
Prep Time: 30 mins
Ingredients

- 1 tablespoon olive oil
- 1 onion, chopped
- 4 cloves minced garlic
- 2 carrots, chopped
- 2 jalapeños, chopped
- 1 1/2 tablespoons chili powder
- 1 tablespoon cumin
- 1/2 teaspoon ground coriander
- 1 teaspoon dried oregano
- 3/4 teaspoons salt
- 1 (15 ounces) can crushed tomatoes
- 1 (28 ounces) can fire roasted diced tomatoes
- 2 cups brown or green lentils
- 4 cups vegetable broth
- 1 teaspoon fresh lime juice
- 1/2 cup chopped fresh cilantro

Directions

1. Preheat olive oil in the insert of the Instant Pot.
2. Stir in garlic, onion, jalapenos, and carrots.
3. Sauté for 4 minutes then add all the spices.
4. Stir in all the remaining ingredients except cilantro and lime juice.
5. Seal the Instant Pot lid and turn the pressure valve to sealing position.
6. Select Manual mode for 15 minutes at high pressure
7. Once done, release the pressure completely then remove the lid.
8. Add cilantro and lime juice.
9. Serve warm.

Nutrition Calories per serving: 225 Carbohydrate: 43.3g Protein: 5.1g Fat: 4.1g Sugar: 3.2g Sodium: 36mg

Quinoa Enchiladas

Serves: 4
Prep Time: 30 mins
Ingredients

Enchilada Sauce:
- 3 tablespoons oil
- 3 tablespoons all-purpose flour
- 1 tablespoon chili powder
- 1 1/2 teaspoons cumin
- 1/2 teaspoon oregano
- 1/2 teaspoon garlic powder
- 1/4 teaspoon salt
- 1/8 teaspoon cinnamon
- 1/4 teaspoon cayenne pepper
- 1 (15 ounces) can crushed tomatoes
- 1 cup of water

Enchilada ingredients:
- 2 bell peppers, chopped
- 1 medium onion, chopped
- 1 cup enchilada sauce
- 1 medium zucchini, chopped
- 1 cup uncooked quinoa
- 3/4 cup water
- 1 (15 ounces) can black beans, drained and rinsed
- 1 (15 ounces) can corn, drained and rinsed
- 1 (4 ounces) can diced jalapeños
- 1/4 cup fresh cilantro
- 4 corn tortillas, cut into strips
- 1 cup shredded cheddar cheese

Directions

1. To make the sauce heat oil in a saucepan on medium heat.

2. Add flour and stir cook for 4 minutes until golden in color.
3. Stir in all the spices and cook for 1 minute.
4. Finally, add water and tomatoes, stir cook for 7 minutes until it thickens
5. Keep 1 cup of the sauce aside for this recipe and preserve the rest.
6. Preheat olive oil in the insert of the Instant Pot on sauté mode.
7. Add zucchini, onion, salt and bell peppers, sauté until soft.
8. Stir in quinoa and cook for a minute.
9. Pour in water and 1 cup of the enchilada sauce.
10. Seal the Instant Pot lid and turn the pressure valve to sealing position.
11. Select Manual mode for 1 minute at high pressure
12. Once done, release the pressure completely then remove the lid.
13. Add cheese, cilantro, corn, black beans, corn tortillas, and jalapeno.
14. Serve warm with extra enchilada sauce.
15. Enjoy.

Nutrition Calories per serving: 492 Carbohydrate: 33.9g Protein: 25.4g Fat: 28.3g Sugar: 1.8g Sodium: 497mg

Maple Bourbon Chili

Serves: 4
Prep Time: 40 mins
Ingredients

- 1 tablespoon cooking oil
- 1 small yellow onion, thinly sliced
- 2-3 cloves garlic minced
- 4 cups sweet potatoes, peeled and cubed
- 2 cups vegetable broth
- 1 1/2 tablespoon chili powder
- 2 teaspoons cumin
- 1/2 teaspoon paprika
- 1/4 teaspoon cayenne pepper
- 2 (15) ounce cans kidney beans, drained and rinsed
- 1 (15) ounce can diced tomatoes
- 1/4 cup bourbon
- 2 tablespoons maple syrup
- salt and pepper, to taste
- a few fresh sprigs of cilantro
- 2 green onions, diced
- 3 small corn tortillas, toasted and sliced

Directions
1. Preheat oil in the insert of the instant pot on sauté mode.
2. Add onions and sauté for 5 minutes until soft.
3. Stir in garlic and stir cook for 30 seconds.
4. Add chili powder, sweet potatoes, paprika, cumin, and cayenne pepper.
5. Stir cook for 1 minute then add maple syrup, tomatoes, beans, broth, and bourbon.
6. Seal the Instant Pot lid and turn the pressure valve to sealing position.
7. Select Soup mode for 15 minutes at high pressure
8. Once done, release the pressure completely then remove the lid.
9. Serve the black beans mixture in warmed tortillas, green onions, and cilantro.
10. Serve warm.

Nutrition Calories per serving: 475 Carbohydrate: 17.6g Protein: 3.7g Fat: 8.2g Sugar: 1.1g Sodium: 158mg

Smoky Pecan Brussels Sprouts

Serves: 2
Prep Time: 15 mins
Ingredients

- 2 cups small baby brussels sprouts
- 1/4 cup water
- 1/2 teaspoon liquid smoke
- 1/4 cup chopped pecans
- 2 tablespoons maple syrup
- salt - to taste

Directions
1. Add water, liquid smoke, and Brussels sprouts to the insert of the Instant Pot.
2. Seal the Instant Pot lid and turn the pressure valve to sealing position.
3. Select Manual mode for 2 minutes at high pressure
4. Once done, release the pressure completely then remove the lid.
5. Switch the Instant pot to sauté mode.
6. Add pecans, salt, and maple syrup.
7. Sauté until the liquid is reduced.
8. Serve warm.

Nutrition Calories per serving: 336 Carbohydrate: 20.6g Protein: 16.4g Fat: 3.8g Sugar: 4.1g Sodium: 661mg

Thai Butternut Squash Curry

Serves: 4
Prep Time: 20 mins
Ingredients
- 1/3 cup Thai red curry paste
- 2 cans (14 ounces) coconut milk
- 1-2 cups low sodium veggie broth
- 1 tablespoon fish sauce
- 1 tablespoon creamy peanut butter
- 4 cups cubed the butternut squash
- 1 stick cinnamon
- 1-inch fresh ginger, grated
- juice from 1 lime
- 2 cups shredded kale
- 1-pound wide egg noodles, boiled and drained
- 1/4 cup fresh cilantro, schopped
- 1 pomegranate, arils for serving

Directions
1. Add coconut milk, fish sauce, 1 cup broth, curry paste and peanut butter to the insert of the Instant Pot.
2. Mix well and add ginger, cinnamon, lime juice, and butternut squash.
3. Adjust seasoning with salt and pepper.
4. Seal the Instant Pot lid and turn the pressure valve to sealing position.
5. Select Manual mode for 8 minutes at high pressure
6. Once done, release the pressure completely then remove the lid.
7. Switch the Instant pot to sauté mode.
8. Add kale and cilantro, stir cook for 5 minutes.
9. Toss in cooked noodles and mix gently.
10. Garnish with cilantro and pomegranate arils.
11. Enjoy.

Nutrition Calories per serving: 166 Carbohydrate: 14.5g Protein: 3.9g Fat: 11.4g Sugar: 6.1g Sodium: 149mg

Spiced Quinoa and Cauliflower Rice Bowls

Serves: 2
Prep Time: 40 mins
Ingredients

- 1 tablespoon olive oil
- 1 large onion, chopped
- 1 cup uncooked quinoa, rinsed
- 2 garlic cloves, minced
- 1-inch fresh ginger, grated
- 1 teaspoon ground turmeric
- 1 teaspoon ground cumin
- 1 teaspoon ground coriander
- 2 cups vegetable broth, divided
- 12 oz firm tofu, cut into ½ inch cubes
- 2 bell peppers, chopped
- 1 lb. (4 cups) cauliflower rice
- ½ cup fresh cilantro leaves
- ¼ cup toasted sliced almonds
- 2-4 tablespoons lemon juice
- salt and pepper, to taste

Directions

1. Preheat oil in the insert of the Instant Pot on sauté mode.
2. Add onions and sauté for 3 minutes.
3. Stir in ginger, garlic, and quinoa.
4. Cook for 2 minutes then add spices, salt, and pepper.
5. Stir cook for 30 seconds then add 2 tablespoons broth to deglaze the pot.
6. Add bell pepper, remaining broth and tofu.
7. Seal the Instant Pot lid and turn the pressure valve to sealing position.
8. Select Manual mode for 1 minute at high pressure
9. Once done, release the pressure completely then remove the lid.
10. Add cauliflower rice and place the Instant Pot lid to cook the rice in an existing heat.
11. Stir in cilantro, lemon juice, and almond slices.
12. Enjoy.

Nutrition Calories per serving: 200 Carbohydrate: 38.2g Protein: 5.9g Fat: 3.1g Sugar: 3.3g Sodium: 893mg

Portobello Pot Roast

Serves: 4
Prep Time: 20 mins
Ingredients:
- 1.25 pounds Yukon gold potatoes, diced
- 1-pound baby belle mushrooms
- 2 large carrots, peeled and diced
- 2 cups frozen pearl onions
- 4 cloves garlic, peeled and minced
- 3 sprigs fresh thyme
- 3 cups vegetable stock, divided
- 1/2 cup dry red
- 3 tablespoons tomato paste
- 2 tablespoons Worcestershire
- 2 tablespoons cornstarch
- kosher salt and black pepper
- Chopped fresh parsley

Directions

1. Toss potatoes, carrots, mushrooms, garlic, onion, thyme, wine, Worcestershire sauce and 2.5 cups stock in the insert of the Instant Pot.
2. Seal the Instant Pot lid and turn the pressure valve to sealing position.
3. Select Manual mode for 20 minutes at high pressure
4. Once done, release the pressure completely then remove the lid.
5. Mix a ½ cup of the remaining stock with corn-starch and pour this mixture into the pot.
6. Switch the Instant pot to sauté mode.
7. Cook for 3 minutes until it thickens.
8. Garnish with parsley.
9. Enjoy.

Nutrition Calories per serving: 422 Carbohydrate: 72g Protein: 14.5g Fat: 5.5g Sugar: 5.5g Sodium: 296g

Indian Spinach and Tofu

Serves: 4
Prep Time: 20 mins
Ingredients

- 1-pound extra-firm tofu
- 5 tablespoons vegetable oil, divided
- 1 medium yellow onion, chopped
- 1-inch (1/2 ounce) piece ginger, smashed
- 3 cloves garlic, minced
- 1 (15.5-oz) can diced tomatoes and their liquid
- 1/4 cup water
- 1/2 teaspoon ground black pepper
- 1/4 teaspoon cayenne pepper
- 1 teaspoon salt
- 16-ounce bag frozen chopped spinach
- 2 teaspoons garam masala
- 1/4 cup coconut milk

Directions

1. Squeeze the liquid out of the tofu and pat it dry.
2. Slice and dice the tofu. Keep it aside.
3. Preheat 2 tablespoons oil in the insert of the Instant Pot on sauté mode.
4. Add onion and sauté for 10 minutes until brown.
5. Meanwhile, heat a tablespoon of cooking oil in a pan and sear the tofu for 3 minutes per side.
6. Stir in ginger and garlic to the pot and sauté for 2 minutes.
7. Stir in seared tofu, water, black pepper, tomatoes, salt, and cayenne pepper.
8. Mix gently then add spinach.
9. Seal the Instant Pot lid and turn the pressure valve to sealing position.
10. Select Manual mode for 5 minutes at high pressure
11. Once done, release the pressure completely then remove the lid.
12. Add coconut milk and garam masala.
13. Mix well and serve warm.

Nutrition Calories per serving: 269 Carbohydrate: 51.7g Protein: 13g Fat: 2g Sugar: 18.2g Sodium: 420mg

Pumpkin Walnut Chili

Serves: 4
Prep Time: 50 mins
Ingredients

Pumpkin Chili

- 1 28-ounce can fire-roasted tomatoes
- ½ onion, minced
- 3 cloves garlic, minced
- 2 poblano peppers, chopped
- 2–3 chipotle peppers, chopped
- 2 cups walnuts, chopped
- 1 cup red lentils
- 1 cup bulgur
- 2 tablespoons chili powder
- 1 tablespoon smoked paprika
- 1 tablespoon salt
- 6 cups water or broth
- 1 cup pumpkin puree
- 2 or 3 14-ounce cans black beans, rinsed and drained

Directions

1. Add all the ingredients for the chili to the insert of the Instant Pot.
2. Seal the Instant Pot lid and turn the pressure valve to sealing position.

3. Select Soup mode for 30 minutes at high pressure
4. Once done, release the pressure completely then remove the lid.
5. Add black beans, pumpkin, to the pot.
6. Mix well and adjust the seasoning with salt and pepper.
7. Garnish as desired.
8. Serve warm.

Nutrition Calories per serving: 146 Carbohydrate: 32.2g Protein: 3.4g Fat: 2.6g Sugar: 0.5g Sodium: 93mg

Pork and Beef Recipes

Pork Carnitas

Serves: 4
Prep Time: 35 mins
Ingredients
- 1 tablespoon ghee
- 1 pound bone-in pork shoulder
- ½ teaspoon garlic powder
- Salt and black pepper, to taste
- 1 orange, juiced

Directions
1. Season the pork with garlic powder, salt and black pepper.
2. Put the seasoned pork, ghee and orange in the pressure cooker.
3. Cook for about 25 minutes on HIGH pressure.
4. Release the pressure naturally and dish out to serve.

Nutrition
Calories: 284 Carbs: 6.7g Fats: 19.4g Proteins: 19.7g Sodium: 274mg Sugar: 5.4g

Easy Beef Briskets

Serves: 6
Prep Time: 45 mins
Ingredients
- 1 tablespoon butter
- 2 pounds beef brisket
- 2 garlic cloves, minced
- Salt and black pepper, to taste
- 1 small onion, sliced

Directions
1. Heat butter in a large wok and add onions and garlic.
2. Sauté for about 3 minutes and add beef briskets, salt and black pepper.
3. Cover the lid and cook for about 30 minutes on medium-low heat.
4. Dish out the brisket and cut into desired slices on a cutting board to serve.

Nutrition
Calories: 304 Carbs: 1.4g Fats: 11.4g Proteins: 46.1g Sodium: 114mg Sugar: 0.5g

Bacon Swiss Pork Chops

Serves: 8
Prep Time: 55 mins

Ingredients

- 12 bacon strips, cut in half
- 8 pork chops, bone-in
- 2 tablespoons butter
- Salt and black pepper, to taste
- 1 cup Swiss cheese, shredded

Directions

1. Season the pork chops with salt and black pepper.
2. Put the butter and seasoned pork chops in a wok.
3. Cook for about 3 minutes on each side and add bacon.
4. Cook, covered for about 15 minutes on medium-low heat and add cheese.
5. Cover the lid again and cook for about 5 minutes until the cheese is melted.
6. Stir well and dish out to serve.

Nutrition

Calories: 483 Carbs: 0.7g Fats: 40g Proteins: 27.7g Sodium: 552mg Sugar: 0.2g

Mozzarella-stuffed Meatballs

Serves: 4
Prep Time: 25 mins
Ingredients

- 1 tablespoon dried basil
- 25 oz. ground beef
- Salt and black pepper, to taste
- Butter, for frying
- 4 oz. mozzarella cheese, cubed

Directions

1. Mix together beef, basil, salt and black pepper in a large bowl and knead well with a little cold water.
2. Make flat patties out of this mixture and place a cheese cube inside each patty.
3. Cover the patty around the cheese cube and roll into a ball.
4. Heat butter in a frying pan on medium heat and drop the patties into it.
5. Cook until the patties are golden brown and dish out to serve.

Nutrition

Calories: 435 Carbs: 1g Fats: 18.9g Proteins: 61.8g Sodium: 307mg Sugar: 0g

Jamaican Pork Roast

Serves: 4
Prep Time: 2 hours
Ingredients

- 1 tablespoon butter
- 1 pound pork shoulder
- ¼ cup beef broth
- Salt and black pepper, to taste
- ¼ cup Jamaican Jerk spice blend

Directions

1. Preheat the oven to 360 degrees F and lightly grease a baking dish.
2. Keep the pork soaked in the beef broth for about 1 hour.
3. Brush the pork with the melted butter and sprinkle with Jamaican Jerk spice blend, salt and black pepper.
4. Place on the baking dish and transfer in the oven.
5. Bake for about 1 hour and dish out to serve.

Nutrition
Calories: 359 Carbs: 0.1g Fats: 27.2g Proteins: 26.7g Sodium: 145mg Sugar: 0g

Ground Beef and Green Beans

Serves: 4
Prep Time: 30 mins
Ingredients
- 9 oz. fresh green beans, trimmed
- 10 oz. ground beef
- 3½ oz. butter
- 1/3 cup crème fraiche
- Salt and black pepper, to taste

Directions
1. Heat 2 tablespoons of butter in a large pan and add ground beef.
2. Cook until brown and sprinkle with salt and black pepper.
3. Reduce the heat and add the remaining butter, green beans, salt and black pepper.
4. Cook for about 5 minutes, stirring occasionally, and top with crème fraiche to serve.

Nutrition
Calories: 356 Carbs: 5.5g Fats: 26.9g Proteins: 23.5g Sodium: 202mg Sugar: 0.9g

Citrus Pork

Serves: 8
Prep Time: 45 mins
Ingredients
- 2 tablespoons butter
- 2 pounds pork shoulder roast, boneless
- 1 tablespoon lemon juice
- Salt and black pepper, to taste
- 1 tablespoon lemon zest, freshly grated

Directions
1. Preheat the oven to 380 degrees F and lightly grease a baking dish.
2. Mix together butter, lemon juice, lemon zest, salt and black pepper in a bowl.
3. Scrub the pork with this mixture and place on the baking dish.
4. Transfer in the oven and bake for about 30 minutes.
5. Dish out to serve hot.

Nutrition
Calories: 317 Carbs: 0.2g Fats: 26g Proteins: 19.1g Sodium: 96mg Sugar: 0.1g

Low Carb Beef Medallions

Serves: 2
Prep Time: 35 mins
Ingredients
- 3 medium shallots, finely chopped
- 1 pound beef tenderloin, sliced into ½ inch pieces
- ¼ cup olive oil
- Salt and black pepper, to taste

Directions
1. Season the beef pieces with salt and black pepper.
2. Heat olive oil in a skillet and add shallots and beef.
3. Cook for about 20 minutes on medium-low heat until cooked.

4. Dish out and serve hot.

Nutrition
Calories: 519 Carbs: 7g Fats: 36g Proteins: 46g Sodium: 117mg Sugar: 1.5g

Paprika Mushroom Pork

Serves: 8
Prep Time: 35 mins
Ingredients
- 2 tablespoons butter
- 2 pounds pork loin
- ¾ cup sour cream
- Salt and black pepper, to taste
- 1 cup white mushrooms

Directions
1. Season the pork with salt and black pepper.
2. Heat butter in a wok and add pork.
3. Sauté for about 3 minutes and add sour cream and mushrooms.
4. Cover the lid and cook for about 15 minutes.
5. Dish out and serve hot.

Nutrition
Calories: 348 Carbs: 1.2g Fats: 23.2g Proteins: 32g Sodium: 103mg Sugar: 0.2g

Beef Taco Casserole

Serves: 6
Prep Time: 45 mins
Ingredients
- 2 tablespoons taco seasoning
- 2 pounds ground beef
- 1 cup salsa
- 8 oz cheddar cheese, shredded
- 16 oz cottage cheese

Directions
1. Preheat the oven to 400 degrees F and grease a large casserole dish.
2. Combine beef and taco seasoning in a bowl and transfer to the casserole dish.
3. Place into the oven and bake for about 20 minutes.
4. Remove from the oven and break up the beef into small pieces.
5. Mix together the salsa, cottage cheese and cheddar cheese in a bowl.
6. Top the casserole dish with the salsa mixture and return to the oven.
7. Bake for about 20 more minutes and dish out to serve hot.

Nutrition
Calories: 522 Carbs: 6.6g Fats: 24g Proteins: 66.8g Sodium: 921mg Sugar: 1.8g

Bacon Garlic Pork Loin

Serves: 6
Prep Time: 25 mins
Ingredients
- ¼ cup olive oil
- 2 pounds pork loin
- 6 bacon slices, thickly cut
- Salt and black pepper, to taste
- 6 garlic cloves, minced

Directions

1. Scrub the pork loin with the minced garlic, salt and black pepper.
2. Wrap the pork with the bacon slices and fasten with a toothpick.
3. Heat olive oil in a skillet and add bacon wrapped pork.
4. Cook for about 15 minutes, flipping occasionally.
5. Dish out and serve immediately

Nutrition

Calories: 545 Carbs: 1.3g Fats: 37.4g Proteins: 48.5g Sodium: 533mg Sugar: 0g

Lime Chili Beef Briskets

Serves: 4
Prep Time: 1 hour 15 mins
Ingredients

- 4 green chilies, chopped
- 1 pound beef briskets
- 1 tablespoon lime juice
- Salt, to taste
- 1 cup homemade chicken broth

Directions

1. Season the beef briskets with lime juice and salt.
2. Transfer the seasoned beef briskets in the slow cooker along with green chilies and chicken broth.
3. Set the slow cooker on LOW and cook for about 8 hours.
4. Dish out and serve hot.

Nutrition

Calories: 222 Carbs: 0.8g Fats: 7.4g Proteins: 35.7g Sodium: 305mg Sugar: 0.4g

Pesto Parmesan Pork Chops

Serves: 6
Prep Time: 7 hours 40 mins
Ingredients

- 1 cup Parmesan cheese, shredded
- ½ cup parsley, chopped
- 6 pork chops, boneless
- 6 tablespoons pesto sauce
- Salt and black pepper, to taste

Directions

1. Season the pork chops with parsley, salt and black pepper.
2. Drizzle with pesto sauce and place in the slow cooker.
3. Cover the lid and cook on LOW for about 7 hours.
4. Open the lid and top with parsley and Parmesan cheese.
5. Cook for about 30 minutes and dish out to serve hot.

Nutrition

Calories: 386 Carbs: 2g Fats: 30.5g Proteins: 25.7g Sodium: 329mg Sugar: 1g

Beef Fajitas

Serves: 5
Prep Time: 45 mins
Ingredients

- 2 bell peppers, sliced
- 2 tablespoons fajita seasoning
- 1½ pounds beef, sliced
- 1 onion, sliced
- 2 tablespoons butter

Directions
1. Heat butter in the skillet and add onions and bell peppers.
2. Sauté for about 3 minutes and add beef and fajita seasoning.
3. Cover the lid and cook on medium-low heat for about 30 minutes.
4. Dish out and serve hot.

Nutrition
Calories: 330 Carbs: 8.2g Fats: 13.2g Proteins: 42.1g Sodium: 334mg Sugar: 3.3g

Mustard Pork Chops

Serves: 4
Prep Time: 1 hour
Ingredients
- 2 tablespoons butter
- 4 pork chops
- 2 tablespoons Dijon mustard
- Salt and black pepper, to taste
- 1 tablespoon fresh rosemary, coarsely chopped

Directions
1. Preheat the oven to 360 degrees F and lightly grease a baking dish.
2. Marinate the pork chops with rosemary, Dijon mustard, salt and black pepper.
3. Drizzle with butter and place on the baking dish.
4. Bake for about 45 minutes and dish out to serve warm.

Nutrition
Calories: 315 Carbs: 1g Fats: 26.1g Proteins: 18.4g Sodium: 186mg Sugar: 0.1g

Ground Beef and Brussels Sprouts

Serves: 2
Prep Time: 1 hour 40 mins
Ingredients
- 5 oz. ground beef
- 4½ oz. Brussels sprouts
- ¼ cup mayonnaise
- 1½ oz. butter
- Salt and black pepper, to taste

Directions
1. Heat 3 tablespoons of butter in a large pan on medium heat and stir in beef.
2. Cook until brown in color and season with salt and black pepper.
3. Decrease the heat and add remaining butter, Brussels sprouts, salt and black pepper.
4. Cook for about 8 minutes, stirring occasionally and top with mayonnaise to serve.

Nutrition
Calories: 356 Carbs: 5.5g Fats: 26.9g Proteins: 23.5g Sodium: 202mg Sugar: 0.9g

Pork with Carrots

Serves: 8

Prep Time: 7 hours 20 mins
Ingredients
- 1 large onion, thinly sliced
- 2 pounds pork shoulder roast, boneless
- 4 medium carrots, peeled and sliced lengthwise
- Salt and black pepper, to taste
- 1 teaspoon dried oregano, crushed

Directions
1. Sprinkle the pork shoulder with salt, black pepper and dried oregano.
2. Transfer the seasoned pork in a bowl and keep aside for about 3 hours.
3. Place onions and carrots in a slow cooker and add the pork.
4. Cover the lid and set the slow cooker on LOW.
5. Cook for about 7 hours and dish out to serve hot.

Nutrition
Calories: 312 Carbs: 4.9g Fats: 23.1g Proteins: 19.6g Sodium: 97mg Sugar: 2.3g

Garlic Creamy Beef Steak

Serves: 6
Prep Time: 45 mins
Ingredients
- 4 garlic cloves, minced
- ½ cup butter
- 2 pounds beef top sirloin steaks
- 1½ cup cream
- Salt and freshly ground black pepper, to taste

Directions
1) Rub the beef top sirloin steaks with garlic, salt and black pepper.
2) Marinate the beef with cream and butter and keep aside.
3) Preheat the grill and transfer the steaks on it.
4) Grill for about 15 minutes on each side and serve hot.

Nutrition
Calories: 353 Carbs: 3.9g Fats: 24.1g Proteins: 31.8g Sodium: 298mg Sugar: 1.2g

Ketogenic Beef Sirloin Steak

Serves: 3
Prep Time: 35 mins
Ingredients
- ½ teaspoon garlic powder
- 3 tablespoons butter
- 1 pound beef top sirloin steaks
- 1 garlic clove, minced
- Salt and freshly ground black pepper, to taste

Directions
1) Put butter and beef sirloin steaks in a large grill pan.
2) Cook for about 2 minutes on each side to brown the steaks.
3) Add garlic clove, garlic powder, salt, and black pepper and cook for about 15 minutes on each side on medium-high heat.
4) Transfer the steaks in a serving platter and serve hot.

Nutrition
Calories: 246 Carbs: 2g Fats: 13.1g Proteins: 31.3g Sodium: 224mg Sugar: 0.1g

Beef Fajitas

Serves: 3
Prep Time: 8 hours 20 mins
Ingredients
- 1 bell pepper, sliced
- 1 tablespoon butter
- 1 pound beef, sliced
- 1 onion, sliced
- 1 tablespoon fajita seasoning

Directions
1) Place the butter in the bottom of the slow cooker and add onions, fajita seasoning, bell pepper, and beef.
2) Set the slow cooker on LOW and cook for about 8 hours.
3) Dish out the delicious beef fajitas and serve hot.

Nutrition
Calories: 353 Carbs: 8.5g Fats: 13.4g Proteins: 46.7g Sodium: 304mg Sugar: 3.6g

Mexican Taco Casserole

Serves: 3
Prep Time: 40 mins
Ingredients
- ½ cup cottage cheese
- ½ cup cheddar cheese, shredded
- 1 pound ground beef
- 1 tablespoon taco seasoning
- ½ cup salsa

Directions
1) Mix together the ground beef and taco seasoning in a bowl.
2) Stir in the cottage cheese, cheddar cheese and salsa.
3) Preheat the oven to 400 degrees F and grease a baking dish.
4) Transfer the ground beef mixture in the baking dish and top with cheese mixture.
5) Bake for about 30 minutes and serve warm.

Nutrition
Calories: 409 Carbs: 5.7g Fats: 16.5g Proteins: 56.4g Sodium: 769mg Sugar: 1.9g

Beef Roast

Serves: 6
Prep Time: 1 hour
Ingredients
- 1 cup onion soup
- 2 pounds beef roast
- 1 cups beef broth
- Salt and freshly ground black pepper, to taste

Directions
1) Put the beef roast in the pressure cooker and then add beef broth, onion soup, salt, and black pepper.
2) Secure the lid and cook at high pressure for about 50 minutes.
3) Release the pressure naturally and dish onto a serving platter.

Nutrition
Calories: 349 Carbs: 2.9g Fats: 18.8g Proteins: 39.9g Sodium: 480mg Sugar: 1.2g

Keto Minced Meat

Serves: 4
Prep Time: 30 mins
Ingredients

- 1 pound ground lamb meat
- 2 tablespoons butter
- 1 cup onions, chopped
- ½ teaspoon turmeric powder
- 1 teaspoon salt
- ½ teaspoon cayenne pepper
- 1 tablespoon garlic, minced
- 1 tablespoon ginger, minced
- ½ teaspoon ground coriander
- ½ teaspoon cumin powder

Directions

1) Put the butter, garlic, ginger, and onions in a pot and sauté for about 3 minutes.
2) Add ground meat and all the spices. Next, lock the lid.
3) Cook for about 20 minutes on medium-high heat and present in a large serving bowl.

Nutrition
Calories: 304 Carbs: 4.8g Fats: 21.1g Proteins: 21.8g Sodium: 705mg Sugar: 1.3g

Beef Curry

Serves: 9
Prep Time: 2 hours
Ingredients

- 2½ pounds chuck roast, cubed into 1-inch size
- ½ cup beef broth
- Salt and black pepper, to taste
- 3 tablespoons Thai red curry paste
- 2 tablespoons butter
- 2½ cups coconut milk
- ¼ cup fresh cilantro, chopped

Directions

1) Put butter and curry paste in a large pan on low heat.
2) Sauté for about 3 minutes and stir in coconut milk and beef broth.
3) Simmer for about 5 minutes and add beef.
4) Cook for about 5 minutes on high heat until boiled.
5) Lower the heat and simmer, covered for about 1 hour while occasionally stirring.
6) Transfer the beef into a bowl with a slotted spoon and keep the pan aside.
7) Remove the fats from top of the curry and return the pan to medium heat.
8) Stir in the beef and simmer for about 30 minutes on low heat.
9) Garnish with cilantro and season with salt to serve.

Nutrition
Calories: 470 Carbs: 4.8g Fats: 30.5g Proteins: 43.5g Sodium: 414mg Sugar: 2.3g

Grilled Beef Steak

Serves: 6
Prep Time: 25 mins
Ingredients

- 2 teaspoons dried rosemary, crushed
- 2 pounds beef top sirloin steaks
- ¼ cup unsalted butter
- 3 garlic cloves, minced
- Salt and black pepper, to taste

Directions

1) Preheat the grill and grease the grill grate.

2) Rub the steaks generously with rosemary, salt, and black pepper.
3) Grill the steaks for about 5 minutes on each side.
4) Melt butter in a pan on medium-low heat and add garlic.
5) Transfer the steaks in serving plates and coat the steaks evenly with melted butter.
6) Keep aside for about 5 minutes and serve hot.

Nutrition
Calories: 352 Carbs: 0.8g Fats: 17.2g Proteins: 46.1g Sodium: 155mg Sugar: 0g

2-Meat Chili

Serves: 8
Prep Time: 45 mins
Ingredients

- 1 pound grass-fed ground beef
- ½ of small yellow onion, chopped
- 2 garlic cloves, minced
- 1 tablespoon ground cumin
- Salt and freshly ground black pepper, to taste
- ½ cup cheddar cheese, shredded
- 1 tablespoon olive oil
- 1 pound ground pork
- 3 medium tomatillos, chopped
- 2 jalapeño peppers, chopped
- 1 (6-ounce) can sugar-free tomato sauce
- 1 tablespoon chili powder
- ¼ cup water

Directions
1) Heat the oil in a pressure cooker and add beef and pork.
2) Cook for about 5 minutes on medium heat and add the remaining ingredients, except cheese.
3) Lock the lid and cook for about 30 minutes at high pressure.
4) Release the pressure naturally and top with cheddar cheese.

Nutrition
Calories: 259 Carbs: 5.4g Fats: 12.5g Proteins: 29.9g Sodium: 253mg Sugar: 1.2g

Keto Low Carb Meat Balls

Serves: 6
Prep Time: 35 mins
Ingredients

- 2 tablespoons Parmesan cheese, grated
- 1 egg
- Salt and ground black pepper to taste
- 1 (14 ounce) can tomato sauce
- 2 pounds ground beef
- 1 teaspoon dried oregano
- 2 tablespoons olive oil
- 1 tablespoon flaxseed meal
- ½ cup water

Directions
1) Mix ground beef, flaxseed, oregano, Parmesan cheese, egg, salt, and black pepper in a bowl until well mixed.
2) Roll the mixture into small balls and keep aside.
3) Heat oil in a non-stick skillet and add meatballs in batches until brown in color.
4) Add water and cook for about 8 minutes on medium-low heat.
5) Dish in a bowl and serve hot.
Nutrition
Calories: 384 Carbs: 4.4g Fats: 17.3g Proteins: 50.9g Sodium: 543mg Sugar: 2.9g

Jamaican Jerk Pork Roast

Serves: 3
Prep Time: 35 mins
Ingredients

- 1 pound pork shoulder
- 1 tablespoon butter
- 1/8 cup Jamaican jerk spice blend
- 1/8 cup beef broth

Directions

1) Season the pork with Jamaican jerk spice blend.
2) Put the butter and seasoned pork in the pot and cook for about 5 minutes.
3) Add beef broth and lock the lid.
4) Cook for about 20 minutes on low heat and dish out in a serving platter.

Nutrition

Calories: 477 Carbs: 0g Fats: 36.2g Proteins: 35.4g Sodium: 162mg Sugar: 0g

Bacon Swiss Pork Chops

Serves: 4
Prep Time: 25 mins
Ingredients

- 4 pork chops, bone-in
- ½ cup Swiss cheese, shredded
- 6 bacon strips, cut in half
- 1 tablespoon butter
- Salt and freshly ground black pepper, to taste

Directions

1) Season the pork chops with salt and black pepper.
2) Put butter and seasoned pork chops in the skillet and cook for about 6 minutes.
3) Stir in bacon strips and cook for about 8 minutes.
4) Top with Swiss cheese and cook on low heat for about 5 minutes.
5) Remove from heat and dish on a platter.

Nutrition

Calories: 483 Carbs: 0.7g Fats: 40g Proteins: 27.7g Sodium: 552mg Sugar: 0.2g

Pork Carnitas

Serves: 3
Prep Time: 25 mins
Ingredients

- 1 orange, juiced
- 1 tablespoon butter
- 1 pound pork shoulder, bone-in
- ½ teaspoon garlic powder
- Salt and freshly ground black pepper, to taste

Directions

1) Season the pork with salt and black pepper.
2) Put butter and garlic powder in the pot and sauté for about 1 minute.
3) Add seasoned pork and sauté for about 3 minutes.
4) Pour orange juice and secure the lid.
5) Cook for about 15 minutes on medium-high heat and dish out.
6) Shred with the help of a fork and immediately serve.

Nutrition

Calories: 506 Carbs: 7.6g Fats: 36.3g Proteins: 35.9g Sodium: 130mg Sugar: 5.8g

Mustard Pork Chops

Serves: 4
Prep Time: 40 mins
Ingredients

- 2 tablespoons Dijon mustard
- 2 tablespoons butter
- 4 pork chops
- 1 tablespoon fresh rosemary, coarsely chopped
- Salt and freshly ground black pepper, to taste

Directions

1) Marinate the pork chops with fresh rosemary, Dijon mustard, salt, and black pepper for about 3 hours.
2) Put the butter and marinated pork chops in a non-stick skillet and cover the lid.
3) Cook for about 30 minutes on medium-low heat and dish to serve hot.

Nutrition
Calories: 315 Carbs: 1g Fats: 26.1g Proteins: 18.4g Sodium: 186mg Sugar: 0.1g

Zesty Pork Chops

Serves: 4
Prep Time: 35 mins
Ingredients

- 3 tablespoons lemon juice
- 4 tablespoons butter
- 4 pork chops, bone-in
- 1 cup picante sauce
- 2 tablespoons low-carb flour mix

Directions

1) Mix picante sauce and orange in a bowl and keep aside.
2) Coat the chops with flour and keep aside.
3) Put the oil and pork chops in the pressure cooker.
4) Close the lid and cook for about 15 minutes at high pressure.
5) Naturally release the pressure for 10 minutes and dish to serve hot.

Nutrition
Calories: 284 Carbs: 1g Fats: 19.5g Proteins: 24.8g Sodium: 150mg Sugar: 0.3g

Greek Pork Gyros

Serves: 4
Prep Time: 40 mins
Ingredients

- 1 pound pork meat, ground
- 4 garlic cloves
- 1 teaspoon rosemary
- ¾ teaspoons salt
- ¼ teaspoon black pepper
- ½ small onion, chopped
- 1 teaspoon dried oregano
- 1 teaspoon ground marjoram
- ¾ cup water

Directions

1) Put onions, ground lamb meat, garlic, marjoram, rosemary, salt, and black pepper in a food processor and process until well combined.
2) Press Meat mixture into the Loaf Pan until very tight and compact.
3) Cover tightly with tin foil and poke some holes in the foil.

4) Preheat the oven to 390 degrees F and transfer the loaf pan in the oven.
5) Bake for about 25 minutes and dish to serve hot.

Nutrition
Calories: 242 Carbs: 2.4g Fats: 15.2g Proteins: 21.4g Sodium: 521mg Sugar: 0.4g

Crispy Parmesan Crusted Pork Chops

Serves: 4
Prep Time: 30 mins
Ingredients
- ½ teaspoon salt
- ½ teaspoon onion powder
- 4 thick pork chops, center cut boneless
- ¼ teaspoon pepper
- 1 teaspoon smoked paprika
- ¼ teaspoon chili powder
- 1 cup pork rind crumbs
- 2 large eggs
- 3 tablespoons parmesan cheese, grated

Directions
1) Preheat the Air fryer to 400 degrees F.
2) Season pork chops with salt and black pepper.
3) Mix together parmesan cheese, pork rind crumbs, and seasonings in a bowl.
4) Whisk the eggs in another bowl and dip each pork chop into the egg mixture first, and then in the crumb mixture.
5) Place pork chops in the air fryer basket and cook for about 20 minutes.
6) Dish out and serve with your favorite dip.

Nutrition
Calories: 271 Carbs: 1.2g Fats: 12.3g Proteins: 38.5g Sodium: 605mg Sugar: 0.4g

Roasted Pork

Serves: 12
Prep Time: 2 hours 25 mins
Ingredients
- 2 teaspoons garlic powder
- ½ teaspoon sea salt
- 4 pounds pork
- 3 teaspoons thyme, dried
- 1 tablespoon Chimichurri sauce, for serving

Directions
1) Preheat the oven at 360 degrees F and wrap a baking sheet with foil.
2) Season the lamb breast with garlic powder, dried thyme, and salt.
3) Arrange the lamb onto the baking sheet and bake for about 1 hour.
4) Increase the temperature of the oven to 440 degrees F and transfer the baking sheet inside the oven.
5) Cook for about 1 hour and dish out the lamb breast onto a serving plate.
6) Top with lemon wedges and chimichurri sauce before serving hot.

Nutrition
Calories: 286 Carbs: 0.6g Fats: 11.3g Proteins: 42.6g Sodium: 200mg Sugar: 0.1g

Fabulous Grilled Pork

Serves: 12

Prep Time: 27 mins
Ingredients
- 2 garlic cloves, minced
- 2 tablespoons paprika
- 2 teaspoons fresh lemon zest, grated finely
- 2 tablespoons red chili powder
- 2 tablespoons ground coffee
- 4 (1½-pound) grass-fed pork
- Salt and freshly ground black pepper, to taste

Directions
1) Preheat the grill and grease the grill grate.
2) Mix together all the ingredients, except steaks, in a bowl and marinate the steaks in this mixture for about 1 hour.
3) Grill the steaks for about 7 minutes on each side.
4) Remove from grill onto a cutting board and cut the steaks in desired slices.
5) Serve hot.

Nutrition
Calories: 457 Carbs: 1.6g Fats: 20.7g Proteins: 62.4g Sodium: 174mg Sugar: 0.2g

Dinner Pork Tenderloin

Serves: 6
Prep Time: 1 hour 10 mins
Ingredients
- 3 garlic cloves, minced
- Salt and freshly ground black pepper, to taste
- 1 (2-pound) grass-fed center-cut pork tenderloin roast
- 1 tablespoon fresh rosemary, minced and divided
- 1 tablespoon olive oil

Directions
1) Preheat the oven to 400 degrees F and grease a large shallow roasting pan.
2) Place beef into the roasting pan and mix with the garlic, rosemary, salt, and black pepper.
3) Drizzle with oil and roast for about 1 hour.
4) Remove from the oven and cut the tenderloin in desired slices to serve hot.

Nutrition
Calories: 343 Carbs: 0.9g Fats: 18g Proteins: 42g Sodium: 93mg Sugar: 0g

Roast and Potatoes

Serves: 6
Prep Time: 1hr 30 mins
Ingredients
- 3 pounds beef chuck roast
- 1 tablespoon oil
- 1 teaspoon salt
- 1 teaspoon onion powder
- 1 teaspoon garlic powder
- 1/2 teaspoon black pepper
- 1/2 teaspoon smoked paprika optional
- 1-pound baby red potatoes
- 4 large carrots, chopped into large chunks
- 1 large yellow onion, chopped
- 4 cups beef broth
- 2 tablespoons Worcestershire sauce
- 1/4 cup water
- 2 tablespoons corn starch

Directions
1. Select Sauté mode on you Instant Pot.
2. Season the roast with garlic powder, salt, pepper, smoked paprika, and onion powder.
3. Add a drizzle of oil to the Instant pot then place the roast in the pot.
4. Cook the chuck roast for 4 minutes per side until brown.
5. Add potatoes, carrots, onion, Worcestershire sauce, and beef broth.
6. Secure and seal the lid. Select the manual mode for 60 minutes at high pressure.
7. Once done, release the pressure completely then remove the lid.
8. Transfer the roast, onions, carrots, and potatoes to a platter.
9. Shred the roast using 2 forks into small chunks.
10. Switch the Instant pot to the Soup mode.
11. Mix corn-starch with water in a bowl then pour it into the pot.
12. Stir cook the mixture until it thickens.
13. Return the veggies and beef to the sauce.
14. Adjust seasoning with salt, pepper and garlic powder.
15. Garnish with thyme and parsley.
16. Enjoy.

Nutrition Calories per serving: 579 Carbohydrate: 14g Protein: 70.1g Fat: 25.5g Sugar: 5.3g Sodium: 314mg

Beef Bourguignon

Serves: 6
Prep Time: 60 mins
Ingredients:
- 6 slices bacon, chopped roughly
- 3 pounds chuck beef, cut into chunks
- 1 cup red cooking wine
- 2 cups beef broth
- 1/2 cup tomato sauce
- 1 beef bouillon cube, crushed
- 1 tablespoon oil
- 1/4 cup flour
- 2 large carrots, cut into 2-inch pieces
- 1 white onion, chopped
- 1 tablespoon minced garlic
- 2 tablespoons fresh thyme, chopped
- 1-pound baby potatoes
- 8 ounces fresh mushrooms, sliced
- 1-2 teaspoons salt or to taste
- 1/2 teaspoon pepper
- chopped parsley for garnish

Directions
1. Preheat oil in the Instant Pot on Sauté mode.
2. Add bacon and sear it for 4 minutes per side.
3. Transfer the crispy bacon to a plate lined with a paper towel.
4. Add beef to the instant pot and sear it for 4 minutes per side.
5. Pour in red wine and deglaze the pot and let it simmer for 5 minutes.
6. Stir in tomato sauce, beef broth and bouillon.
7. Add flour, carrots, bacon, onions, mushroom, potatoes, thyme, salt, pepper, and garlic.
8. Seal and secure the Instant Pot lid then select Manual mode for 45 minutes at high pressure.
9. Once done, release the pressure completely then remove the lid.
10. Switch the Instant pot to sauté mode.
11. Stir cook the sauce until it thickens.
12. Garnish with parsley.
13. Serve warm.

Nutrition Calories per serving: 797 Carbohydrate: 4.9g Protein: 62g Fat: 56.8g Sugar: 0.8g Sodium: 547mg

Beef and Broccoli

Serves: 2
Prep Time: 40 mins
Ingredients
- 1-pound boneless beef chuck roast cubed
- 1 cup beef broth
- 1/2 cup low-sodium soy sauce
- 1/3 cup dark brown sugar
- 1 tablespoon sesame oil
- 3 cloves garlic, minced
- 2-3 cups fresh broccoli florets, blanched
- 2 tablespoons cornstarch
- 3 tablespoons water

Directions
1. Add beef cubes to the insert of the Instant Pot.
2. Mix beef broth with soy sauce, sesame oil, garlic and brown sugar in a bowl.
3. Pour this sauce mixture over the beef.
4. Seal and secure the Instant Pot lid then select Manual mode for 24 minutes at high pressure.
5. Once done, release the pressure completely then remove the lid.
6. Mix corn-starch with water and pour this mixture into the pot.
7. Switch the pot to the Sauté mode and cook until the sauce thickens.
8. Add blanched broccoli to the beef and mix gently.
9. Serve warm.

Nutrition Calories per serving: 449 Carbohydrate: 16.3g Protein: 20.1g Fat: 33.3g Sugar: 10.7g Sodium:316mg

Korean Beef

Serves: 6
Prep Time: 50 mins
Ingredients
- 1/2 cup reduced-sodium soy sauce
- 1/3 cup brown sugar packed
- 1/4 cup reduced-sodium beef broth
- 5 cloves garlic minced
- 2 tablespoons sesame oil
- 2 tablespoons rice vinegar
- 2 tablespoons freshly grated ginger
- 2-4 tablespoons gochujang sauce
- 1/2 teaspoon onion powder
- 1/2 teaspoon pepper
- 3-4-pound boneless beef chuck roast cut into 1-inch cubes

Directions
1. Place the beef cubes in the insert of the Instant Pot.
2. Mix rest of the ingredients in a bowl.
3. Pour this mixture over the beef cubes.
4. Seal the Instant Pot lid and turn the pressure valve to sealing position.
5. Select Meat mode for 40 minutes at high pressure
6. Once done, release the pressure completely then remove the lid.
7. Serve warm.

Nutrition Calories per serving: 325 Carbohydrate: 22.5g Protein: 24.4g Fat: 16.2g Sugar: 10.3g Sodium: 727mg

Mongolian Beef

Serves: 2
Prep Time: 40 mins
Ingredients:

- 1.5 pounds flank steak, sliced
- 1 tablespoon cornstarch
- 1 tablespoon extra olive oil
- 1/2 cup brown sugar 0
- 10 cloves garlic, minced
- 1 tablespoon fresh ginger, minced
- 1/2 cup lite soy sauce

garnish:

- 1/4 cup green onions, chopped

- 1 cup of water
- 1 tablespoon rice wine
- 1 teaspoon red pepper flakes
- cornstarch slurry:
- 2 tablespoons cornstarch
- 1/2 cup water

- 1 teaspoon sesame seeds

Directions

1. Preheat oil in the insert of the Instant Pot on Sauté mode.
2. Mix beef slices with 1 tablespoon corn-starch to coat well.
3. Sear the coated beef in the Instant pot for 3 minutes per side.
4. Pour in ½ cup water, ginger, garlic, water, red pepper flakes, rice wine, soy sauce, and brown sugar.
5. Mix well to combine all the ingredients well.
6. Seal the Instant Pot lid and turn the pressure valve to sealing position.
7. Select Manual mode for 8 minutes at high pressure
8. Once done, release the pressure completely then remove the lid.
9. Mix corn-starch with water and pour this mixture into the pot.
10. Switch the Instant pot to the Sauté mode.
11. Stir cook the beef until the sauce thickens.
12. Garnish with sesame seeds and green onions.
13. Devour.

Nutrition Calories per serving: 408 Carbohydrate: 13.4g Protein: 58.6g Fat: 15.3g Sugar: 3.5g Sodium: 304mg

Italian Beef

Serves: 6
Prep Time: 60 mins
Ingredients

- 3 1/2 pounds boneless beef chuck
- 4 tablespoons butter
- 1 large red onion, peeled and sliced
- 6 cloves garlic, peeled and minced
- 20 pepperoncini peppers
- 1/4 cup pepperoncini juices

- 1/2 cup Worcestershire sauce
- 1 cup beef broth
- 2 tablespoons brown sugar
- 1 tablespoon dried Italian seasoning
- 1/2 teaspoon crushed red pepper

Directions

1. Melt butter in the insert of the Instant Pot on Sauté mode.
2. Add garlic and onions, sauté for 5 minutes.
3. Place beef chunks in the Instant Pot and add Worcestershire sauce, pepper juice, broth, sugar, red pepper, Italian seasoning, and pepperoncini.
4. Seal the Instant Pot lid and turn the pressure valve to sealing position.
5. Select Manual mode for 50 minutes at high pressure
6. Once done, release the pressure completely then remove the lid.

7. Shred the beef using two forks and adjust seasoning with salt and pepper.
8. Garnish with provolone cheese.
9. Serve warm.

Nutrition Calories per serving: 356 Carbohydrate: 0.6g Protein: 57.5g Fat: 12.1g Sugar: 0.1g Sodium: 512mg

Beef Barbacoa

Serves: 4
Prep Time: 60 mins
Ingredients
- 2 tablespoons vegetable oil
- 2 lb. beef stew meat
- 1 cup beef broth
- 2 tablespoons canned chipotle chile in adobo, finely chopped
- 3 cloves garlic, finely chopped
- 1 package (1 oz) taco seasoning mix
- 1 teaspoon ground cumin
- 1 teaspoon ground coriander
- ¼ teaspoon salt
- 2 cups chopped red onions

Directions
1. Preheat oil in the insert of the Instant Pot on sauté mode.
2. Add beef and sear it for 4 minutes per side until brown.
3. Stir in chile, broth, taco seasoning, garlic, coriander, salt, and cumin.
4. Seal the Instant Pot lid and turn the pressure valve to sealing position.
5. Select Manual mode for 45 minutes at high pressure
6. Once done, release the pressure completely then remove the lid.
7. Shred the beef using 2 forks and cook the mixture on sauté mode until it is reduced slightly.
8. Serve warm.

Nutrition Calories per serving: 343 Carbohydrate: 4.8g Protein: 28.7g Fat: 22.5g Sugar: 1.3g Sodium: 676mg

Beef Burgundy

Serves: 2
Prep Time: 50 mins
Ingredients
- 1/2 pounds top sirloin cubed
- 1 teaspoon salt plus additional, to taste
- Fresh ground black pepper to taste
- 4 tablespoons vegetable oil divided
- 3 slices uncooked bacon chopped
- 1 cup diced white or yellow onion
- 4 carrots, peeled and chopped into 1" chunks
- 1 tablespoon minced garlic
- 2 tablespoons tomato paste
- 2 cups full-bodied red wine
- 2 1/2 cups low-sodium beef broth
- 1 tablespoon fresh thyme leaves
- 2 bay leaves
- 3 tablespoons softened butter
- 3 tablespoons all-purpose flour
- 9 ounces cremini mushrooms quartered or halved
- 2 tablespoons minced fresh Italian parsley optional

Directions
1. Preheat oil in the insert of the Instant Pot on sauté mode.
2. Add beef cubes with salt and pepper to the pot.
3. Sauté for 5 minutes then transfer to a plate.

4. Sauté bacon in the pot until crispy then transfer to a plate.
5. Now add carrots and onion to the pot. Sauté for 4 minutes.
6. Stir in salt, pepper, tomato paste, and garlic.
7. Sauté for 1 minute then add wine. Stir cook for 4 minutes.
8. Add beef broth, bay leaves, and thyme.
9. Seal the Instant Pot lid and turn the pressure valve to sealing position.
10. Select Manual mode for 15 minutes at high pressure
11. Once done, release the pressure completely then remove the lid.
12. Mix butter with flour in a small bowl.
13. Add butter-flour mixture to the beef.
14. Mix well then add mushrooms to the pot.
15. Switch the Instant pot to sauté mode.
16. Stir cook for 5 minutes.
17. Discard the bay leaves then add salt and pepper.
18. Serve warm.

Nutrition Calories per serving: 482 Carbohydrate: 8.3g Protein: 74.8g Fat: 14.7g Sugar: 2.6g Sodium: 466mg

Beef and Squash Stew

Serves: 2
Prep Time: 40 mins
Ingredients

- 1 lb. beef chuck, well trimmed, cut into 2-in. pieces
- 1 tablespoon all-purpose flour
- 1 tablespoon olive oil
- 1 large onion, chopped
- 4 cloves garlic, smashed
- 8 sprigs thyme, plus leaves for serving
- kosher salt and pepper
- 1 12-oz bottle beer
- 1/2 butternut squash, peeled and seeded, diced
- 3 medium carrots (about 12 oz), sliced
- 3 cups beef stock
- 1 cup pearled barley

Directions

1. Mix beef with flour to coat well and shake off the excess.
2. Preheat oil in the insert of the Instant Pot.
3. Add coated beef and sear it for 6 minutes from all the side.
4. Once browned, transfer the beef to a plate.
5. Add thyme, garlic, onion, sprigs, salt, and pepper to the Instant Pot.
6. Stir cook for 6 minutes then pours in the beer.
7. Add beef, carrots, stock, barley, and squash to the pot.
8. Seal the Instant Pot lid and turn the pressure valve to sealing position.
9. Select Manual mode for 16 minutes at high pressure
10. Once done, release the pressure completely then remove the lid.
11. Serve warm.

Nutrition Calories per serving: 664 Carbohydrate: 4.8g Protein: 56.9g Fat: 44.8g Sugar: 0.8g Sodium: 1061mg

Beef and Broccoli Ramen

Serves: 2
Prep Time: 30 mins
Ingredients

- 1 tablespoon sesame oil
- 1 package fast fry steak cut into 1-inch pieces
- 4 cloves garlic, minced
- 1 tablespoon fresh minced ginger
- 1 cup beef broth
- 1/4 cup low-sodium soy sauce
- 2 tablespoons oyster sauce
- 1 tablespoon chili sauce
- 3 packages ramen noodles
- 2 heads broccoli, steamed

Directions
1. Thoroughly mix steak with sesame oil, ginger, garlic, soy sauce, chili sauce, oyster sauce, noodles, and broth in a large bowl.
2. Add this mixture to the insert of the Instant Pot.
3. Seal the Instant Pot lid and turn the pressure valve to sealing position.
4. Select Manual mode for 15 minutes at high pressure
5. Once done, release the pressure completely then remove the lid.
6. Meanwhile, steam the broccoli in a steamer for 2 minutes then drain it.
7. Add broccoli to the beef mixture and mix gently.
8. Serve warm after 5 minutes.
9. Devour.

Nutrition Calories per serving: 649 Carbohydrate: 4.1g Protein: 23.9g Fat: 59g Sugar: 1.2g Sodium: 753mg

Coconut Pork

Serves: 6
Prep Time: 50 mins
Ingredients
- 1 tablespoon coconut oil
- 1/2 medium yellow onion, chopped
- 3 tablespoons freshly grated turmeric
- 2 tablespoons freshly grated ginger
- 3 cloves garlic, minced
- 1/2 teaspoon cinnamon
- 1/4 teaspoon cardamom
- Salt and pepper to taste
- 1 cup crushed canned tomatoes
- 1 can (15oz.) Light coconut milk
- 2.5 pounds boneless pork shoulder cut into 4 to 6 large pieces
- Fresh cilantro for garnish

Directions
1. Preheat coconut oil in the insert of your Instant pot on sauté mode.
2. Add onions and sauté for 5 minutes then stir in garlic, ginger, turmeric, cardamom, cinnamon, salt, and pepper.
3. Stir cook for 1 minute then add coconut milk and crush tomatoes.
4. Place pork in the cooking mixture.
5. Seal the Instant Pot lid and turn the pressure valve to sealing position.
6. Select Meat/ Stew mode for 30 minutes at high pressure
7. Once done, release the pressure completely then remove the lid.
8. Switch the Instant pot to sauté mode and shred the pork using two forks.
9. Cook the pork sauce until it thickens.
10. Garnish with cilantro.
11. Serve.

Nutrition Calories per serving: 380 Carbohydrate: 6.3g Protein: 48.1g Fat: 17g Sugar: 3.4g Sodium: 466mg

Pork Tenderloin with Gravy

Serves: 6
Prep Time: 50 mins
Ingredients

- 3-pound Smithfield prime pork tenderloin
- 1/2 teaspoon garlic powder
- 1/2 teaspoon kosher salt
- 1/4 teaspoon ground ginger
- 1/4 teaspoon dried thyme
- 1/4 teaspoon black pepper
- 1 tablespoon olive oil
- 2 cups chicken broth
- 2 tablespoons fresh lemon juice
- 1 tablespoon low sodium soy sauce
- 3 tablespoons cornstarch + 3 tablespoons cold water
- salt and pepper

Directions

1. Pat dry the tenderloin with paper towel then cut it into half.
2. Thoroughly mix salt, ginger, thyme, garlic powder, and pepper in a small bowl.
3. Rub this mixture liberally over the pork.
4. Preheat oil in the insert of the Instant Pot on sauté mode.
5. Cook one half of the pork at a time in the heated oil for 3 minutes per side.
6. Transfer the cooked pork to the cutting board.
7. Add broth to the pot and deglaze the insert.
8. Stir in soy sauce and lemon juice.
9. Place the trivet over broth mixture and arrange seared pork over it.
10. Seal the Instant Pot lid and turn the pressure valve to sealing position.
11. Select Manual mode for 6 minutes at high pressure
12. Once done, release the pressure completely then remove the lid.
13. Transfer the pork to the cutting board and slice it.
14. Switch the Instant pot to sauté mode.
15. Mix corn-starch with water and pour this slurry into the pot.
16. Cook the mixture until it thickens.
17. Add the sliced pork then serve.
18. Enjoy.

Nutrition Calories per serving: 381 Carbohydrate: 6.3g Protein: 39.1g Fat: 21.5g Sugar: 3.5g Sodium: 628mg

Sweet Balsamic Pork

Serves: 4
Prep Time: 40 mins
Ingredients

- 1 1.5-2 lb. pork tenderloin, cut into four pieces

Sauce

- 3 garlic cloves, chopped
- 1/4 cup brown sugar
- 1/4 cup balsamic vinegar
- 1/4 cup water
- 1 tablespoon olive oil

- 1 tablespoon tamari
- 1 tablespoon rosemary, chopped
- 1 tablespoon corn starch

Directions

1. Combine all the ingredients for pork sauce in a bowl except for corn-starch.
2. Preheat olive oil in the insert of your Instant Pot.
3. Rub the pork with salt and pepper then place it in the Instant Pot.

4. Sear the meat for 2 3 minutes per side. Pour in the prepared sauce.
5. Seal the Instant Pot lid and turn the pressure valve to sealing position.
6. Select Meat/ Stew mode for 20 minutes at high pressure
7. Once done, release the pressure naturally then remove the lid.
8. Mix corn-starch with 1 tablespoon water in a bowl then pour it into the pot.
9. Cook more on sauté mode for few minutes until it thickens.
10. Enjoy.

Nutrition Calories per serving: 340 Carbohydrate: 7.1g Protein: 29.5g Fat: 21.3g Sugar: 4.3g Sodium: 179mg

5-Ingredients Pulled Pork

Serves: 6
Prep Time: 1hr. 40 mins
Ingredients

- 2 tablespoons butter
- 3 to 4 lb. boneless pork shoulder, trimmed; cut in 3 pieces
- 1 cup chicken broth
- 2 tablespoons packed brown sugar
- 2 tablespoons soy sauce
- 10 cloves garlic, finely chopped
- 1 teaspoon salt

Directions
1. Melt butter in the insert of the instant pot on Sauté mode.
2. Add pork and cook for 4 minutes per side until brown.
3. Thoroughly mix broth with soy sauce, garlic, salt, and brown sugar.
4. Pour this mixture over the pork.
5. Seal the Instant Pot lid and turn the pressure valve to sealing position.
6. Select Manual mode for 90 minutes at high pressure
7. Once done, release the pressure completely then remove the lid.
8. Remove the pork and shred it using forks.
9. Return this pork to the cooking liquid.
10. Serve warm.

Nutrition Calories per serving: 358 Carbohydrate: 3.1g Protein: 50.6g Fat: 15g Sugar: 1.8g Sodium:411mg

Pork Roast

Serves: 4
Prep Time: 1hr. 40 mins
Ingredients

Spice Rub
- 2 tablespoons brown sugar
- 1/2 tablespoon garlic powder
- 1 teaspoon onion powder
- 1.5 teaspoons coarse salt
- 1/2 teaspoon cinnamon
- 1 teaspoon dried thyme
- 1/2 teaspoon pepper

Sauce
- 2 lb. Pork shoulder roast
- 1/4 cup olive oil, divided
- 2 cloves garlic, minced
- 1/2 cup dry red wine
- 1 cup broth
- 2 sprigs fresh rosemary
- 2 large carrots, chopped into 1.5-inch chunks
- 2 large potatoes, chopped into chunks
- 1/2 yellow onion, chopped
- 1/2 cup balsamic vinegar
- 2 tablespoons corn starch

Directions

1. Mix thoroughly all the dry spices in a small bowl.
2. Liberally rub this mixture over the pork roast and let it sit.
3. Preheat half of the olive oil in the insert of the Instant Pot on Sauté mode.
4. Place pork roast in the pot and cook for 3 minutes per side until brown.
5. Transfer the pork to a plate and heat the remaining oil in the Instant Pot.
6. Add onion and garlic to the heated oil, sauté for 3 minutes.
7. Stir in wine, broth, rosemary and mix well.
8. Place the trivet over this broth mixture and arrange the roast over it.
9. Seal the Instant Pot lid and turn the pressure valve to sealing position.
10. Select Manual mode for 70 minutes at high pressure
11. Once done, release the pressure completely then remove the lid.
12. Add potatoes and carrots to the pot.
13. Seal the Instant Pot lid again and turn the pressure valve to sealing position.
14. Select Manual mode for 3 minutes at high pressure
15. Once done, release the pressure completely then remove the lid.
16. Discard rosemary after removing the trivet, veggies, and roast from the top.
17. Add balsamic vinegar to the sauce in the pot.
18. Mix well then drizzle corn starch over with constant stirring.
19. Switch the Instant pot to sauté mode and cook for 4 minutes until it thickens.
20. Add pork roast to the sauce along with vegetables.
21. Place veggies and pork roast back into the Instant Pot insert.
22. Serve warm.

Nutrition Calories per serving: 533 Carbohydrate: 1.2g Protein: 69.1g Fat: 23.7g Sugar: 0.6g Sodium: 382mg

Pulled Pork

Serves: 6
Prep Time: 60 mins
Ingredients

- 1 tablespoon packed brown sugar
- 2 teaspoons paprika
- 2 teaspoons garlic powder
- 2 teaspoons onion powder
- 1 teaspoon salt
- 1 teaspoon pepper
- 1/2 teaspoon cumin
- 1/4 teaspoon cayenne, optional
- 3-pound boneless pork roast, cut into chunks
- 2 tablespoons olive oil
- 1/3 cup apple cider vinegar
- 2 cups barbecue sauce, divided
- 1 1/4 cup chicken or beef broth
- 1 teaspoon hot pepper sauce, optional

Directions

1. Thoroughly mix brown sugar, garlic powder, onion powder, salt, cumin, pepper, cayenne and paprika in a bowl.
2. Toss the pork cubes with the spice mixture to coat well. Keep it aside.
3. Preheat half of the oil in the insert of the Instant Pot on Sauté mode.
4. Add pork to the pot in batches and cook for 5 minutes per side.
5. Transfer the sear pork to a plate and keep it aside.
6. Whisk barbecue, apple cider vinegar and one cup broth in a container.
7. Add a ¼ cup of the broth to the Instant Pot to deglaze the insert.
8. Return the set pork to the pot and pour the barbecue sauce mixture on top.
9. Seal the Instant Pot lid and turn the pressure valve to sealing position.
10. Select Manual mode for 40 minutes at high pressure

11. Once done, release the pressure completely then remove the lid.
12. Serve fresh.
13. Devour.

Nutrition Calories per serving: 579 Carbohydrate: 14g Protein: 70.1g Fat: 25.5g Sugar: 5.3g Sodium: 314mg

Barbecue Pulled Pork Sandwiches

Serves: 6
Prep Time: 1hr. 30 mins
Ingredients
- 3 tablespoons light brown sugar
- 2 teaspoons hot paprika
- 1 teaspoon mustard powder
- 1/2 teaspoon ground cumin
- kosher salt and freshly ground pepper
- one 4-pound boneless pork shoulder, cut into 6 chunks
- 2 teaspoons vegetable oil
- 1/2 cup apple cider vinegar, plus more to taste
- 3 tablespoons tomato paste
- 12 hamburger potato buns
- 1 cup barbecue sauce, for serving
- 4 cups coleslaw, for serving

Directions
1. Mix mustard powder, paprika, 1 tablespoon brown sugar, cumin, salt and pepper in a bowl.
2. Season the pork with this spice's mixture liberally.
3. Preheat oil in the insert of the Instant Pot on Sauté mode.
4. Add pork to the pot in batches and cook each for 5 minutes per side.
5. Transfer the seared pork to a plate and keep it aside.
6. Add 2 ¾ cups water, vinegar, 2 tablespoons brown sugar, 2 and tomato paste to the pot.
7. Mix well then return the pork to the pot.
8. Seal the Instant Pot lid and turn the pressure valve to sealing position.
9. Select Manual mode for 60 minutes at high pressure
10. Once done, release the pressure completely then remove the lid.
11. Switch the Instant pot to sauté mode.
12. Cook the mixture for 15 minutes until reduced.
13. Adjust seasoning with salt and pepper. Shred the pork using forks.
14. Serve warm with buns, sauce, and coleslaw.

Nutrition Calories per serving: 427 Carbohydrate: 6.8g Protein: 27.4g Fat: 23g Sugar: 2.3g Sodium: 536mg

Pork Vindaloo

Serves: 4
Prep Time: 60 mins
Ingredients
- 4 tablespoons oil of choice
- 1 teaspoon cumin seeds
- ½ teaspoon black mustard seeds
- 2 onions, diced
- 1 serrano pepper or green chili, minced

Spices
- 4 teaspoons paprika
- 2 teaspoons salt

- 2 pounds pork shoulder, cut into 1.5-inch cubes
- 3 tablespoons minced garlic
- 1 tablespoon minced ginger

- 1 teaspoon coriander powder
- ½ teaspoon cinnamon

- ½ teaspoon ground cardamom
- ½ teaspoon black pepper
- ¼ – ½ teaspoon cayenne, adjust to taste
- 4 tablespoons white vinegar
- A ¾ cup of water
- Cilantro, garnish

Directions
1. Preheat oil in the insert of the Instant Pot on sauté mode.
2. Add mustard seeds and cumin, sauté for 1 minute until seeds pop.
3. Stir in serrano pepper and onions, sauté for 10 minutes.
4. Add ginger, garlic, and pork, sauté for 4 minutes.
5. Stir in all the spices, water, and vinegar.
6. Seal the Instant Pot lid and turn the pressure valve to sealing position.
7. Select Manual mode for 25 minutes at high pressure
8. Once done, release the pressure completely then remove the lid.
9. Switch the Instant pot to sauté mode and cook for 10 minutes.
10. Garnish with cilantro.
11. Serve right away.

Nutrition Calories per serving: 224 Carbohydrate: 10.1g Protein: 26g Fat: 9.2g Sugar: 6.6g Sodium: 451mg

Pork Tenderloin with Garlic Herb Rub
Serves: 2
Prep Time: 40 mins
Ingredients
- 1 cup low sodium chicken broth
- 1 tablespoon balsamic vinegar
- 1 lb. pork tenderloin
- 1 teaspoon garlic powder
- 1 teaspoon dried parsley
- 1/2 teaspoon seasoning salt
- 1/4 teaspoon onion powder
- 1/4 teaspoon black pepper

glaze:
- 2-3 tablespoons honey
- 1 tablespoon ketchup
- 1 tablespoon water
- 1 tablespoon corn starch

Directions
1. Pour balsamic vinegar and chicken broth into the insert of the Instant Pot.
2. Place trivet over the broth and arrange the tenderloin over the trivet.
3. Mix garlic powder with parsley, onion powder, black pepper, and salt in a container.
4. Sprinkle this spice mixture over both sides of the tenderloin.
5. Seal the Instant Pot lid and turn the pressure valve to sealing position.
6. Select Manual mode for 7 minutes at high pressure
7. Once done, release the pressure completely then remove the lid.

Glaze:
8. Transfer the tenderloin to a plate after removing the trivet.
9. Switch the Instant pot to sauté mode.
10. Add ketchup and honey to the pot.
11. Mix corn-starch with water and pour this mixture into the pot.
12. Stir cook this mixture for 3 minutes until it thickens.
13. Pour this sauce over the pork tenderloin.
14. Serve warm.

Nutrition Calories per serving: 616 Carbohydrate: 22.2g Protein: 74.3g Fat: 23.8g Sugar: 8g Sodium: 792mg

Hawaiian Pineapple Pork

Serves: 4
Prep Time: 50 mins
Ingredients
- 1 can (20 oz) pineapple chunks in pineapple juice
- 2 tablespoons water
- 1 tablespoon cornstarch
- 3 tablespoons honey
- 2 tablespoons soy sauce
- 2 tablespoons brown sugar
- 1 tablespoon grated ginger
- 3 garlic cloves, minced
- 2 tablespoons olive oil, separated
- 1 onion, chopped
- 1 red pepper, chopped
- 2 lb. Boneless pork stew meat
- Kosher salt and black pepper
- 1 teaspoon oregano
- Parsley for garnishing

Directions
1. Separate the pineapple chunks from the juice and keep their juice aside.
2. Combine water with pineapple juice, corn-starch, soy sauce, honey, ginger, brown sugar and garlic in a small bowl.
3. Preheat 1 tablespoon oil in the insert of the Instant Pot on Sauté mode.
4. Toss in red peppers and onions, sauté for 3 minutes.
5. Transfer these veggies to a plate.
6. Add more oil to the Instant Pot then place pork meat in it.
7. Cook until the meat loses its pink color then add oregano and pineapple.
8. Adjust seasoning with salt and pepper, mix well.
9. Seal the Instant Pot lid and turn the pressure valve to sealing position.
10. Select Manual mode for 10 minutes at high pressure
11. Once done, release the pressure completely then remove the lid.
12. Add sautéed veggies to the pork and mix gently.
13. Garnish with parsley.
14. Serve warm.

Nutrition Calories per serving: 445 Carbohydrate: 24.3g Protein: 32g Fat: 25.5g Sugar: 15.7g Sodium: 430mg

Sauces and Dressings Recipes

Keto Hollandaise

Serves: 4
Prep Time: 15 mins
Ingredients
- 2 tablespoons fresh lemon juice
- Dash hot sauce
- 4 egg yolks
- ½ cup butter, melted
- 1 pinch sea salt and cayenne pepper

Directions
1. Whisk together egg yolks and lemon juice in a bowl thoroughly.
2. Boil water in a saucepan and place the bowl of eggs mixture over top of the saucepan above water.

3. Whisk in the melted butter slowly and remove from heat.
4. Stir in the hot sauce, sea salt, and cayenne pepper to serve.

Nutrition
Calories: 262 Carbs: 1.3g Fats: 27.6g Proteins: 3g Sodium: 177mg Sugar: 0.3g

Chipotle Mayonnaise

Serves: 4
Prep Time: 10 mins
Ingredients
- ½ tablespoon chipotle powder
- 1 cup mayonnaise
- 1 tablespoon tomato paste

Directions
1. Mix together the tomato paste, mayonnaise, and chipotle powder in a small bowl.
2. Refrigerate for about 30 minutes and serve with your favorite snacks.

Nutrition
Calories: 234 Carbs: 14.8g Fats: 19.7g Proteins: 0.9g Sodium: 430mg Sugar: 4.3g

Keto Ranch Sauce

Serves: 8
Prep Time: 10 mins
Ingredients
- ½ cup crème fraiche
- 1 cup mayonnaise
- 2 tablespoons ranch seasoning

Directions
1. Mix together crème fraiche, mayonnaise. and ranch seasoning in a bowl.
2. Serve with your favorite snacks or as a dressing on a salad.

Nutrition
Calories: 173 Carbs: 7.4g Fats: 14.9g Proteins: 1.4g Sodium: 420mg Sugar: 1.9g

Homemade Mayonnaise

Serves: 4
Prep Time: 10 mins
Ingredients
- 1 tablespoon Dijon mustard
- 2 teaspoons white wine vinegar
- 1 egg yolk
- 1 cup avocado oil
- Salt and black pepper, to taste

Directions
1. Whisk together egg yolk and mustard with a stick blender in a bowl.
2. Slowly add avocado oil and white wine vinegar.
3. Season with salt and black pepper and mix well.
4. Refrigerate for about 30 minutes and serve.

Nutrition
Calories: 91 Carbs: 3.5g Fats: 8.4g Proteins: 1.5g Sodium: 49mg Sugar: 0.2g

Poppy Seed Salad Dressing

Serves: 8
Prep Time: 15 mins
Ingredients

- 2 tablespoons Swerve
- ¾ cup mayonnaise
- 2 tablespoons apple cider vinegar
- ½ teaspoon sea salt
- 1 tablespoon poppy seeds

Directions

1. Mix together poppy seeds with rest of the ingredients in a small bowl.
2. Refrigerate for about 30 minutes and use it as a dressing for your salad.

Nutrition
Calories: 94 Carbs: 6.1g Fats: 7.9g Proteins: 0.4g Sodium: 274mg Sugar: 1.6g

Blue Cheese Dressing

Serves: 16
Prep Time: 5 mins
Ingredients

- ½ cup sour cream
- Garlic salt and black pepper, to taste
- 1 cup blue cheese, crumbled
- ½ cup mayonnaise
- ½ teaspoon lemon juice

Directions

1. Mix together all the ingredients except half of blue cheese.
2. Put the mixture into an immersion blender and blend well.
3. Stir in rest of the blue cheese and use it as a dressing for your salad.

Nutrition
Calories: 74 Carbs: 2.3g Fats: 6.4g Proteins: 2.1g Sodium: 174mg Sugar: 0.5g

Honey Mustard Dressing

Serves: 8
Prep Time: 5 mins
Ingredients

- ¼ cup water
- ½ cup full fat sour cream
- ¼ cup Dijon mustard
- 1 tablespoon honey
- 1 tablespoon apple cider vinegar

Directions

1. Whisk together honey and mustard with all the other ingredients in a bowl.
2. Refrigerate for about 30 minutes and use it as a dressing for your salad.

Nutrition
Calories: 44 Carbs: 3.2g Fats: 3.3g Proteins: 0.8g Sodium: 96mg Sugar: 2.3g

Creamy Garlic Salad Dressing

Serves: 10
Prep Time: 5 mins
Ingredients

- 2/3 cup mayo
- 10 garlic cloves, chopped
- 1 can coconut cream
- ½ teaspoon salt
- 1 tablespoon tomato paste

Directions
1. Mix together all the ingredients in a bowl.
2. Refrigerate for about 30 minutes and use it as a dressing for your salad

Nutrition
Calories: 156 Carbs: 2g Fats: 16g Proteins: 6.5g Sodium: 204mg Sugar: 0.1g

Peanut Sauce

Serves: 4
Prep Time: 5 mins
Ingredients
- 3 tablespoons coconut aminos
- 3 tablespoons lime juice
- ½ cup salted creamy peanut butter
- 2 tablespoons maple syrup
- 2 tablespoons chili sauce

Directions
1. Mix together coconut aminos, lime juice, peanut butter, maple syrup, and chili sauce in a bowl.
2. Add some water to attain the desired consistency and refrigerate for about 1 hour.
3. Serve with your favorite snacks.

Nutrition
Calories: 229 Carbs: 16.1g Fats: 16.3g Proteins: 8.1g Sodium: 352mg Sugar: 9.2g

Eggs and Dairy Recipes

Scrambled Eggs

Serves: 2
Prep Time: 15 mins
Ingredients
- 1 tablespoon butter
- Salt and black pepper, to taste
- 4 eggs, whisked
- 1 tablespoon milk

Directions
1) Combine together milk, eggs, salt, and black pepper in a medium bowl.
2) Put butter in a pan over medium-low heat and add the whisked eggs mixture slowly.
3) Stir continuously for about 4 minutes and dish onto a serving plate.

Nutrition
Calories: 151 Carbs: 0.7g Fats: 11.6g Proteins: 11.1g Sodium: 144mg Sugar: 0.7g

Pepperoni Omelet

Serves: 8
Prep Time: 15 mins

Ingredients
- 30 pepperoni slices
- 8 tablespoons cream
- 4 tablespoons butter
- 12 eggs
- Salt and freshly ground black pepper, to taste

Directions
1) Whisk together the eggs in a bowl and add the remaining ingredients.
2) Put butter in a pan and add the egg mixture.
3) Cook for about 2 minutes and flip the sides.
4) Cook for another 2 minutes and dish out in a serving plate.

Nutrition
Calories: 141 Carbs: 0.6g Fats: 11.3g Proteins: 8.9g Sodium: 334mg Sugar: 0.5g

Eggs Stuffed with Avocado and Watercress

Serves: 3
Prep Time: 15 mins
Ingredients
- ½ medium ripe avocado, peeled, pitted and chopped
- ¼ tablespoon fresh lemon juice
- 3 organic eggs, boiled, peeled and cut in half lengthwise
- ¼ cup fresh watercress, trimmed
- Salt, to taste

Directions
1) Place a steamer basket at the bottom of the pot and pour water.
2) Put the watercress on the trivet and pour water in the pressure cooker.
3) Place the trivet in the cooker and lock the lid.
4) Cook for about 3 minutes at high pressure and then release the pressure quickly.
5) Drain the watercress completely and keep aside.
6) Remove the egg yolks and transfer into a bowl.
7) Mash watercress, lemon juice, avocado and salt completely with a fork.
8) Place the egg whites in a plate and stuff the egg whites with the watercress mixture.
9) Serve immediately.

Nutrition
Calories: 132 Carbs: 3.3g Fats: 10.9g Proteins: 6.3g Sodium: 65mg Sugar: 0.5g

Cheesy Mini Frittatas

Serves: 3
Prep Time: 25 mins
Ingredients
- 4 tablespoons cheddar cheese, shredded
- ¼ cup unsweetened almond milk
- 3 organic eggs
- 1 scallion, chopped
- ¼ teaspoon lemon pepper seasoning
- 2 cooked bacon slices, crumbled
- Salt and black pepper, to taste
- 1 medium zucchini, finely chopped

Directions
1) Preheat the oven to 400 degrees F and grease the silicone moulds.
2) Whisk together eggs and stir in the remaining ingredients, mixing well.
3) Pour the eggs mixture into the silicone moulds and transfer the moulds in the oven.

4) Bake for about 15 minutes and remove from the oven to serve.

Nutrition
Calories: 185 Carbs: 3.5g Fats: 13.2g Proteins: 13.6g Sodium: 435mg Sugar: 1.6g

Keto Coconut Pancakes

Serves: 4
Prep Time: 15 mins
Ingredients
For Pancakes
- 4 eggs
- ¼ cup full-fat coconut milk
- ¼ cup melted ghee or grass-fed butter
- ½ tablespoon salt
- ½ tablespoon baking powder
- ¼ cup coconut flour

For Keto Caramel Sauce
- ¼ cup grass-fed butter
- ¼ cup full-fat coconut milk
- ½ tablespoon pure vanilla extract
- 1 pinch salt

Directions
For Pancakes
1) Take a non-stick skillet and heat butter or ghee in it at a low flame.
2) Now take a bowl and add butter, salt, milk, vanilla, and eggs to it.
3) Whisk and add coconut flour and baking powder. Keep whisking until a smooth mixture is formed.
4) Pour the batter to heated skillet and cook until the edges rise.
5) Flip and cook from the other side for a minute.
6) Add a bit of butter in between the batches to make the edges crispy.
7) Serve after topping with your favorite ones.

For Keto Caramel Sauce
1) Melt the butter in a small sauce pan until it turns brown and bubbly in appearance.
2) Add coconut milk and keep stirring until you achieve the thickness you desire.
3) Remove when it is boiled and add vanilla and salt to it.
4) Drizzle it over the pancakes to serve.
5) This sauce is in its best flavor, if used the same day.

Nutrition
Calories: 267 Carbs: 7.4g Fats: 24g Proteins: 7g Sodium: 943mg Sugar: 1.1g

Nut Porridge

Serves: 4
Prep Time: 25 mins
Ingredients
- 4 teaspoons coconut oil, melted
- 1 cup pecan, halved
- 1 cup water
- 1 cup coconut milk
- 2 tablespoons stevia
- 1 cup cashew nuts, raw and unsalted

Directions
1) Place the cashew nuts and pecans in the food processor and pulse until chunked.
2) Put the chunked nuts into the pot and stir in coconut oil, stevia and water.
3) Cook for about 5 minutes on high heat and reduce the heat to low.
4) Simmer for about 10 minutes and dish out to serve.

Nutrition
Calories: 260 Carbs: 12.7g Fats: 22.9g Proteins: 5.6g Sodium: 9mg Sugar: 1.8g

Lemon Mousse

Serves: 4
Prep Time: 25 mins
Ingredients
- 1 cup heavy cream
- ¼ cup fresh lemon juice
- 1 teaspoon lemon liquid stevia
- 8-ounce cream cheese, softened
- ¼ teaspoon salt

Directions
1) Preheat the oven to 360 degrees F and grease 4 ramekins.
2) Mix together lemon liquid stevia, cream cheese, lemon juice, heavy cream, and salt in a bowl.
3) Pour the mixture into the ramekins and transfer the ramekins into the oven.
4) Bake for about 12 minutes and pour into the serving glasses.
5) Refrigerate for at least 2 hours and serve chilled.

Nutrition
Calories: 305 Carbs: 2.7g Fats: 31g Proteins: 5g Sodium: 299mg Sugar: 0.5g

Vanilla Yogurt

Serves: 12
Prep Time: 13 hours
Ingredients
- ½ tablespoon pure vanilla extract
- 2 scoops stevia
- ½ cup full-fat milk
- ¼ cup yogurt starter
- 1 cup heavy cream

Directions
1) Pour milk into the slow cooker and set it on low for about 2 hours.
2) Whisk vanilla extract, stevia and heavy cream in the slow cooker.
3) Allow the yogurt to sit and set the slow cooker on LOW to cook for about 3 hours.
4) Mix the yogurt starter with full-fat milk and return this mixture to the slow cooker.
5) Lock the lid of the slow cooker again and wrap it in two small towels.
6) Let the wrapped slow cooker to sit for about 8 hours and allow the yogurt to culture.
7) Dish out in a serving bowl or alternatively, store it by refrigerating.

Nutrition
Calories: 292 Carbs: 8.2g Fats: 26.2g Proteins: 5.2g Sodium: 86mg Sugar: 6.6g

Low Carb Blueberry Muffins

Serves: 6
Prep Time: 55 mins
Ingredients
- 2 cups fresh blueberries
- 1 teaspoon cream of tartar
- ¼ cup coconut oil
- 4 eggs
- 1 pinch salt
- 1 teaspoon baking soda
- 1 teaspoon lemon juice
- 1/3 cup coconut flour
- 1 cup almonds, ground
- ½ cup coconut yogurt

Directions
1) Separate eggs yolks and heat oven to 350 degrees F.
2) Take a bowl and mix lemon juice, coconut oil, and egg yolks.
3) Add baking soda, ground almonds, flax seeds, salt, coconut flour, and coconut yogurt to it and mix.
4) Use an electric egg beater to beat egg whites and add tartar cream after 30 seconds.
5) Fold egg whites into dough first and then add blueberries.
6) Line a non-stick muffin tray and grease it with coconut oil.
7) Bake in an oven for 30-35 minutes. Remove from heat and cool for 10 minutes before removing tins.
8) Muffins can be frozen for two months and kept at room temperature for four days.

Nutrition
Calories: 278 Carbs: 16.7g Fats: 21.1g Proteins: 8.8g Sodium: 280mg Sugar: 6.9g

Keto Quiche

Serves: 8
Prep Time: 25 mins
Ingredients
- 8 large eggs
- ¼ cup greens
- ¼ cup onions
- ¼ pound bacon
- ½ tablespoon salt
- 1 cup full-fat coconut milk
- 1 cup nut flour
- ¼ cup nutritional yeast
- ¼ cup coconut oil

Directions
1) Heat oven up to 400°F and grease an 8" pan lightly.
2) Mix the flour with coconut oil, eggs, and salt to form dough.
3) Press this dough into spring form pan in a way that the crust rises to the sides. Then poke holes with a fork.
4) Place spring form pan on a sheet pan to allow baking for 10 minutes.
5) Add bacons or greens according to your desire.
6) Bake for 30-40 minutes at a temp of 350 degrees F.
7) Slice when cooled.

Nutrition
Calories: 347 Carbs: 13.8g Fats: 27.5g Proteins: 15.4g Sodium: 847mg Sugar: 5.6g

Desserts

Gingerbread Bread Pudding

Serves: 6
Prep Time: 40 mins
Ingredients
- 6 cups cubed French bread
- 3 eggs
- 1.5 cups milk
- 1/3 cup brown sugar
- 2 tablespoons molasses
- 1 teaspoon vanilla extract
- 1 teaspoon cinnamon
- 1 teaspoon ginger (dried)
- 1/2 cup chopped pecans
- 1.5 cups water
- almond butter, chocolate chips & pecans for topping, optional

Directions
1. whisk eggs with molasses, brown sugar, milk, ginger, cinnamon and pecan in a bowl.
2. Add bread cubes to the mixture and let them sit for 5 minutes.
3. Spread these cubes in a greased 1.5-quart glass dish.
4. Pour 1.5 cup water into the insert of the Instant Pot.
5. Place trivet over the water and spread the aluminum foil over it.
6. Keep the glass dish over the foil.
7. Seal the Instant Pot lid and turn the pressure valve to sealing position.
8. Select Manual mode for 20 minutes at high pressure
9. Once done, release the pressure completely then remove the lid.
10. Allow it to cook for 5 minutes then serve.

Nutrition Calories per serving: 317 Carbohydrate: 20g Protein: 6g Fat: 23.9g Sugar: 13.1g
  Sodium: 246mg

Rice Pudding

Serves: 2
Prep Time: 30 mins
Ingredients
- 1 cup arborio rice
- 1 1/2 cups water
- 1/4 teaspoon salt
- 2 cups whole milk, divided
- 1/2 cup sugar
- 2 eggs
- 1/2 teaspoon vanilla extract
- 3/4 cup raisins

Directions
1. Mix rice, salt, and water in the insert of the Instant Pot.
2. Seal the Instant Pot lid and turn the pressure valve to sealing position.
3. Select Manual mode for 3 minutes at high pressure
4. Once done, release the pressure completely then remove the lid.
5. Stir in 1.5 cups milk and sugar, mix well.
6. Whisk eggs with ½ cup milk and vanilla in a bowl.
7. Pour this mixture into the pot through a sieve.
8. Switch the Instant Pot to sauté mode and cook the mixture until it boils.
9. Add raisins and cook until it thickens.
10. Serve as desired.

Nutrition Calories per serving: 377 Carbohydrate: 27.8g Protein: 4.6g Fat: 27.8g Sugar:
  25.6g Sodium: 33mg

Pumpkin Pie Pudding

Serves: 2
Prep Time: 40 mins
Ingredients
- 2 eggs
- 1/2 cup heavy whipping cream
- 3/4 cup erythritol
- 15 ounces canned pumpkin puree
- 1 teaspoon pumpkin pie spice
- 1 teaspoon vanilla
- for finishing
- 1/2 cup heavy whipping cream

Directions
1. Whisk all the ingredients for the pudding in a bowl.
2. Pour this mixture into a 6-inch pan.

3. Add 1.5 cups water to the insert of the Instant Pot.
4. Place the steamer trivet over the water.
5. Keep the pumpkin pie pan over the trivet.
6. Cover this pan aluminon foil.
7. Seal the Instant Pot lid and turn the pressure valve to sealing position.
8. Select Manual mode for 20 minutes at high pressure
9. Once done, release the pressure completely then remove the lid.
10. Allow it to cool and refrigerate for 8 hours.
11. Serve with whipped cream on top.

Nutrition Calories per serving: 366 Carbohydrate: 21.5g Protein: 10.3g Fat: 26.7g Sugar: 12.3g Sodium: 293mg

Oreo Cheesecake

Serves: 8
Prep Time: 60 mins
Ingredients

- 12 whole Oreo cookies, crushed into crumbs
- 2 tablespoons salted butter, melted
- 16 ounces cream cheese, room temperature
- 1/2 cup granulated sugar
- 2 large eggs, room temperature
- 1 tablespoon all-purpose flour
- 1/4 cup heavy cream
- 2 teaspoons pure vanilla extract
- 8 whole Oreo cookies, coarsely chopped
- 1 cup whipped cream or whipped topping
- chocolate sauce, optional

Directions

1. Layer a 7-inch pan with a foil sheet and grease it with cooking spray.
2. Add 12 Oreos and butter to a food processor and pulse until it forms a crumbly mixture.
3. Spread this mixture in the greased pan and press it well.
4. Place the crust in the freezer for 15 minutes.
5. Beat cream cheese with sugar, eggs in an electric mixer.
6. Stir in flour, vanilla, and heavy cream, mix well until smooth.
7. Fold in 8 chopped Oreos then spread this filling in the frozen crust.
8. Cover the batter with a foil sheet.
9. Pour 1.5 cups water into the insert of the instant pot.
10. Place the trivet over it and keep the cake pan over it.
11. Seal the Instant Pot lid and turn the pressure valve to sealing position.
12. Select Manual mode for 35 minutes with high pressure settings.
13. Once done, release the pressure completely then remove the lid.
14. Allow the cake to cool then refrigerate overnight.
15. Slice and serve with favorite topping.
16. Enjoy.

Nutrition Calories per serving: 295 Carbohydrate: 63.7g Protein: 3.3g Fat: 3.9g Sugar: 35.8g Sodium: 88mg

Apple Cake

Serves: 6
Prep Time: 1hr. 10 mins
Ingredients

- 3 cups peeled and diced apples any variety

- 1/2 tablespoon ground cinnamon
- 2 tablespoons sugar
- 1-1/2 cups flour
- 1/2 tablespoon baking powder
- 1/2 teaspoon fine sea salt
- 1/2 cup vegetable oil
- 3/4 cup sugar
- 2 tablespoons orange juice
- 1 teaspoon vanilla extract
- 2 large eggs room temperature

Directions
1. Grease a 7-inch pan with cooking spray and dust it with flour.
2. Toss chopped apples with cinnamon and 2 tablespoons sugar in a suitable container.
3. Mix flour with salt and baking powder in a separate bowl.
4. Whisk eggs, oil, sugar, vanilla and orange juice in a mixer.
5. Stir in flour mixture and mix until smooth.
6. Spread half of this batter in the pan and top it with half of the chopped apples evenly.
7. Spread the remaining batter over the apples and top it with remaining apples and juices then cover the pan with aluminum foil.
8. Pour water in the insert of the Instant Pot.
9. Place trivet over it and keep the cake pan over it.
10. Seal the Instant Pot lid and turn the pressure valve to sealing position.
11. Select Manual mode for 60 minutes at high pressure
12. Once done, release the pressure completely then remove the lid.
13. Allow the cake to cool then slice.
14. Serve.

Nutrition Calories per serving: 471 Carbohydrate: 29.4g Protein: 9g Fat: 35.5g Sugar: 19.1g Sodium: 368mg

Vegan Chocolate Cake

Serves: 6
Prep Time: 40 mins
Ingredients
- ¾ cup all-purpose flour
- ½ cup raw sugar or vegan sugar of choice
- ¼ cup unsweetened cocoa powder
- ½ teaspoon baking soda
- ½ teaspoon baking powder
- ¼ teaspoon salt
- ½ cup plant milk
- ¼ cup oil
- ½ teaspoon pure vanilla extract
- 1 teaspoon distilled white or apple cider vinegar

Directions
1. Layer, a 6-inch pan with aluminum foil, then grease it with cooking oil.
2. Lastly, dust the pan with flour and set it aside.
3. Mix all the dry ingredients in a bowl and pass it through a sieve.
4. Whisk in vinegar and milk, mix well and let it sit for 1 minute.
5. Add all the remaining ingredients for batter and mix well using a hand blender until smooth.
6. Pour this fillling mixture into the prepared pan and cover it with foil sheet.
7. Place trivet over it and keep the cake pan over it.
8. Seal the Instant Pot lid and turn the pressure valve to sealing position.
9. Select Manual mode for 20 minutes at high pressure
10. Once done, release the pressure completely then remove the lid.
11. Allow the cake to cool then slice.
12. Enjoy

Nutrition Calories per serving: 383 Carbohydrate: 67.8g Protein: 3.7g Fat: 13.2g Sugar: 41g Sodium: 128mg

Chocolate Pots De Crème

Serves: 6
Prep Time: 40 mins
Ingredients:

- 1/2 cup whole milk
- 5 large egg yolks
- 1/4 cup sugar
- pinch of salt

- 8 ounces bittersweet chocolate, melted
- 1 1/2 cups heavy cream
- whipped cream and grated chocolate

Directions

1. Simmer cream with milk in a saucepan.
2. Whisk egg yolks with salt, and sugar in a mixing bowl.
3. Gradually stir in cream milk mixture.
4. Stir in chocolate slowly and blend well until smooth.
5. Divide the mixture into 6 custard cups.
6. Pour 1.5 cups water to the insert of the Instant Pot.
7. Place trivet over it and keep 3 custard cups over it.
8. Seal the Instant Pot lid and turn the pressure valve to sealing position.
9. Select Manual mode for 6 minutes at high pressure
10. Once done, release the pressure completely then remove the lid.
11. Cook the remaining 3 cups of the custard cups in the same way.
12. Allow them to cool then refrigerate for 4 hours.
13. Serve warm.

Nutrition Calories per serving: 377 Carbohydrate: 27.8g Protein: 4.6g Fat: 27.8g Sugar: 25.6g Sodium: 33mg

Banana Bread

Serves: 6
Prep Time: 60 mins
Ingredients

- 3 ripe bananas, mashed
- 1/2 cup butter, softened
- 1/2 cup brown sugar
- 1/2 cup white sugar
- 2 eggs, beaten
- 1 teaspoon vanilla

- 1/4 cup buttermilk
- 2 cups all-purpose flour, sifted
- 1 teaspoon baking soda
- 1 teaspoon baking powder
- 1/4 teaspoon cinnamon
- 1/2 teaspoon salt

Directions

1. Grease a suitably sized baking pan with cooking spray and keep it aside.
2. Mash banana flesh in a bowl using a fork.
3. Beat cream with sugars and butter in a mixer.
4. Add vanilla, and eggs while beating this mixture.
5. Stir in bananas, sour cream and mix well using a spoon.
6. Continue adding all the dry ingredients while mixing the mixture.
7. Mix until smooth then pour the batter into the prepared pan.
8. Cover the pan with a foil sheet.
9. Pour 1.5 cups water into the insert the Instant Pot.

10. Place trivet over it and keep the cake pan over it.
11. Seal the Instant Pot lid and turn the pressure valve to sealing position.
12. Select Manual mode for 47 minutes at high pressure
13. Once done, release the pressure completely then remove the lid.
14. Allow the bread to cool then refrigerate for 4 hours.
15. Garnish as desired.
16. Slice and serve.

Nutrition Calories per serving: 248 Carbohydrate: 41g Protein: 7.6g Fat: 24g Sugar: 8g Sodium: 195mg

New York-Style Cheesecake

Serves: 6
Prep Time: 40 mins
Ingredients
Graham cracker crust:
- 3 tablespoons sugar
- 5 tablespoons butter
- 9 large graham crackers, pulsed into crumbs

- 2 tablespoons ground pecans
- 1/4 teaspoon cinnamon

Cheesecake filling:
- 12 ounces cream cheese
- 1/4 teaspoon kosher salt
- 2 teaspoons lemon zest
- 2 teaspoons vanilla extract

- 1 tablespoon cornstarch
- 1/2 cup 2 tablespoons granulated sugar
- 2 large eggs + 1 egg yolk
- 1/2 cup sour cream

Directions
1. Grease a 7-inch pan with cooking spray then line it with parchment paper.
2. Crush crackers with pecans, cinnamon, butter and sugar in a food processor.
3. Spread this mixture into the prepared pan and press it firmly.
4. Beat cream cheese with sugar in an electric mixer until smooth.
5. Whisk in egg, egg yolk, lemon zest, salt, vanilla, and sour cream, while beating the mixture.
6. Pour this filling mixture into the pressed crust in the pan.
7. Cover this filling with aluminum foil.
8. Pour 1.5 cup water into the insert the Instant Pot.
9. Place trivet over it and keep the cake pan over it.
10. Seal the Instant Pot lid and turn the pressure valve to sealing position.
11. Select Manual mode for 25 minutes at high pressure
12. Once done, release the pressure completely then remove the lid.
13. Allow the cake to cool then refrigerate for 4 hours.
14. Garnish with cream or berries.
15. Serve fresh.

Nutrition Calories per serving: 223 Carbohydrate: 17.8g Protein: 6.5g Fat: 21.2g Sugar: 15.4g Sodium: 195g

Turtle Cheesecake

Serves: 6
Prep Time: 50 mins

Ingredients

- 3/4 cup crushed chocolate cookies
- 2 tablespoons unsalted butter - melted
- 16 ounces cream cheese - room temperature
- 2/3 cup granulated sugar
- 2 eggs
- 1/4 cup sour cream
- 1 teaspoon pure vanilla extract
- Whiskey caramel sauce
- 1/2 cup pecans

Directions

1. Grease a 7-inch pan with cooking spray then line it with parchment paper.
2. Crush cookies in a food processor and mix well butter.
3. Spread this crust mixture into the prepared pan and press it firmly.
4. Beat cream cheese with sugar in an electric mixer until smooth.
5. Whisk in eggs, vanilla, and sour cream, while beating the mixture.
6. Pour this sour cream mixture into the prepared crust in the pan.
7. Cover this filling with aluminum foil.
8. Pour 1.5 cup water into the insert the Instant Pot.
9. Place trivet over it and keep the cake pan over it.
10. Seal the Instant Pot lid and turn the pressure valve to sealing position.
11. Select Manual mode for 35 minutes with high pressure setting.
12. Once done, release the pressure completely then remove the lid.
13. Allow the cake to cool then refrigerate for 4 hours.
14. Garnish with pecans and caramel sauce.
15. Slice and serve.

Nutrition Calories per serving: 227 Carbohydrate: 51.4g Protein: 0.9g Fat: 0.5g Sugar: 40.6gg Sodium: 9mg

Bread Baking for Beginners Recipes

Keto Bread

Serves: 6
Prep Time: 5 hours 10 mins
Ingredients

- 6 large eggs, separated
- ¼ teaspoon cream of tartar
- 6 drops liquid stevia
- 1½ cups almond flour
- ¼ cup butter, melted
- 3 teaspoons baking powder
- 1 pinch pink salt

Directions

1. Preheat oven to 365 degrees F and grease a loaf pan.
2. Whisk together egg whites with cream of tartar.
3. Put 1/3 of the beaten egg whites, egg yolks, butter, baking powder, liquid stevia, salt, and almond flour in a food processor and process until combined.
4. Stir in the remaining 2/3 of the egg whites and process until completely incorporated.
5. Pour mixture into the loaf pan and transfer in the oven.
6. Bake for about 30 minutes and dish out to serve hot.

Nutrition

Calories: 310 Carbs: 7.7g Fats: 26g Proteins: 12.4g Sodium: 207mg Sugar: 0.4g

Macadamia Nut Bread

Serves: 5
Prep Time: 40 mins
Ingredients

- 5 large eggs
- 5 oz macadamia nuts
- ¼ cup coconut flour
- ½ teaspoon apple cider vinegar
- ½ teaspoon baking soda

Directions

1. Preheat oven to 350 degrees F and grease a standard-size bread pan.
2. Put macadamia nuts and eggs in a food processor and pulse until combined.
3. Add coconut flour, apple cider vinegar, and baking soda and pulse until incorporated.
4. Pour this mixture in the bread pan and transfer in the oven.
5. Bake for about 40 minutes and dish out to serve.

Nutrition
Calories: 299 Carbs: 8.3g Fats: 27.1g Proteins: 9.3g Sodium: 197mg Sugar: 1.7g

Cauliflower Bread with Garlic & Herbs

Serves: 18
Prep Time: 1 hour
Ingredients

- 10 large eggs, separated
- 1¼ cups coconut flour
- 3 cups cauliflower, finely chopped
- ¼ teaspoon cream of tartar
- 1½ tablespoons gluten-free baking powder
- 1 teaspoon sea salt
- 6 cloves garlic, minced
- 1 tablespoon fresh parsley, chopped
- 6 tablespoons butter, melted
- 1 tablespoon fresh rosemary, chopped

Directions

1. Preheat the oven to 350 degrees F and line a loaf pan with parchment paper.
2. Steam the riced cauliflower and keep aside to dry out completely.
3. Whisk together egg whites, and cream of tartar in a bowl and keep aside.
4. Place the baking powder, coconut flour, sea salt, egg yolks, butter, garlic, whipped egg whites and cauliflower in a food processor.
5. Process until combined and add in the parsley and rosemary.
6. Transfer the batter into the loaf pan and transfer in the oven.
7. Bake for about 50 minutes and slice to serve.

Nutrition
Calories: 115 Carbs: 7.4g Fats: 7.5g Proteins: 5.1g Sodium: 372mg Sugar: 0.6g

Keto Banana Walnut Bread

Serves: 8
Prep Time: 1 hour 10 mins
Ingredients

- 2 cups almond flour
- ½ cup walnuts
- Coconut oil, for greasing
- 3 medium bananas, sliced
- 3 large eggs
- ¼ cup olive oil
- 1 teaspoon baking soda

Directions

1. Preheat oven to 360 degrees F and grease a loaf pan with coconut oil.
2. Place all ingredients in a bowl and mix until well combined
3. Pour mixture into the loaf pan and transfer in the oven.
4. Bake for about 1 hour and slice to serve.

Nutrition

Calories: 333 Carbs: 17g Fats: 27.5g Proteins: 10.7g Sodium: 186mg Sugar: 6.6g

Sesame Seed Keto Bread

Serves: 8
Prep Time: 55 mins
Ingredients

- 7 large eggs, separated
- 1 teaspoon baking powder
- 2 cups sesame seed flour
- ½ cup butter, melted

Directions

1. Preheat the oven to 355 degrees F and line a bread loaf tin with baking paper.
2. Whisk egg whites in a bowl and keep aside.
3. Mix together sesame seed flour, egg yolks, butter, and baking powder in another bowl.
4. Fold in the egg whites into sesame seed flour mixture until a uniform color is formed.
5. Pour the mixture in the bread loaf tin and transfer in the oven.
6. Bake for about 45 minutes and slice to serve.

Nutrition

Calories: 368 Carbs: 10g Fats: 30g Proteins: 17g Sodium: 227mg Sugar: 0.3g

Fluffy Keto Buns

Serves: 4
Prep Time: 45 mins
Ingredients

- 2 tablespoons ground psyllium husks
- 2 egg yolks
- ½ tablespoon apple cider vinegar
- Salt and black pepper, to taste
- ¼ cup coconut flour
- 4 egg whites
- 1 teaspoon gluten free baking powder
- 1 cup water
- 1 teaspoon dried thyme
- 1 teaspoon dried oregano

Directions

1. Preheat the oven to 350 degrees and grease a baking sheet.
2. Whisk together eggs in a bowl and keep aside.
3. Mix together rest of the ingredients in another bowl and add whisked egg whites.
4. Form four rolls of equal size from the dough and arrange on the baking sheet.
5. Transfer in the oven and bake for about 40 minutes.
6. Remove from your oven and serve warm.

Nutrition

Calories: 86 Carbs: 8.7g Fats: 3.1g Proteins: 6g Sodium: 237mg Sugar: 0.3g

Buttery Low Carb Flatbread

Serves: 4

Prep Time: 30 mins
Ingredients
Wet Ingredients
- 2 tablespoons coconut flour
- 1 cup almond flour
- 2 teaspoons xanthan gum

Dry Ingredients
- 1 tablespoon olive oil
- 1 tablespoon water

- ½ teaspoon salt
- ½ teaspoon baking powder

- 1 tablespoon butter, melted
- 1 whole egg + 1 egg white

Directions
1. Preheat the oven to 375 degrees and grease a baking sheet.
2. Mix together the dry ingredients in a bowl until well combined.
3. Add the egg and egg white and fold gently into the flour mixture to form a dough.
4. Add water and mix the dough to allow the xanthan gum and flour to absorb the moisture.
5. Divide the dough in 4 equal parts and press each part to flatten.
6. Arrange the flatbread on the baking sheet and transfer in the oven.
7. Bake for about 20 minutes and dish out to serve.

Nutrition
Calories: 250 Carbs: 11g Fats: 20.1g Proteins: 8.7g Sodium: 474mg Sugar: 0.1g

Garlic and Herb Focaccia Bread

Serves: 8
Prep Time: 30 mins
Ingredients
Wet Ingredients
- 1 tablespoon lemon juice
- 2 eggs

- 2 teaspoons olive oil + 2 tablespoons olive oil, to drizzle

Dry Ingredients
- 1 teaspoon flaky salt
- ½ teaspoon xanthan gum
- ¼ cup coconut flour
- 1 cup almond flour

- 1 teaspoon garlic powder
- ½ teaspoon baking soda
- ½ teaspoon baking powder

Directions
1. Preheat the oven to 350 degrees F and line a baking tray with parchment.
2. Mix together the dry ingredients in a bowl and keep aside.
3. Whisk together the wet ingredients until combined and mix with the dry ingredients.
4. Make a dough and flatten it with a spatula.
5. Arrange the focaccia on the baking tray and transfer in the oven.
6. Cover and bake for about 10 minutes.
7. Drizzle with olive oil and bake uncovered for about 15 more minutes.
8. Remove from the oven and serve warm.

Nutrition
Calories: 162 Carbs: 7g Fats: 13.4g Proteins: 5g Sodium: 425mg Sugar: 0.2g

Coconut Bread

Serves: 5
Prep Time: 1 hour

Ingredients
- ¼ teaspoon salt
- ½ cup coconut flour
- ¼ teaspoon baking soda
- 6 eggs
- ¼ cup unsweetened almond milk
- ¼ cup coconut oil, melted

Directions
1. Preheat the oven to 350 degrees F and grease a loaf pan.
2. Mix together the coconut flour, baking soda and salt in a bowl.
3. Combine the eggs, milk, and coconut oil in another bowl.
4. Slowly add the wet ingredients into the dry ingredients and mix until combined.
5. Pour the mixture into the prepared loaf pan and transfer in the oven.
6. Bake for about 50 minutes and dish out to serve.

Nutrition
Calories: 219 Carbs: 8.5g Fats: 17.5g Proteins: 8.3g Sodium: 262mg Sugar: 0.4g

Keto Mug Bread

Serves: 2
Prep Time: 15 mins
Ingredients
- ¼ cup almond flour
- 1 egg
- 1 tablespoon coconut flour
- 1 tablespoon coconut oil
- ¼ teaspoon baking powder

Directions
1. Preheat the oven to 350 degrees F and grease a mug.
2. Put all ingredients into a mug and mix with a fork until combined.
3. Transfer the mug in the oven and bake for about 8 minutes.
4. Serve immediately.

Nutrition
Calories: 190 Carbs: 6g Fats: 16g Proteins: 6.3g Sodium: 36mg Sugar: 0.2g

Simple Cakes Recipes

Buttery Chocolate Cake

Serves: 6
Prep Time: 1 hour
Ingredients
- 3½ oz. butter
- 7 oz. sugar-free dark chocolate
- 3½ oz. cream
- Erythritol, to taste
- 4 eggs, separated

Directions
1. Preheat the oven to 350 degrees F and grease a baking pan with some butter.
2. Mix the remaining butter with chocolate and microwave for about 2 minutes.
3. Add Erythritol, egg yolks, and cream to the chocolate mixture.
4. Whisk egg whites in another bowl until foamy and add to the creamy chocolate mixture.
5. Pour the batter into the baking pan and transfer in the oven.
6. Bake for about 45 minutes and remove from the oven.

7. Allow it cool for 5 minutes and then refrigerate it for about 4 hours to serve.

Nutrition

Calories: 173 Carbs: 9.4g Fats: 16.2g Proteins: 3.3g Sodium: 42mg Sugar: 0.2g

Italian Pecan Cake

Serves: 8
Prep Time: 1 hour
Ingredients
Cake

- 1 cup Swerve
- 1 teaspoon vanilla essence
- ½ cup coconut, shredded
- ½ cup butter, softened
- 4 large eggs, separated
- ½ cup heavy cream
- ½ cup pecans, chopped
- 2 teaspoons baking powder
- 1½ cups almond flour
- ¼ teaspoon tartar cream
- ¼ cup coconut flour
- ½ teaspoon salt

Frosting

- ½ cup heavy whipping cream
- 1 teaspoon vanilla essence
- 8 ounces cream cheese, softened
- ½ cup butter, softened
- 1 cup powdered Swerve

Garnish

- 2 tablespoons pecans, chopped and lightly toasted
- 2 tablespoons coconut, shredded and lightly toasted

Directions

1. **Cake:** Preheat the oven to 330 degrees F and grease 2 baking pans of 8 inches each.
2. Whisk together egg yolks, butter, cream, Swerve, and vanilla essence in a bowl.
3. Combine almond flour, coconut flour, chopped pecans, baking powder, salt, and coconut.
4. Add the flour mixture to the egg yolk mixture and combine well.
5. Whisk together egg whites in a bowl until foamy and add this to the flour mixture.
6. Divide the mixture into the baking pans and transfer in the oven.
7. Bake for about 45 minutes and remove from the oven..
8. **Frosting:** Put all ingredients for frosting in a mixer and process until frothy.
9. Top the icing mixture over 1 cake and place the other cake over it.
10. Spread the rest of the icing on the top of the upper cake.
11. Garnish it with pecans and coconut.
12. Dish out to slice and serve.

Nutrition

Calories: 267 Carbs: 8.4g Fats: 44.5g Proteins: 3.1g Sodium: 217mg Sugar: 2.3g

Citrus Cream Cake

Serves: 4
Prep Time: 1 hour 15 mins
Ingredients
For Cake

- 4 whole eggs
- 1¼ cups almond flour
- ¼ teaspoon lemon essence
- ¾ teaspoons baking powder
- ¾ teaspoons vanilla essence
- ¼ cup butter, unsalted softened
- ¾ cup erythritol
- ¼ teaspoon salt
- 4 ounces cream cheese

For Cream Frosting

- 1½ tablespoons heavy whipping cream
- 1/8 cup erythritol
- ¼ teaspoon vanilla essence

Directions
1. Preheat the oven to 350 degrees F and grease a baking pan.
2. Mix together butter, Erythritol, and cream cheese in a bowl.
3. Stir in eggs, vanilla essence, and lemon essence and mix well.
4. Whisk in baking powder, almond flour, and salt.
5. Pour the mixture into a baking pan and transfer in the oven.
6. Bake for about 1 hour and remove from the oven.
7. Mix together all ingredients for cream frosting in a bowl and spread on the cake.
8. Refrigerate the cake for about 1 hour and serve chilled.

Nutrition
Calories: 255 Carbs: 2.5g Fats: 23.4g Proteins: 7.9g Sodium: 112mg Sugar: 12.5g

Layered Cream Cake

Serves: 8
Prep Time: 45 mins
Ingredients
For Cream Cheese Icing:
- ½ cup butter, softened
- 2 tablespoons heavy cream
- 8 oz. cream cheese softened
- ½ cup powdered Swerve
- 1 teaspoon vanilla essence

For Carrot Cake Layers:
- ¾ cup Erythritol
- 14 tablespoons butter, melted
- ½ cup coconut flour
- 2 teaspoons baking powder
- 1¼ cups carrots, shredded
- 5 eggs large
- 2 teaspoons vanilla essence
- ¼ teaspoon unsweetened coconut, shredded
- ¼ teaspoon salt
- 1¾ cups almond flour
- 1½ teaspoons cinnamon, ground

Directions
1. **For Cream Cheese Icing:** Mix together all ingredients for the cream cheese icing until foamy and keep aside.
2. **For Carrot Cake Layers:** Preheat the oven to 350 degrees F and grease 2 baking pans.
3. Whisk together eggs with Erythritol in a bowl and keep aside.
4. Mix together almond flour, coconut flour, salt, cinnamon, and baking powder in another bowl.
5. Combine the two mixtures and stir in coconut, butter and carrots.
6. Divide the cake mixture into 2 baking pans and transfer in the oven.
7. Bake for about 30 minutes and remove from the oven to cool.
8. Top the icing mixture over 1 cake and place the other cake over it.
9. Spread the rest of the icing on the top of the upper cake.
10. Dish out to slice and serve.

Nutrition
Calories: 307 Carbs: 7g Fats: 29g Proteins: 6g Sodium: 122mg Sugar: 1g

Molten Lava Cake

Serves: 3
Prep Time: 20 mins
Ingredients

- 2 ounces unsalted butter
- 2 tablespoons powdered Erythritol
- 4 fresh strawberries
- 2 ounces 70% dark chocolate
- 2 organic eggs
- 1 tablespoon almond flour

Directions

1. Preheat the oven to 350 degrees F and lightly grease 2 ramekins.
2. Mix chocolate with butter in a microwave-safe bowl and microwave for about 2 minutes.
3. Whisk together eggs in a bowl and add chocolate mixture, Erythritol, and almond flour until combined.
4. Divide the mixture evenly into 2 ramekins and transfer in the oven.
5. Bake for about 10 minutes and remove from the oven.
6. Keep aside for about 2 minutes and then invert the cakes carefully onto serving plates.
7. Garnish with the strawberries and serve.

Nutrition

Calories: 312 Carbs: 15.3g Fats: 27.8g Proteins: 5.5g Sodium: 151mg Sugar: 2.1g

Matcha Roll Cake

Serves: 10
Prep Time: 30 mins
Ingredients
For Cake:

- ½ cup powdered Swerve
- ¼ cup psyllium husk powder
- 1 cup almond flour
- ¼ cup matcha powder
- 1 teaspoon organic baking powder

For Filling:

- 1 packet unflavored gelatin
- ¼ cup powdered Swerve
- 4 tablespoons water

- ½ teaspoon salt
- ½ cup heavy whipping cream
- 1 teaspoon organic vanilla extract
- 3 large organic eggs
- 4 tablespoons butter, melted

- 2 cups heavy whipping cream
- 2 teaspoons organic vanilla extract

Directions

1. Preheat oven to 350 degrees F and lightly grease a baking sheet.
2. **For Cake:** Mix together almond flour, matcha powder, Swerve, baking powder, psyllium husk, and salt in a bowl.
3. Sift the almond flour mixture into a second bowl.
4. Combine rest of the ingredients in a bowl and mix with the almond flour mixture to form a thick dough.
5. Place the dough onto the baking sheet and roll into an even rectangle.
6. Transfer in the oven and bake for about 10 minutes.
7. Remove from the oven and allow to cool.
8. Roll the warm cake gently with the help of parchment paper and keep aside.
9. **For filling:** Put gelatin in water and microwave for about 20 seconds.
10. Remove from microwave and beat the gelatin mixture until smooth.
11. Place gelatin mixture and remaining ingredients in bowl and beat until cream becomes stiff.
12. Layer the whipped cream evenly over cooled cake and roll the cake gently.

13. Freeze for about 10 minutes and cut into desired sized slices to serve.
Nutrition
Calories: 257 Carbs: 13.1g Fats: 22.5g Proteins: 7.4g Sodium: 194mg Sugar: 6.2g

Allspice Almond Cake

Serves: 8
Prep Time: 40 mins
Ingredients
For Cake:
- 5 tablespoons butter softened
- 2 tablespoons unsweetened almond milk
- 2 tablespoons coconut flour
- 1½ teaspoons cinnamon, ground
- ½ cup almonds

For Cream Cheese Frosting:
- 2 tablespoons butter, softened
- ¼ cup Erythritol
- 4 oz. cream cheese, softened

- ½ cup Erythritol
- 4 large eggs
- 1 teaspoon vanilla
- 1½ cups almond flour
- 1 tablespoon baking powder
- ¼ teaspoon ground allspice

- 1 teaspoon vanilla
- 1 tablespoon heavy cream

Directions
1. Preheat the oven to 350 degrees F and lightly grease a baking pan.
2. Mix erythritol with butter in a bowl until foamy.
3. Whisk in eggs, vanilla and milk and slowly add coconut flour, spices, almond flour, and baking powder.
4. Stir in the almonds to this mixture and pour this batter in the baking pan.
5. Transfer in the oven and bake for about 25 minutes.
6. Remove from the oven and place it over a wire rack.
7. Meanwhile, beat cream cheese frosting ingredients in a bowl until creamy.
8. Layer the frosting evenly over the cake and refrigerate for 30 minutes.
9. After ten minutes spread the frosting over the cake evenly.
10. Slice and serve to enjoy.

Nutrition
Calories: 331 Carbs: 9.2g Fats: 38.5g Proteins: 2.1g Sodium: 283mg Sugar: 3g

Double Layer Cream Cake

Serves: 8
Prep Time: 45 mins
Ingredients
First Layer
- ¼ cup Erythritol, powdered
- 1 tablespoon gelatin
- 2 large eggs
- 3 tablespoons coconut flour

Second Layer
- 8 oz. cream cheese
- 8 tablespoons butter
- ½ teaspoon vanilla essence

- 1 teaspoon baking powder
- 8 tablespoons butter
- ½ teaspoon vanilla essence

- 2 large eggs
- Liquid Stevia, to taste

Directions

1. Preheat the oven to 350 degrees F and lightly grease an 8-inch springform pan.
2. **First layer:** Whisk together eggs, vanilla and butter in a bowl and add gelatin, baking powder and coconut flour.
3. Combine well and keep this mixture aside.
4. **Second Layer:** Mix butter with cream cheese and add eggs, Stevia, and vanilla essence.
5. Beat well until the mixture is smooth.
6. Spread the first layer in the pan and top evenly with batter from the second layer.
7. Transfer in the oven and bake for about 25 minutes.
8. Remove from the oven and allow it to cool.
9. Refrigerate for about 3 hours in a wrapped plastic sheet and slice to serve.

Nutrition
Calories: 336 Carbs: 9.1g Fats: 34.5g Proteins: 5.1g Sodium: 267mg Sugar: 0.2g

Chunky Carrot Cake

Serves: 8
Prep Time: 45 mins
Ingredients
- ¾ cup butter
- ½ teaspoon pineapple extract
- 2½ cups almond flour
- ½ teaspoon sea salt
- 1 cup pecans, chopped
- ¾ cup Erythritol
- 1 teaspoon vanilla essence
- 4 large eggs
- 2 teaspoons gluten-free baking powder
- 2 teaspoons cinnamon
- 2½ cups carrots, grated

Directions
1. Preheat the oven at 350 degrees F and grease two 9-inch baking dishes.
2. Mix Erythritol, cream, vanilla essence, and pineapple extract in a bowl.
3. Whisk in eggs one by one, then add cinnamon, baking powder, salt and flour to mix well.
4. Stir in pecans and carrots and divide the entire batter in the two pans.
5. Transfer in the oven and bake for about 30 minutes.
6. Remove the cakes from the pans and allow them to cool slightly.
7. Dish out to slice and serve.

Nutrition
Calories: 359 Carbs: 8.5g Fats: 34g Proteins: 7.5g Sodium: 92mg Sugar: 2g

Zesty Lemon Cake

Serves: 8
Prep Time: 1 hour
Ingredients
For Cake
- 5 eggs
- ½ cup coconut flour
- ¼ cup Swerve
- Juice from ½ lemon
- ½ teaspoon lemon zest
- ½ teaspoon salt
- ½ cup butter, melted
- ½ teaspoon xanthan gum

For Icing
- 3 tablespoons swerve
- ½ teaspoon lemon zest
- 1 cup cream cheese
- 1 teaspoon vanilla essence

Directions

1. Preheat the oven at 340 degrees F and grease a loaf pan.
2. Whisk egg whites using an electric mixer until it forms stiff peaks.
3. Mix together the remaining ingredients in another bowl and combine with egg whites.
4. Pour the batter to the loaf pan and transfer in the oven.
5. Bake for about 45 minutes and dish out.
6. Meanwhile, prepare the topping by beating icing ingredients in the electric mixer.
7. Place the baked cake on the wire rack and allow it to cool.
8. Layer the cream cheese icing over the cake and evenly spread it.
9. Refrigerate for about 30 minutes and cut into slices to enjoy.

Nutrition
Calories: 251 Carbs: 4.3g Fats: 24.5g Proteins: 5.9g Sodium: 142mg Sugar: 0.5g

Perfect Cookies Recipes

Chocolate Chip Butter Cookies

Serves: 8
Prep Time: 25 mins
Ingredients
- ⅓ cup butter, unsalted
- 2 large eggs
- ⅛ teaspoon salt
- ¼ cup coconut flour
- 3 tablespoons Swerve
- 3 tablespoons sugar-free chocolate chips
- ¼ teaspoon vanilla essence

Directions
1. Preheat the oven at 350 degrees F and grease a cookie sheet.
2. Mix salt, Swerve and coconut flour in a bowl.
3. Beat the vanilla essence, butter, and eggs in a mixer.
4. Stir in the flour mixture to the eggs mixture to combine.
5. Add chocolate chips and spoon this mixture on a cookie sheet.
6. Bake the cookies in the oven for 15 minutes and allow it to cool before serving.

Nutrition
Calories: 198 Carbs: 4.5g Fats: 19.2g Proteins: 3.4g Sodium: 142mg Sugar: 3.3g

Buttery Energy Cookies

Serves: 8
Prep Time: 15 mins
Ingredients
- 3 tablespoons butter
- 1 cup almond flour
- 2 tablespoons erythritol
- Pinch of salt
- 1 teaspoon vanilla essence

Directions
1. Preheat the oven at 350 degrees F and grease a cookie sheet.
2. Put all ingredients in a bowl and whisk until well combined.
3. Divide the cookie dough into small cookies and arrange on the cookie sheet.
4. Transfer the cookie sheet in the oven and bake for about 12 minutes.
5. Refrigerate to chill for about 1 hour and serve.

Nutrition

Calories: 114 Carbs: 3.1g Fats: 9.6g Proteins: 3.5g Sodium: 155mg Sugar: 1.4g

Cream Dipped Cookies

Serves: 8
Prep Time: 40 mins
Ingredients
- ½ cup cacao nibs
- ½ cup almond butter
- 2 large eggs
- ¼ teaspoon salt
- 1 cup almond flour

- ½ cup coconut flakes, unsweetened
- 1/3 cup Erythritol
- ¼ cup butter, melted
- Stevia, to taste

Glaze:
- 1/8 teaspoon xanthan gum
- ½ teaspoon vanilla essence

- ¼ cup heavy whipping cream
- Stevia, to taste

Directions
1. Preheat the oven at 350 degrees F and grease a cookie sheet.
2. Combine all the dry ingredients in a bowl.
3. Beat eggs, Stevia almond butter, butter, and vanilla essence in another bowl.
4. Stir in the almond flour mixture and mix well.
5. Make cookies on a cookie sheet by dropping the batter with spoon.
6. Press each cookie to flatten it and transfer in the oven.
7. Bake for about 25 minutes and keep aside.
8. Combine the glaze ingredients in a saucepan and cook until the sauce thickens.
9. Once the cookies are done, pour this cooked glaze over the cookies equally.
10. Allow this glaze to set for about 15 minutes and enjoy.

Nutrition

Calories: 192 Carbs: 2.2g Fats: 17.4g Proteins: 4.7g Sodium: 135mg Sugar: 1.4g

Keto Coconut Cookies

Serves: 18
Prep Time: 35 mins
Ingredients
- ½ cup butter
- ½ tablespoon heavy cream
- 6 tablespoons coconut flour
- 1 teaspoon baking powder
- ½ teaspoon salt
- ¾ cup Splenda

- 3 eggs
- 1 teaspoon almond milk
- ½ cup unsweetened coconut flakes
- ¼ cup almond flour
- 1 teaspoon baking soda

Directions
1. Preheat the oven to 350 degrees F and grease lightly a baking sheet.
2. Mix together Splenda, butter, heavy cream, eggs, and almond milk in a bowl until smooth.
3. Combine coconut flakes, coconut flour, almond flour, baking powder, baking soda, and salt in another bowl.
4. Combine both mixtures until dough comes together.
5. Drop spoonfuls of cookie dough onto the baking sheet and transfer in the oven.
6. Bake for about 18 minutes and cool to serve.

Nutrition
Calories: 98 Carbs: 3.3g Fats: 8.9g Proteins: 2g Sodium: 211mg Sugar: 0g

Vanilla Cream Cheese Cookies

Serves: 8
Prep Time: 30 mins
Ingredients
- 2 oz. plain cream cheese
- 2 teaspoons vanilla essence
- ¼ teaspoon sea salt
- ¼ cup butter
- ½ cup erythritol
- 1 large egg white
- 3 cups almond flour

Directions
1. Preheat the oven to 350 degrees F and grease lightly a cookie sheet.
2. Put butter, cream cheese, egg white, and vanilla essence in a blender and blend until smooth.
3. Add Erythritol, flour, and salt, and mix well until smooth.
4. Divide the dough into small cookies on the cookie sheet and transfer in the oven.
5. Bake for about 15 minutes and allow the cookies to cool to serve.

Nutrition
Calories: 195 Carbs: 4.5g Fats: 14.3g Proteins: 3.2g Sodium: 125mg Sugar: 0.5g

Peanut Butter Cookies

Serves: 6
Prep Time: 1 hour
Ingredients
- ½ cup Swerve
- ½ cup peanut butter
- 1 egg

Directions
1. Preheat the oven to 350 degrees F and grease a baking sheet.
2. Mix together all ingredients in a bowl until thoroughly combined.
3. Scoop out dough with a cookie scoop and form balls.
4. Arrange on the baking sheet and press with a fork.
5. Transfer in the oven and bake for about 15 minutes.
6. Allow the cookies to cool for about 10 minutes.

Nutrition
Calories: 82 Carbs: 2.5g Fats: 6g Proteins: 3g Sodium: 65mg Sugar: 1g

Coconut Vanilla Cookies

Serves: 4
Prep Time: 20 mins
Ingredients
- ¾ teaspoon baking powder
- 1/6 cup coconut oil
- 2 large eggs
- ½ teaspoon vanilla essence
- 6 tablespoons coconut flour
- 1/8 teaspoon salt
- 3 tablespoons butter
- 6 tablespoons Swerve
- ½ tablespoon coconut milk

Directions
1. Preheat the oven to 375 degrees F and grease a cookie sheet.
2. Put all the wet ingredients in a food processor and process.
3. Stir in the remaining ingredients and mix well.
4. Divide the dough into small cookies and arrange on the cookie sheet.
5. Transfer in the oven and bake for about 10 minutes.
6. Allow the cookies to cool and serve.

Nutrition
Calories: 151 Carbs: 1.5g Fats: 14.7g Proteins: 0.8g Sodium: 53mg Sugar: 0.3g

Cinnamon Snickerdoodle Cookies

Serves: 8
Prep Time: 25 mins
Ingredients
Cookies:
- 2 teaspoons vanilla essence
- ½ cup almond milk
- 2 eggs
- 1 cup almond butter
- ¼ cup coconut oil, solid, at
- 1½ cups monk fruit sweetener
- 1 cup coconut flour
- 2 teaspoons tartar cream
- 1 teaspoon cinnamon
- 1¾ cups almond flour
- 1 teaspoon baking soda
- 1/8 teaspoon pink Himalayan salt

Topping:
- 1 tablespoon cinnamon
- 3 tablespoons monk fruit sweetener

Directions
1. Preheat the oven to 350 degrees F and grease a cookie sheet.
2. Add the wet ingredients of the cookies to a blender and beat well.
3. Stir in the dry mixture and combine well.
4. Place this batter in the refrigerator for 20 minutes to set.
5. Make small balls from this mixture.
6. Mix cinnamon and monk fruit in a shallow plate.
7. Roll these balls into this cinnamon mixture to coat well.
8. Place these balls on a baking sheet and transfer in the oven.
9. Bake for about 12 minutes and dish out to serve.

Nutrition
Calories: 252 Carbs: 7.2g Fats: 17.3g Proteins: 5.2g Sodium: 153mg Sugar: 0.3g

Nutmeg Gingersnap Cookies

Serves: 8
Prep Time: 25 mins
Ingredients
- ¼ cup butter, unsalted
- 1 teaspoon vanilla essence
- 2 cups almond flour
- 1 cup Erythritol
- 1 large egg
- ¼ teaspoon salt
- ¼ teaspoon nutmeg, ground
- ½ teaspoon cinnamon, ground
- 2 teaspoons ginger, ground
- ¼ teaspoon cloves, ground

Directions
1. Preheat the oven to 350 degrees F and grease a cookie sheet.

2. Beat the wet ingredients in an electric mixer.
3. Stir in the leftover ingredients and mix until smooth.
4. Divide the dough into small cookies and arrange on the cookie sheet spoon by spoon.
5. Transfer in the oven and bake for about 12 minutes.
6. Dish out to serve and enjoy.

Nutrition
Calories: 78 Carbs: 5.4g Fats: 7.1g Proteins: 2.3g Sodium: 15mg Sugar: 0.2g

Vanilla Shortbread Cookies

Serves: 6
Prep Time: 25 mins
Ingredients
- 6 tablespoons butter
- 1 teaspoon vanilla essence
- 2½ cups almond flour
- ½ cup erythritol

Directions
1. Preheat the oven to 350 degrees F and grease a cookie sheet.
2. Beat Erythritol with butter until frothy.
3. Stir in flour and vanilla essence while beating the mixture.
4. Divide this batter and arrange on a cookie sheet in small cookies.
5. Transfer in the oven and bake for about 15 minutes.
6. Dish out to serve and enjoy.

Nutrition
Calories: 288 Carbs: 9.6g Fats: 25.3g Proteins: 7.6g Sodium: 74mg Sugar: 0.1g

Biscuits, Muffins and Scones Recipes

Cranberry Jalapeño "Cornbread" Muffins

Serves: 12
Prep Time: 40 mins
Ingredients
- 1/3 cup Swerve
- ½ teaspoon salt
- ½ cup butter, melted
- 1 cup fresh cranberries, cut in half
- 1 jalapeño, seeds removed, sliced into 12 slices, for garnish
- 1 cup coconut flour
- 1 tablespoon baking powder
- 7 large eggs, lightly beaten
- 1 cup unsweetened almond milk
- 3 tablespoons jalapeño peppers, minced
- ½ teaspoon vanilla extract

Directions
1. Preheat the oven to 330 degrees F and line muffin tins with parchment paper.
2. Whisk together Swerve, baking powder, coconut flour, and salt in a bowl thoroughly.
3. Add eggs, butter, vanilla extract, and almond milk and mix well.
4. Stir in jalapeños and cranberries and pour into the muffin tins.
5. Transfer in the oven and bake for about 30 minutes.
6. Dish out to serve and enjoy.

Nutrition
Calories: 160 Carbs: 8.6g Fats: 11.9g Proteins: 5.2g Sodium: 236mg Sugar: 0.6g

Almond Flour Biscuits

Serves: 12
Prep Time: 25 mins
Ingredients
- 2 teaspoons gluten-free baking powder
- 2 cups almond flour
- ½ teaspoons sea salt
- 1/3 cup butter
- 2 large eggs, beaten

Directions
1. Preheat the oven to 360 degrees F and grease a cookie sheet lightly.
2. Mix together dry ingredients in a large bowl and then add in the wet ingredients.
3. Scoop spoonfuls of the dough onto the cookie sheet and flatten with your fingers slightly.
4. Transfer in the oven and bake for about 15 minutes.
5. Allow to cool on the baking sheet and serve.

Nutrition
Calories: 165 Carbs: 4.2g Fats: 15.3g Proteins: 5.1g Sodium: 255mg Sugar: 0.7g

Maple Nut Scones

Serves: 8
Prep Time: 50 mins
Ingredients
- ½ cup coconut flour
- 2 tablespoons collagen
- 1 tablespoon baking powder
- 1½ cups almond flour
- ¼ cup Swerve
- ½ teaspoon salt
- 1 large egg

Maple Glaze Icing:
- 1 teaspoon maple extract
- 2 teaspoons water
- 2½ tablespoons cold butter, cut into small pieces
- 1 teaspoon molasses
- ½ cup heavy cream
- 2 teaspoons maple extract
- 2/3 cup pecans, coarsely chopped

- ½ cup powdered Erythritol 1 tablespoon half and half

Directions
1. Preheat the oven to 360 degrees F and grease a cookie sheet lightly.
2. Put the dry ingredients into the food processor and pulse until combined.
3. Add the egg, cream, butter, maple extract, molasses, and pecans to pulse again until the dough comes together into a ball.
4. Cut the dough into 8 wedges and arrange on the baking sheet with half an inch between the scones.
5. Transfer in the oven and bake for about 40 minutes.
6. Mix together the maple glaze ingredients and spread on the scones to serve.

Nutrition
Calories: 302 Carbs: 11g Fats: 27g Proteins: 7g Sodium: 208mg Sugar: 2g

Raspberry Muffins

Serves: 12
Prep Time: 15 mins
Ingredients
- 1 cup coconut milk
- 1 cup coconut butter

- ½ cup coconut oil
- 1 teaspoon vanilla essence
- Stevia, to taste
- ¼ cup cacao butter
- ¼ cup freeze-dried raspberries

Directions
1. Preheat the oven to 350 degrees F and grease muffin cups of a tray lightly
2. Put all the ingredients in a food processor and process until smooth.
3. Pour and divide the mixture into the muffin cups.
4. Transfer in the oven and bake for about 30 minutes.
5. Remove from the muffin cups and serve.

Nutrition
Calories: 261 Carbs: 6.1g Fats: 27.1g Proteins: 1.8g Sodium: 10mg Sugar: 2.1g

Keto Drop Biscuits

Serves: 6
Prep Time: 30 mins
Ingredients
- ½ cup coconut cream
- 2 tablespoons water
- ¼ cup psyllium husk, finely ground
- ¼ cup almond flour
- 1 teaspoon xanthan gum
- 7 tablespoons coconut oil
- 1 egg
- 2 teaspoons +1 tablespoon apple cider vinegar
- ¼ cup coconut flour
- 3½ teaspoons baking powder
- ½ teaspoon kosher salt

Directions
1. Preheat the oven to 450 degrees F and grease a baking tray.
2. Whisk together eggs, coconut cream, apple cider vinegar, and water in a medium bowl and keep aside.
3. Add almond flour, coconut flour, flaxseed meal, baking powder, whey protein, xanthan gum, and kosher salt to a food processor and pulse until combined.
4. Stir in the butter along with the egg mixture and pulse until combined.
5. Drop 6 parts of dough onto the baking tray and brush with the melted butter.
6. Transfer in the oven and bake for about 20 minutes.
7. Remove from the oven and serve cooled.

Nutrition
Calories: 245 Carbs: 12.2g Fats: 24.1g Proteins: 3.2g Sodium: 257mg Sugar: 0.7g

Blackberry Scones

Serves: 8
Prep Time: 30 mins
Ingredients
For Scones
- ¼ cup coconut flour
- ¼ teaspoon sea salt
- 1 cup blanched almond flour
- 3 tablespoons erythritol
- ½ teaspoon gluten-free baking powder
- ¼ cup unsweetened almond milk
- 1 large egg
- ½ cup blackberries
- 2 tablespoons coconut oil
- 1 teaspoon vanilla extract

For Glaze

- 1 teaspoon Erythritol
- 1 tablespoon coconut oil
- 2 tablespoons blackberries

Directions
1. Preheat the oven to 350 degrees F and grease a baking sheet.
2. Mix together coconut flour, almond flour, Erythritol, baking powder, and sea salt in a bowl.
3. Whisk together egg, coconut oil, vanilla extract, and almond milk in a small bowl.
4. Fold the blackberries into the dough and place the dough onto the baking sheet.
5. Cut into 8 wedges and transfer in the oven.
6. Bake for about 20 minutes until golden and remove from oven to keep aside.
7. Meanwhile, puree the glaze ingredients in a blender and drizzle over the scones to serve.

Nutrition
Calories: 159 Carbs: 8g Fats: 13g Proteins: 5g Sodium: 200mg Sugar: 3g

Lemon Muffins

Serves: 6
Prep Time: 35 mins
Ingredients
- ¼ cup golden flax meal
- 2 tablespoons poppy seeds
- ¾ cup almond flour
- 1/3 cup Erythritol
- 1 teaspoon organic baking powder
- ¼ cup heavy cream
- ¼ cup salted butter, melted
- 1 teaspoon organic vanilla extract
- 2 teaspoons fresh lemon zest, finely grated
- 3 large organic eggs
- 3 tablespoons fresh lemon juice
- 20 drops liquid Stevia

Directions
1. Preheat the oven to 350 degrees F and grease 6 cups of a muffin tin.
2. Mix together the flax meal, flour, poppy seeds, baking powder, and Erythritol in a bowl.
3. Whisk the eggs, heavy cream and butter in another bowl and mix with the flour mixture.
4. Add lemon juice, vanilla extract, lemon zest, and Stevia and mix well.
5. Pour the mixture evenly into the muffin cups and transfer in the oven.
6. Bake for about 20 minutes and remove from oven.
7. Allow to cool for about 10 minutes and serve.

Nutrition
Calories: 249 Carbs: 14.5g Fats: 21.7g Proteins: 7.9g Sodium: 99mg Sugar: 14.2g

Cheesy Keto Biscuits

Serves: 4
Prep Time: 30 mins
Ingredients
- 1 tablespoon baking powder
- 2 cups almond flour
- 2½ cups Cheddar cheese, shredded
- ¼ cup half-and-half
- 4 eggs

Directions
1. Preheat the oven to 350 degrees F and grease a baking sheet.

2. Mix together almond flour and baking powder in a large bowl.
3. Stir in Cheddar cheese and form a small well in the center of the bowl.
4. Add eggs and half-and-half to the center and mix well until a sticky batter forms.
5. Drop small portions of batter onto the baking sheet and transfer in the oven.
6. Bake for about 20 minutes and dish out to serve.

Nutrition
Calories: 329 Carbs: 7.2g Fats: 27.1g Proteins: 16.7g Sodium: 391mg Sugar: 1g

Keto Scones with Bacon

Serves: 6
Prep Time: 35 mins
Ingredients

- 1½ teaspoons baking soda
- 3 cups almond flour
- ½ teaspoon kosher salt
- 2 large eggs
- 2 tablespoons apple cider vinegar
- 8 slices bacon, diced and cooked until crisp
- 4 tablespoons cold butter, cut into cubes
- 2 tablespoons bacon grease

Directions
1. Preheat the oven to 350 degrees F and grease lightly a baking sheet.
2. Mix together the almond flour, baking soda, and kosher salt in a large bowl.
3. Stir in the cold butter and mix well.
4. Whisk together the eggs, vinegar, and bacon grease in another bowl and add to the flour mixture.
5. Mix well and cut triangles from the dough.
6. Cut into 6 triangles and arrange onto the baking sheet.
7. Transfer in the oven and bake for about 25 minutes to serve.

Nutrition
Calories: 510 Carbs: 12g Fats: 46g Proteins: 18g Sodium: 93mg Sugar: 2.2g

Blueberry Muffins

Serves: 12
Prep Time: 35 mins
Ingredients

- ½ cup Swerve
- ¼ teaspoon salt
- ¼ cup butter, melted
- ¾ cup fresh blueberries
- 2 cups almond flour
- 2 teaspoons organic baking powder
- 3 organic eggs, beaten
- ¼ cup unsweetened almond milk
- 1 teaspoon organic vanilla extract

Directions
1. Preheat the oven to 350 degrees F and grease 12 cups of a muffin tin.
2. Mix together almond flour, salt, Swerve, and baking powder in a bowl.
3. Whisk together the eggs, almond milk, butter, and vanilla extract in another bowl.
4. Combine the egg mixture well with the flour mixture and add blueberries.
5. Pour the mixture evenly into prepared muffin cups and transfer in the oven.
6. Bake for about 20 minutes and remove from the oven.
7. Allow to cool for about 10 minutes and serve.

Nutrition
Calories: 170 Carbs: 5.9g Fats: 13.9g Proteins: 5.5g Sodium: 104mg Sugar: 1g

Easy Tarts and Bars Recipes

Mixed Berries Tart

Serves: 8
Prep Time: 25 mins
Ingredients
Tart crust:
- ¼ cup Erythritol, powdered
- ¼ teaspoon sea salt
- 2¼ cups almond flour
- 5 tablespoons butter, melted

Filling:
- 2 tablespoons erythritol
- 6 oz. mascarpone cheese
- 1/3 cup heavy cream
- ¼ teaspoon lemon zest
- 1 teaspoon vanilla essence

To garnish:
- 6 blueberries
- 6 raspberries
- 6 blackberries

Directions
1. **Crust:** Preheat the oven to 350 degrees F and grease 8 small tart pans with butter.
2. Put butter, almond flour, Erythritol, and salt in a food processor and process until coarse.
3. Divide this mixture into the tart pans and press firmly.
4. Transfer in the oven and bake for about 10 minutes.
5. **Filling:** Put the erythritol and cream in an electric mixer and beat for about 2 minutes.
6. Stir in the cream, lemon zest, and vanilla essence slowly and continue beating until the mixture thickens.
7. Fill this mixture in the baked crust of each tart pan and garnish with the berries.
8. Chill for 10 minutes in the refrigerator to serve and enjoy.

Nutrition
Calories: 237 Carbs: 5g Fats: 22g Proteins: 5g Sodium: 118mg Sugar: 1g

Crunchy Chocolate Bars

Serves: 8
Prep Time: 15 mins
Ingredients
- 1 cup almond butter
- 1½ cups sugar-free chocolate chips
- Stevia, to taste
- 3 cups pecans, chopped
- ¼ cup coconut oil

Directions
1. Preheat the oven to 350 degrees F and grease an 8-inch baking pan.
2. Melt chocolate chips with stevia and coconut oil in a glass bowl.
3. Mix well and add seeds and nuts.
4. Pour this nutty batter into the baking pan and transfer in the oven.
5. Bake for about 10 minutes and remove from the oven to cool.
6. Place the pan in the refrigerator for about 3 hours.
7. Dish out and slice into small bars to serve.

Nutrition
Calories: 316 Carbs: 8.3g Fats: 30.9g Proteins: 6.4g Sodium: 8mg Sugar: 1.8g

Creamy Chocolate Tart

Serves: 8
Prep Time: 40 mins
Ingredients
Crust
- 2 tablespoons Erythritol
- 6 tablespoons coconut flour
- 4 tablespoons butter, melted

- 1 large egg
- 2 (4-inch) tart pans

Filling
- ½ cup heavy whipping cream
- 2 oz. sugar-free chocolate
- ¼ cup Erythritol, powdered

- 1 large egg
- Liquid Stevia, to taste
- 1 oz. cream cheese

Directions
1. Preheat the oven to 350 degrees F and grease 2 (4 inches) tart pans with butter.
2. Put all the ingredients for the crust in a food processor and process until coarse.
3. Divide this mixture into each tart pan and press firmly.
4. Pierce few holes in the crusts with a fork and transfer in the oven.
5. Bake both the crusts for about 12 minutes.
6. Meanwhile, heat cream in a saucepan on medium heat and add chocolate.
7. Cook until it melts and transfer in an immersion blender.
8. Puree this mixture and add egg, cream cheese, Erythritol, and Stevia.
9. Divide this filling into each crust and return both the pans to the oven.
10. Bake for about 15 minutes and allow to cool.
11. Transfer to the refrigerator for about 3 hours to serve chilled.

Nutrition
Calories: 190 Carbs: 5.5g Fats: 17.2g Proteins: 3g Sodium: 28mg Sugar: 2.8g

Lemon Egg Bars

Serves: 8
Prep Time: 1 hour
Ingredients
- 1¾ cups almond flour
- ½ cup butter, melted
- 1 cup Erythritol, powdered

- 3 large eggs
- 3 medium lemons, juiced

Directions
1. Preheat the oven to 350 degrees F and grease an 8-inch baking pan.
2. Whisk together butter, almond flour, Erythritol, and salt in a bowl.
3. Transfer this mixture to a pan and press firmly.
4. Place in the oven and bake for about 20 minutes.
5. Dish out and allow it to cool for 10 minutes at room temperature.
6. Mix the rest of the ingredients in a separate bowl and spread evenly over the baked crust.
7. Bake again for 25 minutes in the oven and slice the bars after removing from oven.
8. Serve and enjoy.

Nutrition
Calories: 282 Carbs: 9.4g Fats: 25.1g Proteins: 8g Sodium: 117mg Sugar: 0.7g

Blackberry Lemon Tart

Serves: 8
Prep Time: 30 mins
Ingredients
- 2 (9" tart molds with loose bottoms)
- 1 tablespoon sliced almonds
- 1 cup blackberries
- 1 cup lemon curd

Almond Flour Pie Crust
- ½ cup coconut flour
- 4 tablespoons cold butter, unsalted
- 1½ cups almond flour
- 4 tablespoons Erythritol, powdered
- 2 eggs

Directions
1. Preheat the oven to 350 degrees F and grease two tart molds.
2. Mix together all the ingredients for almond flour pie crust to form a dough.
3. Divide the dough into two equal sized balls and place in the tart molds.
4. Make a few holes into each dough layer with a fork and transfer in the oven.
5. Bake for about 15 minutes and remove from the oven to cool.
6. Fill both the crusts equally with lemon curd and top with berries, Erythritol, and almond slices.
7. Serve and enjoy.

Nutrition
Calories: 321 Carbs: 8.1g Fats: 12.9g Proteins: 5.4g Sodium: 28mg Sugar: 1.8g

Caramel Bars

Serves: 8
Prep Time: 55 mins
Ingredients
For the Cracker Base:
- 1 cup almond flour
- ¼ teaspoon salt
- ¼ teaspoon baking powder
- 1 egg
- 2 tablespoons grass-fed salted butter, melted

Caramel Sauce:
- ½ cup butter
- ½ cup Swerve
- ½ cup heavy cream
- 1 teaspoon caramel extract
- ¼ teaspoon salt
- ½ teaspoon vanilla essence

Toppings:
- 1 cup pecans, chopped
- 2 cups chocolate chips
- 1 cup coconut, shredded

Directions
1. **Crackers:** Preheat the oven to 300 degrees F and grease a baking pan.
2. Combine baking powder, salt, and almond flour in a bowl.
3. Whisk eggs and butter in a bowl and combine with the flour mixture.
4. Place the dough on the working surface layered with parchment paper.
5. Cut the dough into a rectangle then cover it with a parchment paper.
6. Spread it using a rolling pin into 1/8 inch thick dough sheet.
7. Transfer it to the baking pan and bake for about 35 minutes.
8. Increase the temperature of the oven to 375 degrees F.
9. **Caramel sauce:** Put butter, Swerve, vanilla, cream, and caramel extracts in a saucepan.
10. Combine well and spread the sauce over the baked crackers base.
11. Drizzle chocolate chips, coconut, and pecans over it and transfer in the oven.

12. Bake for another 5 minutes and remove from the pan.
13. Allow it to cool and slice to serve.

Nutrition
Calories: 358 Carbs: 7.4g Fats: 35.2g Proteins: 5.5g Sodium: 178mg Sugar: 1.1g

Strawberry Vanilla Tart

Serves: 3
Prep Time: 25 mins
Ingredients
Coconut crust:
- ¾ cup coconut flour
- ½ cup coconut oil
- 2 eggs

- 1 teaspoon powdered sweetener
- 1 teaspoon vanilla essence

Cream Filling:
- 2 eggs, separated
- 1 cup strawberries
- 1 cup mascarpone

- 1 teaspoon vanilla essence
- 2 tablespoons Stevia, powdered

Directions
1. **Crust:**
2. Preheat the oven to 350 degrees F and grease a baking pan.
3. Whisk together eggs in a bowl and add rest of the ingredients.
4. Spread this dough in between two sheets of parchment paper.
5. Place this dough sheet in a greased pan and pierce holes in it with a fork.
6. Transfer in the oven and bake for about 10 minutes.
7. **Cream Filling:**
8. Whisk the egg whites in an electric mixer until frothy.
9. Stir in mascarpone cream, egg yolks, sweetener, and vanilla and beat for about 3 minutes.
10. Spread this filling evenly in the baked crust and top with Stevia and strawberries.
11. Place the pie in the refrigerator for about 30 minutes and serve hot.

Nutrition
Calories: 236 Carbs: 7.6g Fats: 21.5g Proteins: 4.3g Sodium: 21mg Sugar: 1.4g

Peanut Butter Bars

Serves: 8
Prep Time: 15 mins
Ingredients
Bars
- 2 oz. butter
- ¾ cup almond flour
- ¼ cup Swerve

- ½ teaspoon vanilla extract
- ½ cup peanut butter

Topping
- ½ cup sugar-free chocolate chips

Directions
1. Preheat the oven to 300 degrees F and grease a baking pan.
2. Put all the ingredients for the bars in a bowl and mix well.
3. Spread this mixture in the pan and top with chocolate chips.
4. Transfer in the oven and bake for about 15 minutes.

5. Remove from the oven and transfer the pan in the refrigerator for about 1 hour.
6. Remove the base from pan and slice to serve.

Nutrition
Calories: 214 Carbs: 6.5g Fats: 19g Proteins: 6.5g Sodium: 123mg Sugar: 1.9g

Cheesecake Jam Tarts

Serves: 6
Prep Time: 45 mins
Ingredients
Crust
- ½ cup almond flour
- 1½ tablespoons butter, melted

Filling
- 1 small egg
- ½ teaspoon vanilla essence
- 1/8 teaspoon salt
- 6 oz. cream cheese
- 1/8 cup Erythritol
- ½ tablespoon fresh lemon juice

Toppings
- 1/8 cup strawberry jam, sugar-free
- 1/8 cup blueberries

Directions
1. Preheat the oven to 340 degrees F and grease muffin tins.
2. Mix butter and almond flour in a bowl and pour this mixture into the muffin tin.
3. Transfer in the oven and bake for about 8 minutes.
4. Meanwhile, beat cream cheese in an electric mixture along with an egg.
5. Stir in Erythritol, vanilla essence, salt, and lemon juice and combine well.
6. Divide this filling into the muffin crust and transfer in the oven.
7. Bake the tarts for 20 minutes and allow it to cool after removing from oven.
8. Top with jam and blueberries and refrigerate overnight to serve.

Nutrition
Calories: 175 Carbs: 2.8g Fats: 16g Proteins: 9g Sodium: 8mg Sugar: 1.8g

Chocolate Dipped Granola Bars

Serves: 4
Prep Time: 35 mins
Ingredients
- 3 tablespoons coconut oil
- 1 oz. sesame seeds
- 1½ oz. walnuts
- 1 oz. pumpkin seeds
- 1 teaspoon cinnamon, ground
- 1½ oz. sugar-free dark chocolate
- 1 egg
- 1½ oz. almonds
- ¼ teaspoon flaxseed
- 1 oz. coconut, shredded, unsweetened
- 1 oz. sugar-free dark chocolate
- 2 tablespoons tahini
- ½ pinch sea salt
- ½ teaspoon vanilla essence

Directions
1. Preheat the oven to 340 degrees F and grease a baking pan.
2. Put all the ingredients in a food processor, except chocolate, and coarsely grind.
3. Spread the ground mixture in the baking pan and transfer in the oven.
4. Bake for about 20 minutes and remove from oven.
5. Allow it to cool at room temperature and slice it into small squares.
6. Melt the chocolate in a microwave and pour over the bars.

7. Arrange the bars over a baking sheet and refrigerate them for about 30 minutes to serve.

Nutrition
Calories: 313 Carbs: 9.2g Fats: 28.4g Proteins: 8.1g Sodium: 39mg Sugar: 3.1g

Tasty Pies Recipes

Pumpkin Almond Pie

Serves: 8
Prep Time: 1 hour 15 mins
Ingredients
Almond Flour Pie Crust
- 4 tablespoons butter, melted
- 2 cups almond flour
- 1 teaspoon vanilla

- ½ teaspoon cinnamon
- 1 egg yolk

Pumpkin Spice Filling
- 1 cup heavy cream
- 2 teaspoons pumpkin pie spice
- ⅔ cups Swerve

- 8 ounces cream cheese
- 4 eggs
- 1 teaspoon vanilla
- ¼ teaspoon salt

Directions
1. Preheat the oven to 400 degrees F and grease a pie pan.
2. Mix together all the ingredients for the crust in a bowl and transfer into the pie pan.
3. Press this mixture and transfer into the oven.
4. Bake this crust for about 12 minutes and keep aside.
5. **Filling:** Whisk together eggs and cream cheese until it turns frothy.
6. Add rest of the ingredients and stir well to combine.
7. Spread this filling evenly into the baked crust and return the stuffed pie to the oven.
8. Bake for another 45 minutes and allow to cool for 10 minutes.
9. Slice and enjoy.

Nutrition
Calories: 285 Carbs: 3.5g Fats: 27.3g Proteins: 7.2g Sodium: 165mg Sugar: 0.4g

Key Lime Pie

Serves: 8
Prep Time: 40 mins
Ingredients
For Crust:
- ½ cup coconut flour, sifted
- ¼ cup butter, melted
- ¼ teaspoon salt

- ½ cup almond flour
- ¼ cup Erythritol
- 2 organic eggs

For Filling:
- ½ cup Erythritol
- 2 teaspoons xanthan gum
- 3 organic egg yolks
- 2 tablespoons unsweetened dried coconut

- ¾ cup unsweetened coconut milk
- ¼ cup heavy cream
- 1 teaspoon guar gum
- ¼ teaspoon powdered Stevia
- ½ cup key lime juice

For Topping:

- ½ lime, cut into slices
- 1 cup whipped cream

Directions
1. Preheat the oven to 390 degrees F and grease a 9-inch pie dish.
2. **For crust:** Mix together all ingredients in a bowl to form a dough.
3. Arrange the dough between 2 sheets of wax paper and roll into 1/8-inch thick circle.
4. Place the dough in the pie dish and press firmly.
5. Pierce the bottom and sides of crust with a fork at many places.
6. Transfer in the oven and bake for about 10 minutes.
7. Remove from the oven and allow it to cool.
8. Reset the oven to 350 degrees F.
9. **For filling:** Put coconut milk, heavy cream, egg yolks, lime juice, erythritol, guar gum, xanthan gum and Stevia in a food processor.
10. Pulse until well combined and spread the filling mixture evenly over crust.
11. Transfer in the oven and bake for about 10 minutes.
12. Remove from oven and allow to cool for about 10 minutes.
13. Freeze for about 4 hours and top with whipped cream and lime slices to serve.

Nutrition
Calories: 255 Carbs: 13.1g Fats: 24.8g Proteins: 5.2g Sodium: 147mg Sugar: 8.9g

Meringue Pie

Serves: 10
Prep Time: 1 hour
Ingredients
- 2 tablespoons coconut flour
- 1 tablespoon granulated Swerve
- ¼ teaspoon salt
- 4 tablespoons ice water
- 1¼ cups almond flour
- 2 tablespoons arrowroot starch
- 1 teaspoon xanthan gum
- 5 tablespoons chilled butter, cut into small pieces

For Filling:
- 1½ cups plus 2 tablespoons water, divided
- ¼ teaspoon salt
- 3 tablespoons butter
- 1 tablespoon grass-fed gelatin
- 4 large organic egg yolks
- 1 cup granulated Swerve
- 2 teaspoons fresh lemon zest, grated
- 1/3 cup fresh lemon juice
- ½ teaspoon xanthan gum

For Meringue Topping:
- ¼ teaspoon cream of tartar
- ¼ cup powdered Swerve
- ½ teaspoon organic vanilla extract
- 4 large organic egg whites
- Pinch of salt
- ¼ cup granulated Swerve

Directions
1. Preheat the oven to 335 degrees F and grease a pie pan.
2. **For crust:** Put the flours, butter, arrowroot starch, Swerve, xanthan gum, and salt in a food processor until combined.
3. Add ice water slowly to form a dough and transfer into a pie pan.
4. Press gently and pierce holes in the crust with a fork.
5. Transfer in the oven and bake for about 12 minutes.
6. Remove from the oven and keep aside to cool completely.
7. Reheat the oven to 300 degrees F.

For filling: Whisk together egg yolks in a bowl and slowly add ½ cup of water, beating until well combined.

8. Boil Swerve, salt and lemon zest in 1 cup of the water in a pan.
9. Whisk in the egg yolks mixture slowly into the pan, beating continuously.
10. Lower the heat and cook for about 1 minute, stirring continuously.
11. Remove from the heat and stir in the butter and lemon juice until smooth.
12. Top with xanthan gum and beat vigorously with a wire whisk until well combined.
13. Meanwhile, dissolve the gelatin into remaining 2 tablespoons of water in a small bowl.
14. Keep aside for about 2 minutes and add the gelatin mixture into hot lemon mixture.
15. Beat until well combined and cover the pan to keep aside.

For topping: Whisk together the egg whites, cream of tartar, and salt in a large bowl and beat until frothy.

16. Add the powdered Swerve, granulated Swerve, and vanilla extract slowly until stiff peaks form.
17. Pour the warm filling evenly over the crust and top with meringue.
18. Transfer in the oven and bake for about 20 minutes.
19. Remove from the oven and keep aside to cool.
20. Refrigerate for at least 3 hours and serve chilled.

Nutrition
Calories: 215 Carbs: 7.2g Fats: 18.5g Proteins: 6.7g Sodium: 159mg Sugar: 1.1g

Keto Meat Pie

Serves: 8
Prep Time: 25 mins
Ingredients
The Filling
- 1 garlic clove, finely chopped
- 20 oz. ground beef
- 1 tablespoon dried oregano
- ½ cup water
- ½ yellow onion, finely chopped
- 2 tablespoons butter
- Salt and black pepper, to taste
- 4 tablespoons tomato paste

Pie Crust
- 4 tablespoons sesame seeds
- 1 tablespoon ground psyllium husk powder
- 1 pinch salt
- 4 tablespoons water
- ¾ cup almond flour
- 4 tablespoons coconut flour
- 1 teaspoon baking powder
- 3 tablespoons olive oil
- 1 egg

Topping
- 7 oz. cheddar cheese, shredded
- 8 oz. cottage cheese

Directions
1. Preheat the oven to 350 degrees F and grease a springform pan.
2. Heat olive oil in a pan and add onion and garlic.
3. Sauté for about 3 minutes and add ground beef, dried oregano, salt and black pepper.
4. Cook for about 4 minutes and add tomato paste, psyllium husk powder and water.
5. Lower the heat and allow to simmer for at least 20 minutes.
6. Meanwhile, make the dough for the crust by mixing all the dough ingredients in a food processor.
7. Spread the dough in the pan and transfer in the oven.
8. Bake for about 15 minutes and remove from the oven.
9. Fill the meat in the crust and top with cheese.
10. Transfer in the oven and bake for about 40 minutes.

11. Serve hot.
Nutrition
Calories: 467 Carbs: 12.7g Fats: 30.5g Proteins: 36.9g Sodium: 368mg Sugar: 2.4g

Keto Silk Pie

Serves: 4
Prep Time: 15 mins
Ingredients
For the crust:
- ½ teaspoon baking powder
- 1/3 cup granulated Stevia
- 1½ teaspoons vanilla extract
- 1½ cups almond flour
- 1/8 teaspoon salt
- 3 tablespoons butter
- 1 medium egg
- 1 teaspoon butter, for greasing the pan

For the filling:
- 4 tablespoons sour cream
- ½ cup + 2 teaspoons granulated Stevia
- 16 oz. cream cheese, room temperature
- 4 tablespoons butter
- 1 tablespoon +1 teaspoon vanilla extract
- ½ cup cocoa powder
- 1 cup whipping cream

Directions
1. Preheat the oven to 375 degrees F and grease a 9-inch pie pan with some butter.
2. Combine baking powder, almond flour, salt, and 1/3 cup Stevia in a bowl and add butter.
3. Stir in egg and vanilla extract and knead until the dough forms into a ball.
4. Transfer the dough into the pie pan and spread it covering the bottom and sides of the pan.
5. Pierce the holes in the crust and transfer in the oven.
6. Bake for about 15 minutes and remove crust from the oven to cool.
7. **For the filling:** Place sour cream, cream cheese, butter, vanilla extract, cocoa powder, and ½ cup stevia in a blender.
8. Blend until fluffy and place the whipping cream in a separate bowl.
9. Add 2 teaspoons granulated stevia and 1 teaspoon vanilla extract to the cream and beat to form stiff peaks.
10. Mix the whipped cream mixture into the sour cream mixture.
11. Scoop this mixture into the crust and cover to refrigerate for at least 3 hours before serving.
Nutrition
Calories: 449 Carbs: 9.3g Fats: 43.6g Proteins: 9.5g Sodium: 267mg Sugar: 2.3g

Banana Cream Pie

Serves: 10
Prep Time: 45 mins
Ingredients
Crust
- 1 batch Low Carb Walnut Pie Crust
Banana Cream Filling
- 1/3 cup almond milk
- 1/8 teaspoon xanthan gum
- 2 large eggs
- 1 teaspoon banana extract
- ½ teaspoon Stevia
- 1 cup heavy cream
- 1/3 cup Erythritol
- 2 tablespoons cornstarch
- 3 large egg yolks
- 1 teaspoon vanilla
- 1 pinch salt
- 2 tablespoons butter
For Filling and Topping

- Stevia, to taste
- 1½ cups heavy cream

Directions
1. Preheat the oven to 325 degrees F and grease a 9-inch pie pan.
2. **Banana Cream Filling:** Mix together all the ingredients in a saucepan on medium-low heat.
3. Allow to simmer and remove from heat.
4. Refrigerate overnight and fill in the readymade low carb crust.
5. Transfer it in the oven and bake for about 20 minutes.
6. Dish out and keep aside.
7. Mix Stevia in heavy cream and pour over the pie.
8. Refrigerate at least 4 hours before serving.

Nutrition
Calories: 478 Carbs: 9g Fats: 47g Proteins: 9g Sodium: 145mg Sugar: 3.8g

Chayote Squash Mock Apple Pie

Serves: 16
Prep Time: 1 hour
Ingredients
Crust
- 1½ cups almond flour
- ½ teaspoon salt
- ½ cup butter, melted
- ¾ cup coconut flour
- 4 eggs
- 1 tablespoon whole psyllium husks

Filling
- ¾ cup stevia
- ¼ teaspoon ginger
- 1 tablespoon lemon juice
- 1/3 cup butter cut in small pieces
- 5 medium chayote squash, peeled and sliced
- 1½ teaspoons cinnamon
- 1/8 teaspoon nutmeg
- 1 tablespoon xanthan gum
- 2 teaspoons apple extract

Topping
- 1 tablespoon Stevia
- 1 egg

Directions
1. Preheat the oven to 375 degrees F and grease a 9-inch pie pan.
2. Mix together crust ingredients to form a dough ball.
3. Transfer the dough ball into the pie dish and press firmly.
4. **Filling:** Boil sliced chayote and drain completely.
5. Add Stevia, apple extract, lemon juice, and xanthan gum to cooked chayote squash.
6. Pour chayote mixture into pie pan and top with butter.
7. **Topping:** Brush egg on pie top and sprinkle with Stevia.
8. Bake for about 35 minutes and dish out to serve.

Nutrition
Calories: 187 Carbs: 6.6g Fats: 16.7g Proteins: 2g Sodium: 204mg Sugar: 0.5g

Low-Carb Banoffee Pie

Serves: 12
Prep Time: 40 mins

Ingredients
- 1 cup organic almond flour
- 1 cup Stevia
- 6 tablespoons organic butter
- 2 cups + 2 tablespoons organic heavy cream
- 1 tablespoon banana flavor

Directions
1. Preheat the oven to 300 degrees F and grease a 9-inch pie pan.
2. Melt the butter over low heat and add almond flour and 1/3 cup stevia.
3. Press the dough firmly into a pan and transfer in the oven.
4. Bake the crust for about 20 minutes and keep aside.
5. Put ¾ cup + 2 tablespoons of the heavy cream and 2/3 cup Stevia in a saucepan and stir well.
6. Boil this mixture on a medium heat stirring constantly until the mixture thickens.
7. Remove the pan from heat and add banana flavor.
8. Allow to cool in the fridge and spread the toffee on the crust.
9. Top with the remaining whipped cream and serve chilled.

Nutrition
Calories: 323 Carbs: 11.5g Fats: 27.8g Proteins: 3.3g Sodium: 70mg Sugar: 0g

Brownie Truffle Pie

Serves: 10
Prep Time: 55 mins
Ingredients
Crust:
- 3 tablespoons coconut flour
- 5 tablespoons butter, cut into small pieces
- 1¼ cups almond flour
- 1 tablespoon granulated Swerve
- ¼ teaspoon salt
- 4 tablespoons ice water

Filling:
- 6 tablespoons cocoa powder
- 1 teaspoon baking powder
- ¼ cup melted butter
- ½ cup almond flour
- 6 tablespoons Swerve Sweetener
- 2 large eggs
- 5 tablespoons water
- 1 tablespoon Sukrin Fiber Syrup
- 3 tablespoons sugar-free chocolate chips
- ½ teaspoon vanilla extract

Topping:
- 2 tablespoons Swerve Sweetener
- ½ ounce sugar-free dark chocolate
- 1 cup whipping cream
- ¼ teaspoon vanilla extract

Directions
1. **Crust:** Preheat the oven to 325 degrees F and grease a pie pan.
2. Mix together almond flour, coconut flour, water, Swerve, butter, and salt in a bowl to form a dough.
3. Press evenly into the pie pan and transfer in the oven.
4. Bake for about 12 minutes and remove from the oven.
5. **Filling:** Whisk together the cocoa powder, almond flour, Swerve, and baking powder in a bowl.
6. Add water, eggs, butter, chocolate chips, and vanilla extract until well combined.
7. Pour this batter into the pie crust and transfer in the oven.
8. Bake for about 30 minutes and allow to cool.
9. **Topping:** Mix together cream, vanilla extract, and Swerve in a large bowl.
10. Beat until stiff peaks form and layer over cooled filling.

11. Top with dark chocolate and chill until completely set.

Nutrition
Calories: 374 Carbs: 5.7g Fats: 33.9g Proteins: 8.5g Sodium: 280mg Sugar: 0.8g

Low Carb Grasshopper Pie

Serves: 8
Prep Time: 25 mins
Ingredients
- ½ cup cocoa powder
- ½ teaspoon baking powder
- ¼ cup coconut oil
- 2 tablespoons chocolate syrup
- 2 cups ground flax seeds
- 3 teaspoons Stevia powder
- Pinch of salt
- ½ cup smooth almond butter
- 2 eggs
- Mint ice cream, sugar-free

Directions
1. Preheat the oven to 350 degrees F and grease a large pie dish.
2. Mix together all dry ingredients in a bowl and keep aside.
3. Mix almond butter, eggs, chocolate syrup and coconut oil in another bowl.
4. Combine the two mixtures to form a crumbly dough and press in the pie dish.
5. Transfer in the oven and bake for about 12 minutes.
6. Allow to cool and fill with sugar-free mint ice cream to serve.

Nutrition
Calories: 358 Carbs: 15.2g Fats: 26.5g Proteins: 11g Sodium: 51mg Sugar: 4.3g

Delicious Pizza Recipes

Keto Breakfast Pizza

Serves: 6
Prep Time: 30 mins
Ingredients
- 2 tablespoons coconut flour
- 2 cups cauliflower, grated
- ½ teaspoon salt
- 1 tablespoon psyllium husk powder
- 4 eggs

Toppings:
- Avocado
- Smoked Salmon
- Herbs
- Olive oil
- Spinach

Directions
1. Preheat the oven to 360 degrees and grease a pizza tray.
2. Mix together all ingredients in a bowl, except toppings, and keep aside.
3. Pour the pizza dough onto the pan and mold it into an even pizza crust using hands.
4. Top the pizza with toppings and transfer in the oven.
5. Bake for about 15 minutes until golden brown and remove from the oven to serve.

Nutrition
Calories: 454 Carbs: 16g Fats: 31g Proteins: 22g Sodium: 1325mg Sugar: 4.4g

Coconut Flour Pizza

Serves: 4
Prep Time: 35 mins
Ingredients
- 2 tablespoons psyllium husk powder
- ¾ cup coconut flour
- 1 teaspoon garlic powder
- ½ teaspoon salt
- ½ teaspoon baking soda
- 1 cup boiling water
- 1 teaspoon apple cider vinegar
- 3 eggs

Toppings
- 3 tablespoons tomato sauce
- 1½ oz. Mozzarella cheese
- 1 tablespoon basil, freshly chopped

Directions
1. Preheat the oven to 350 degrees F and grease a baking sheet.
2. Mix coconut flour, salt, psyllium husk powder, and garlic powder until fully combined.
3. Add eggs, apple cider vinegar, and baking soda and knead with boiling water.
4. Place the dough out on a baking sheet and top with the toppings.
5. Transfer in the oven and bake for about 20 minutes.
6. Dish out and serve warm.

Nutrition
Calories: 173 Carbs: 16.8g Fats: 7.4g Proteins: 10.4g Sodium: 622mg Sugar: 0.9g

Mini Pizza Crusts

Serves: 4
Prep Time: 20 mins
Ingredients
- 1 cup coconut flour, sifted
- 8 large eggs, 5 whole eggs and 3 egg whites
- ½ teaspoon baking powder
- Italian spices, to taste
- Salt and black pepper, to taste

For the pizza sauce
- 2 garlic cloves, crushed
- 1 teaspoon dried basil
- ½ cup tomato sauce
- ¼ teaspoon sea salt

Directions
1. Preheat the oven to 350 degrees F and grease a baking tray.
2. Whisk together eggs and egg whites in a large bowl and stir in the coconut flour, baking powder, Italian spices, salt, and black pepper.
3. Make small dough balls from this mixture and press on the baking tray.
4. Transfer in the oven and bake for about 20 minutes.
5. Allow pizza bases to cool and keep aside.
6. Combine all ingredients for the pizza sauce together and sit at room temperature for half an hour.
7. Spread this pizza sauce over the pizza crusts and serve.

Nutrition
Calories: 170 Carbs: 5.7g Fats: 10.5g Proteins: 13.6g Sodium: 461mg Sugar: 2.3g

Keto Pepperoni Pizza

Serves: 4
Prep Time: 40 mins

Ingredients
Crust
- 6 oz. mozzarella cheese, shredded
- 4 eggs

Topping
- 1 teaspoon dried oregano
- 5 oz. mozzarella cheese, shredded
- 1½ oz. pepperoni
- Olives
- 3 tablespoons tomato paste

Directions
1. Preheat the oven to 400 degrees F and grease a baking sheet.
2. Whisk together eggs and cheese in a bowl and spread on a baking sheet.
3. Transfer in the oven and bake for about 15 minutes until golden.
4. Remove from the oven and allow it to cool.
5. Increase the oven temperature to 450 degrees F.
6. Spread the tomato paste on the crust and top with oregano, pepperoni, cheese, and olives on top.
7. Bake for another 10 minutes and serve hot.

Nutrition
Calories: 356 Carbs: 6.1g Fats: 23.8g Proteins: 30.6g Sodium: 790mg Sugar: 1.8g

Thin Crust Low Carb Pizza

Serves: 6
Prep Time: 25 mins
Ingredients
- 2 tablespoons tomato sauce
- 2 ounces low-moisture mozzarella cheese
- 1/8 teaspoon black pepper
- 1/8 teaspoon chili flakes
- 1/8 teaspoon garlic powder
- 1 piece low-carb pita bread

Toppings:
- Bacon, roasted red peppers, spinach, olives, pesto, artichokes, salami, pepperoni, roast beef, prosciutto, avocado, ham, chili paste, Sriracha

Directions
1. Preheat the oven to 450 degrees F and grease a baking dish.
2. Mix together tomato sauce, black pepper, chili flakes, and garlic powder in a bowl and keep aside.
3. Place the low-carb pita bread in the oven and bake for about 2 minutes.
4. Remove from oven and spread the tomato sauce on it.
5. Add mozzarella cheese and top with your favorite toppings.
6. Bake again for 3 minutes and dish out.

Nutrition
Calories: 254 Carbs: 12.9g Fats: 16g Proteins: 19.3g Sodium: 255mg Sugar: 2.8g

BBQ Chicken Pizza

Serves: 4
Prep Time: 30 mins
Ingredients
Dairy Free Pizza Crust
- 6 tablespoons Parmesan cheese

- 6 large eggs
- 3 tablespoons psyllium husk powder

Toppings
- 6 oz. rotisserie chicken, shredded
- 4 oz. cheddar cheese
- 1 tablespoon mayonnaise

- Salt and black pepper, to taste
- 1½ teaspoons Italian seasoning

- 4 tablespoons tomato sauce
- 4 tablespoons BBQ sauce

Directions
1. Preheat the oven to 400 degrees F and grease a baking dish.
2. Place all Pizza Crust ingredients in an immersion blender and blend until smooth.
3. Spread dough mixture onto the baking dish and transfer in the oven.
4. Bake for about 10 minutes and top with favorite toppings.
5. Bake for about 3 minutes and dish out.

Nutrition
Calories: 356 Carbs: 2.9g Fats: 24.5g Proteins: 24.5g Sodium: 396mg Sugar: 0.6g

Buffalo Chicken Crust Pizza

Serves: 6
Prep Time: 25 mins
Ingredients
- 1 cup whole milk mozzarella, shredded
- 1 teaspoon dried oregano
- 2 tablespoons butter
- 1 pound chicken thighs, boneless and skinless
- 1 large egg
- ¼ teaspoon black pepper

- ¼ teaspoon salt
- 1 stalk celery
- 3 tablespoons Franks Red Hot Original
- 1 stalk green onion
- 1 tablespoon sour cream
- 1 ounce bleu cheese, crumbled

Directions
1. Preheat the oven to 400 degrees F and grease a baking dish.
2. Process chicken thighs in a food processor until smooth.
3. Transfer to a large bowl and add egg, ½ cup of shredded mozzarella, oregano, black pepper, and salt to form a dough.
4. Spread the chicken dough in the baking dish and transfer in the oven
5. Bake for about 25 minutes and keep aside.
6. Meanwhile, heat butter and add celery, and cook for about 4 minutes.
7. Mix Franks Red Hot Original with the sour cream in a small bowl.
8. Spread the sauce mixture over the crust, layer with the cooked celery and remaining ½ cup of mozzarella and the bleu cheese.
9. Bake for another 10 minutes, until the cheese is melted

Nutrition
Calories: 172 Carbs: 1g Fats: 12.9g Proteins: 13.8g Sodium: 172mg Sugar: 0.2g

Fresh Bell Pepper Basil Pizza

Serves: 3
Prep Time: 25 mins
Ingredients
Pizza Base
- ½ cup almond flour

- 2 tablespoons cream cheese

- 1 teaspoon Italian seasoning
- ½ teaspoon black pepper
- 6 ounces mozzarella cheese
- 2 tablespoons psyllium husk

Toppings
- 4 ounces cheddar cheese, shredded
- ¼ cup Marinara sauce
- 2/3 medium bell pepper

- 2 tablespoons fresh Parmesan cheese
- 1 large egg
- ½ teaspoon salt

- 1 medium vine tomato
- 3 tablespoons basil, fresh chopped

Directions
1. Preheat the oven to 400 degrees F and grease a baking dish.
2. Microwave mozzarella cheese for about 30 seconds and top with the remaining pizza crust.
3. Add the remaining pizza ingredients to the cheese and mix together.
4. Flatten the dough and transfer in the oven.
5. Bake for about 10 minutes and remove pizza from the oven.
6. Top the pizza with the toppings and bake for another 10 minutes.
7. Remove pizza from the oven and allow to cool.

Nutrition
Calories: 411 Carbs: 6.4g Fats: 31.3g Proteins: 22.2g Sodium: 152mg Sugar: 2.8g

Keto Thai Chicken Flatbread Pizza

Serves: 12
Prep Time: 25 mins
Ingredients
Peanut Sauce
- 2 tablespoons rice wine vinegar
- 4 tablespoons reduced sugar ketchup
- 4 tablespoons pbfit
- 4 tablespoons soy sauce

- 4 tablespoons coconut oil
- ½ lime, juiced
- 1 teaspoon fish sauce

Pizza Base
- ¾ cup almond flour
- 3 tablespoons cream cheese
- ½ teaspoon garlic powder
- 8 oz. mozzarella cheese
- 1 tablespoon psyllium husk powder

- 1 large egg
- ½ teaspoon onion powder
- ½ teaspoon ginger
- ½ teaspoon black pepper
- ½ teaspoon salt

Toppings
- 3 oz. mung bean sprouts
- 2 medium green onions
- 2 tablespoons peanuts

- 2 chicken thighs
- 6 oz. mozzarella cheese
- 1½ oz. carrots, shredded

Directions
1. Preheat oven to 400 degrees F and grease a baking tray.
2. Mix together all peanut sauce ingredients and set aside.
3. Microwave cream cheese and mozzarella cheese for the pizza base for 1 minute.
4. Add eggs, then mix together with all dry ingredients.
5. Arrange dough onto a baking tray and bake for about 15 minutes.
6. Flip pizza and top with sauce, chopped chicken, shredded carrots, and mozzarella.
7. Bake again for 10 minutes, or until cheese has melted.
8. Top with bean sprouts, spring onion, peanuts, and cilantro.

Nutrition
Calories: 268 Carbs: 3.2g Fats: 21g Proteins: 15g Sodium: 94mg Sugar: 0.2g

Apple and Ham Flatbread Pizza

Serves: 8
Prep Time: 15 mins
Ingredients
For the crust:
- ¾ cup almond flour
- ½ teaspoon sea salt
- 2 cups mozzarella cheese, shredded
- 2 tablespoons cream cheese
- 1/8 teaspoon dried thyme

For the topping:
- ½ small red onion, cut into thin slices
- 4 ounces low carbohydrate ham, cut into chunks
- Salt and black pepper, to taste
- 1 cup Mexican blend cheese, grated
- ¼ medium apple, sliced
- 1/8 teaspoon dried thyme

Directions
1. Preheat the oven to 425 degrees F and grease a 12-inch pizza pan.
2. Boil water and steam cream cheese, mozzarella cheese, almond flour, thyme, and salt.
3. When the cheese melts enough, knead for a few minutes to thoroughly mix dough.
4. Make a ball out of the dough and arrange in the pizza pan.
5. Poke holes all over the dough with a fork and transfer in the oven.
6. Bake for about 8 minutes until golden brown and reset the oven setting to 350 degrees F.
7. Sprinkle ¼ cup of the Mexican blend cheese over the flatbread and top with onions, apples, and ham.
8. Cover with the remaining ¾ cup of the Mexican blend cheese and sprinkle with the thyme, salt, and black pepper.
9. Bake for about 7 minutes until cheese is melted and crust is golden brown.
10. Remove the flatbread from the oven and allow to cool before cutting.
11. Slice into desired pieces and serve.

Nutrition
Calories: 179 Carbs: 5.3g Fats: 13.6g Proteins: 10.4g Sodium: 539mg Sugar: 2.1g

Air Fryer Breakfast Recipes

Ham, Spinach & Egg in a Cup

Serves: 8/Prep Time: 35 mins
Ingredients
- 2 tablespoons olive oil
- 2 tablespoons unsalted butter, melted
- 2 pounds fresh baby spinach
- 8 eggs
- 8 teaspoons milk
- 14-ounce ham, sliced
- Salt and black pepper, to taste

Directions
1. Preheat the Airfryer to 360 degrees F and grease 8 ramekins with butter.
2. Heat oil in a skillet on medium heat and add spinach.
3. Cook for about 3 minutes and drain the liquid completely from the spinach.
4. Divide the spinach into prepared ramekins and layer with ham slices.
5. Crack 1 egg over ham slices into each ramekin and drizzle evenly with milk.
6. Sprinkle with salt and black pepper and bake for about 20 minutes.

Nutrition: Calories: 228 Carbs: 6.6g Fats: 15.6g Proteins: 17.2g Sodium: 821mg Sugar: 1.1g

Eggs with Sausage & Bacon

Serves: 2/Prep Time: 25 mins

Ingredients

- 4 chicken sausages
- 4 bacon slices
- 2 eggs
- Salt and freshly ground black pepper, to taste

Directions

1. Preheat the Airfryer to 330 degrees F and place sausages and bacon slices in an Airfryer basket.
2. Cook for about 10 minutes and lightly grease 2 ramekins.
3. Crack 1 egg in each prepared ramekin and season with salt and black pepper.
4. Cook for about 10 minutes and divide sausages and bacon slices in serving plates.

Nutrition Calories: 245 Carbs: 5.7g Fats: 15.8g Proteins: 17.8g Sodium: 480mg Sugar: 0.7g

Tropical Almond Pancakes

Serves: 8/Prep Time: 15 mins

Ingredients

- 2 cups creamy milk
- 3½ cups almond flour
- 1 teaspoon baking soda
- ½ teaspoon salt
- 1 teaspoon allspice
- 2 tablespoons vanilla
- 1 teaspoon cinnamon
- 1 teaspoon baking powder
- ½ cup club soda

Directions

1. Preheat the Air fryer at 290 degrees F and grease the cooking basket of the air fryer.
2. Whisk together salt, almond flour, baking soda, allspice and cinnamon in a large bowl.
3. Mix together the vanilla, baking powder and club soda and add to the flour mixture.
4. Stir the mixture thoroughly and pour the mixture into the cooking basket.
5. Cook for about 10 minutes and dish out in a serving platter.

Nutrition: Calories: 324 Carbs: 12.8g Fats: 24.5g Proteins: 11.4g Sodium: 342mg Sugar: 1.6g

Bacon & Hot Dogs Omelet

Serves: 4/Prep Time: 15 mins

Ingredients

- 4 hot dogs, chopped
- 8 eggs
- 2 bacon slices, chopped
- 4 small onions, chopped

Directions

1. Preheat the Airfryer to 325 degrees F.
2. Crack the eggs in an Airfryer baking pan and beat well.
3. Stir in the remaining ingredients and cook for about 10 minutes until completely done.

Nutrition Calories: 298 Carbs: 9g Fats: 21.8g Proteins: 16.9g Sodium: 628mg Sugar: 5.1g

Toasted Bagels

Serves: 6/Prep Time: 10 mins

Ingredients
- 6 teaspoons butter
- 3 bagels, halved

Directions
1. Preheat the Airfryer to 375 degrees F and arrange the bagels into an Airfryer basket.
2. Cook for about 3 minutes and remove the bagels from Airfryer.
3. Spread butter evenly over bagels and cook for about 3 more minutes.

Nutrition Calories: 169 Carbs: 26.5g Fats: 4.7g Proteins: 5.3g Sodium: 262mg Sugar: 2.7g

Eggless Spinach & Bacon Quiche

Serves: 8/Prep Time: 20 mins

Ingredients
- 1 cup fresh spinach, chopped
- 4 slices of bacon, cooked and chopped
- ½ cup mozzarella cheese, shredded
- 4 tablespoons milk
- 4 dashes Tabasco sauce
- 1 cup Parmesan cheese, shredded
- Salt and freshly ground black pepper, to taste

Directions
1. Preheat the Airfryer to 325 degrees F and grease a baking dish.
2. Put all the ingredients in a bowl and mix well.
3. Transfer the mixture into prepared baking dish and cook for about 8 minutes.
4. Dish out and serve.

Nutrition Calories: 72 Carbs: 0.9g Fats: 5.2g Proteins: 5.5g Sodium: 271mg Sugar: 0.4g

Ham Casserole

Serves: 4/Prep Time: 25 mins

Ingredients
- 4-ounce ham, sliced thinly
- 4 teaspoons unsalted butter, softened
- 8 large eggs, divided
- 4 tablespoons heavy cream
- ¼ teaspoon smoked paprika
- 4 teaspoons fresh chives, minced
- Salt and freshly ground black pepper, to taste
- 6 tablespoons Parmesan cheese, grated finely

Directions
1. Preheat the Airfryer to 325 degrees F and spread butter in the pie pan.
2. Place ham slices in the bottom of the pie pan.
3. Whisk together 2 eggs, cream, salt and black pepper until smooth.
4. Place the egg mixture evenly over the ham slices and crack the remaining eggs on top.
5. Season with paprika, salt and black pepper.
6. Top evenly with chives and cheese and place the pie pan in an Airfryer.
7. Cook for about 12 minutes and serve with toasted bread slices.

Nutrition: Calories: 410 Carbs: 3.9g Fats: 30.8g Proteins: 31.2g Sodium: 933mg Sugar: 0.8g

Sausage & Bacon with Beans

Serves: 12/Prep Time: 30 mins

Ingredients
- 12 medium sausages
- 12 bacon slices
- 8 eggs
- 2 cans baked beans
- 12 bread slices, toasted

Directions
1. Preheat the Airfryer at 325 degrees F and place sausages and bacon in a fryer basket.

2. Cook for about 10 minutes and place the baked beans in a ramekin.
3. Place eggs in another ramekin and the Airfryer to 395 degrees F.
4. Cook for about 10 more minutes and divide the sausage mixture, beans and eggs in serving plates
5. Serve with bread slices.

Nutrition Calories: 276 Carbs: 14.1g Fats: 17g Proteins: 16.3g Sodium: 817mg Sugar: 0.6g

French Toasts

Serves: 4/Prep Time: 15 mins
Ingredients
- ½ cup evaporated milk
- 4 eggs
- 6 tablespoons sugar
- ¼ teaspoon vanilla extract
- 8 bread slices
- 4 teaspoons olive oil

Directions
1. Preheat the Airfryer to 395 degrees F and grease a pan.
2. Put all the ingredients in a large shallow dish except the bread slices.
3. Beat till well combined and dip each bread slice in egg mixture from both sides.
4. Arrange the bread slices in the prepared pan and cook for about 3 minutes per side.

Nutrition Calories: 261 Carbs: 30.6g Fats: 12g Proteins: 9.1g Sodium: 218mg Sugar: 22.3g

Veggie Hash

Serves: 8/Prep Time: 55 mins
Ingredients
- 2 medium onions, chopped
- 2 teaspoons dried thyme, crushed
- 4 teaspoons butter
- 1 green bell pepper, seeded and chopped
- 3 pounds russet potatoes, peeled and cubed
- Salt and freshly ground black pepper, to taste
- 10 eggs

Directions
1. Preheat the Airfryer to 395 degrees F and grease the Airfryer pan with butter.
2. Add bell peppers and onions and cook for about 5 minutes.
3. Add the herbs, potatoes, salt and black pepper and cook for about 30 minutes.
4. Heat a greased skillet on medium heat and add beaten eggs.
5. Cook for about 1 minute on each side and remove from the skillet.
6. Cut it into small pieces and add egg pieces into Airfryer pan.
7. Cook for about 5 more minutes and dish out.

Nutrition Calories: 229 Carbs: 31g Fats: 7.6g Proteins: 10.3g Sodium: 102mg Sugar: 4.3g

Parmesan Garlic Rolls

Serves: 4/Prep Time: 15 mins
Ingredients
- 1 cup Parmesan cheese, grated
- 4 dinner rolls
- 4 tablespoons unsalted butter, melted
- 1 tablespoon garlic bread seasoning mix

Directions
1. Preheat the Airfryer at 360 degrees F and cut the dinner rolls into cross style.
2. Stuff the slits evenly with the cheese and coat the tops of each roll with butter.
3. Sprinkle with the seasoning mix and cook for about 5 minutes until cheese is fully melted.

Nutrition Calories: 391 Carbs: 45g Fats: 18.6g Proteins: 11.7g Sodium: 608mg Sugar: 4.8g

Pickled Toasts

Serves: 4/Prep Time: 25 mins
Ingredients
- 4 tablespoons unsalted butter, softened
- 8 bread slices, toasted
- 4 tablespoons Branston pickle
- ½ cup Parmesan cheese, grated

Directions
1. Preheat the Airfryer to 385 degrees F and place the bread slice in a fryer basket.
2. Cook for about 5 minutes and spread butter evenly over bread slices.
3. Layer with Branston pickle and top evenly with cheese.
4. Cook for about 5 minutes until cheese is fully melted.

Nutrition Calories: 186 Carbs: 16.3g Fats: 12.9g Proteins: 2.6g Sodium: 397mg Sugar: 6.8g

Potato Rosti

Serves: 4/Prep Time: 15 mins
Ingredients
- ½ pound russet potatoes, peeled and grated roughly
- Salt and freshly ground black pepper, to taste
- 3.5 ounces smoked salmon, cut into slices
- 1 teaspoon olive oil
- 1 tablespoon chives, chopped finely
- 2 tablespoons sour cream

Directions
1. Preheat the Airfryer to 360 degrees F and grease a pizza pan with the olive oil.
2. Add chives, potatoes, salt and black pepper in a large bowl and mix until well combined.
3. Place the potato mixture into the prepared pizza pan and transfer the pizza pan in an Airfryer basket.
4. Cook for about 15 minutes and cut the potato rosti into wedges.
5. Top with the smoked salmon slices and sour cream and serve.

Nutrition Calories: 91 Carbs: 9.2g Fats: 3.6g Proteins: 5.7g Sodium: 503mg Sugar: 0.7g

Pumpkin Pancakes

Serves: 8/Prep Time: 20 mins
Ingredients
- 2 squares puff pastry
- 6 tablespoons pumpkin filling
- 2 small eggs, beaten
- ¼ teaspoon cinnamon

Directions
1. Preheat the Airfryer to 360 degrees F and roll out a square of puff pastry.
2. Layer it with pumpkin pie filling, leaving about ¼-inch space around the edges.
3. Cut it up into equal sized square pieces and cover the gaps with beaten egg.
4. Arrange the squares into a baking dish and cook for about 12 minutes.
5. Sprinkle some cinnamon and serve.

Nutrition Calories: 51 Carbs: 5g Fats: 2.5g Proteins: 2.4g Sodium: 48mg Sugar: 0.5g

Simple Cheese Sandwiches

Serves: 4/Prep Time: 10 mins
Ingredients

- 8 American cheese slices
- 8 bread slices
- 8 teaspoons butter

Directions
1. Preheat the Air fryer to 365 degrees F and arrange cheese slices between bread slices.
2. Spread butter over outer sides of sandwich and repeat with the remaining butter, slices and cheese.
3. Arrange the sandwiches in an Air fryer basket and cook for about 8 minutes, flipping once in the middle way.

Nutrition Calories: 254 Carbs: 12.4g Fats: 18.8g Proteins: 9.2g Sodium: 708mg Sugar: 3.9g

Air Fryer Poultry Recipes

Sweet & Sour Chicken Wings

Serves: 4/Prep Time: 20 mins
Ingredients
For Wings Marinade:
- 2 tablespoons fresh lemon juice
- 2 teaspoons garlic, chopped finely
- 2 tablespoons soy sauce
- Salt and black pepper, to taste
- 1 teaspoon dried oregano, crushed
- 16 chicken wings

For Sauce:
- 4 teaspoons scallions, chopped finely
- 2 tablespoons tomato ketchup
- 2 tablespoons chili sauce
- 2 teaspoons brown sugar
- 2 tablespoons vinegar

For Sprinkling:
- 4 tablespoons all-purpose flour

Directions
1. Preheat the air fryer to 355 degrees F and grease Airfryer tray.
2. For marinade: Mix together all ingredients in a large bowl except wings.
3. Add wings and coat generously with marinade.
4. Cover and refrigerate for about 2 hours.
5. Remove the chicken wings from marinade and sprinkle evenly with flour.
6. Place wings in an Airfryer tray and cook for about 6 minutes, flipping once after 3 minutes.
7. Add all sauce ingredients in a bowl and mix until well combined.
8. Remove chicken wings from Air fryer tray and coat generously with sauce.
9. Return the wings in Airfryer and cook for about 3 more minutes.

Nutrition Calories: 120 Carbs: 11.1g Fats: 2.8g Proteins: 11.8g Sodium: 758mg Sugar: 3.7

Breaded Chicken

Serves: 8/Prep Time: 25 mins
Ingredients
- 4 tablespoons vegetable oil
- 2 eggs, beaten
- 1 cup breadcrumbs
- 16 skinless, boneless chicken tenderloins

Directions
1. Preheat the air fryer to 360 degrees F.
2. Beat the eggs in a shallow dish and in another shallow dish, add breadcrumbs and oil.
3. Mix until a crumbly mixture is formed and dip the chicken tenderloins in egg.

4. Coat in the breadcrumbs mixture and marinate for about 2 hours.
5. Place the chicken tenderloins in the Airfryer and cook for about 12 minutes.

Nutrition Calories: 409 Carbs: 9.8g Fats: 16.6g Proteins: 53.2g Sodium: 194mg Sugar: 0.9g

Herbed Duck Legs

Serves: 4/Prep Time: 40 mins
Ingredients
- 1 tablespoon fresh thyme, chopped
- 2 garlic cloves, minced
- 1 tablespoon fresh parsley, chopped
- 2 teaspoons five spice powder
- 4 duck legs
- Salt and freshly ground black pepper, to taste

Directions
1. Preheat the Airfryer to 345 degrees F.
2. Mix together herbs, garlic, five spice powder, salt and black pepper in a bowl.
3. Rub the duck legs generously with garlic mixture.
4. Cook the duck legs in Airfryer for about 25 minutes.
5. Reset the Airfryer to 390 degrees F and cook for about 5 more minutes.

Nutrition Calories: 138 Carbs: 1g Fats: 4.5g Proteins: 22g Sodium: 82mg Sugar: 0g

Whole Spring Chicken

Serves: 8/Prep Time: 45 mins
Ingredients
- 4 teaspoons oyster sauce
- 4 teaspoons dried rosemary, crushed
- Salt and freshly ground black pepper, to taste
- 4 bay leaves
- 2 tablespoons olive oil
- 2 (1½-pounds) spring chicken
- 8 bell peppers, seeded and cut into chunks

Directions
1. Preheat the Airfryer to 355 degrees F and grease an Airfryer grill pan.
2. Mix together oyster sauce, rosemary, salt and black pepper in a bowl.
3. Rub the chicken evenly with rosemary mixture and stuff the chicken cavity with bay leaves.
4. Place the potatoes into an Airfryer grill pan and cook for about 15 minutes.
5. Coat the bell pepper pieces with oil and remove grill pan from Airfryer.
6. Transfer the chicken onto a plate and line the grill pan with bell pepper pieces.
7. Arrange chicken over bell pepper pieces and cook for 15 more minutes.

Nutrition Calories: 394 Carbs: 9.7g Fats: 16.5g Proteins: 50.5g Sodium: 168mg Sugar: 6g

Chicken Wings with Prawn Paste

Serves: 6/Prep Time: 20 mins
Ingredients
- 2 tablespoons prawn paste
- 4 tablespoons olive oil
- 1½ teaspoons sugar
- 2 teaspoons sesame oil
- 1 teaspoon Shaoxing wine
- Corn flour, as required
- 2 teaspoons fresh ginger juice
- 2 pounds mid-joint chicken wings

Directions
1. Mix together all the ingredients in a bowl except wings and corn flour.
2. Add chicken wings and coat generously with marinade.

3. Refrigerate overnight and coat the chicken wings evenly with corn flour.
4. Shake off the excess flour and preheat the air fryer to 360 degrees F.
5. Coat the wings with a little extra oil and arrange the chicken wings in Airfryer basket.
6. Cook for about 8 minutes and dish out.

Nutrition: Calories: 416 Carbs: 11.2g Fats: 31.5g Proteins: 24.4g Sodium: 661mg Sugar: 1.6g

Spicy Green Crusted Chicken

Serves: 6/Prep Time: 40 mins

Ingredients
- 6 teaspoons oregano
- 6 eggs, beaten
- 6 teaspoons parsley
- 4 teaspoons thyme
- Salt and freshly ground black pepper, to taste
- 4 teaspoons paprika
- 1 pound chicken pieces

Directions
1. Preheat the air fryer to 360 degrees F and grease Air fryer basket.
2. Place eggs in a bowl and mix together remaining ingredients in another bowl except chicken pieces.
3. Dip the chicken in eggs and then coat with the dry mixture.
4. Arrange half of the chicken pieces in Air fryer basket and cook for about 20 minutes.
5. Repeat with the remaining mixture and serve.

Nutrition Calories: 218 Carbs: 2.6g Fats: 10.4g Proteins: 27.9g Sodium: 128mg Sugar: 0.6g

Glazed Chicken Tenders

Serves: 4/Prep Time: 10 mins

Ingredients
- 1 cup brown sugar
- 4 skinless, boneless chicken tenders
- 2 cups ketchup
- 4 tablespoons honey

Directions
1. Preheat the air fryer to 355 degrees F.
2. Mix together all ingredients in a bowl except chicken tenders.
3. Add chicken tenders and coat generously with glazed mixture.
4. Arrange the chicken tenderloins in Airfryer basket and cook for about 10 minutes.

Nutrition Calories: 458 Carbs: 83g Fats: 4.4g Proteins: 27.2g Sodium: 1388mg Sugar: 79.7g

Mongolian Chicken

Serves: 2/Prep Time: 20 mins

Ingredients
- ½ pound boneless chicken, cubed
- ¼ tablespoon corn starch
- 1 egg
- ½ medium yellow onion, sliced thinly
- 1½ teaspoons garlic, minced
- 2 curry leaves
- ¼ teaspoon curry powder
- ½ teaspoon sugar
- Pinch of black pepper
- ½ tablespoon light soy sauce
- 1 tablespoon olive oil
- 1 green chili, chopped
- ½ teaspoon fresh ginger, grated
- ½ tablespoon chili sauce
- ¼ teaspoon salt
- ¼ cup evaporated milk

Directions
1. Mix together egg, chicken, corn starch and soy sauce in a bowl.

2. Cover for about 1 hour and then pat with paper towels to dry.
3. Preheat the Airfryer to 390 degrees F and grease an Airfryer basket.
4. Place the chicken in an Airfryer basket and cook for about 10 minutes.
5. Heat oil in a skillet on medium heat and add green chili, onions, garlic and ginger.
6. Sauté for about 2 minutes and add chicken, chili sauce, curry powder, sugar, salt and black pepper.
7. Mix until well combined and add evaporated milk.
8. Cook for about 4 minutes and dish out.

Nutrition Calories: 387 Carbs: 15g Fats: 20.3g Proteins: 39.3g Sodium: 1785mg Sugar: 8.4g

Creamy Chicken Tenders

Serves: 8/Prep Time: 20 mins
Ingredients
- 2 pounds chicken tenders
- 4 tablespoons olive oil
- 1 cup cream
- Salt and freshly ground black pepper, to taste
- 1 cup feta cheese

Directions
1. Season chicken tenders with salt and black pepper in a bowl.
2. Preheat the air fryer to 340 degrees F.
3. Put the chicken tenderloins and oil in Air fryer basket.
4. Top with feta cheese and cream and cook for about 15 minutes.
5. Reset the Air fryer to 390 degrees F and cook for about 5 more minutes.

Nutrition Calories: 344 Carbs: 1.7g Fats: 21.1g Proteins: 35.7g Sodium: 317mg Sugar: 1.4g

Mirin Coated Chicken Kebabs

Serves: 8/Prep Time: 15 mins
Ingredients
- 2 tablespoons mirin
- ½ cup light soy sauce
- 2 teaspoons garlic salt
- 8 (4-ounce) skinless, boneless chicken thighs, cubed into 1-inch size
- 2 teaspoons sugar
- 10 scallions, cut into 1-inch pieces lengthwise

Directions
1. Mix together mirin, soy sauce, garlic salt and sugar in a large baking dish.
2. Thread green onions and chicken onto pre-soaked wooden skewers.
3. Place the skewers into the baking dish and coat with marinade generously.
4. Cover and refrigerate for about 1 hour.
5. Preheat the air fryer to 355 degrees F and place the skewers in a fryer basket.
6. Cook for about 12 minutes and dish out.

Nutrition: Calories: 161 Carbs: 5.6g Fats: 4.1g Proteins: 26g Sodium: 370mg Sugar: 3.2g

Mexican Style Chicken

Serves: 8/Prep Time: 45 mins
Ingredients
- 2 pounds skinless, boneless chicken breasts
- 4 bay leaves
- 2 small yellow onions, chopped
- 6 garlic cloves, chopped
- 1 poblano pepper
- 2 (14½-ounce) cans diced tomatoes

- 2 (10-ounce) cans rotel tomatoes
- Salt, to taste
- 20 corn tortillas, cut into diamond slices
- 2 tablespoons olive oil
- 8 tablespoons feta cheese, crumbled
- ½ cup sour cream
- 4 red onions, sliced

Directions
1. Put the bay leaves and chicken in a pan of water and cook for about 20 minutes.
2. Dish out the chicken breasts in a bowl and keep aside to cool.
3. Shred the chicken with 2 forks.
4. Put the onions, garlic, poblano pepper and tomatoes in a food processor and pulse until smooth.
5. Transfer the sauce into a skillet on medium-high heat and bring to a boil.
6. Reduce the heat to medium-low and cook for about 10 minutes.
7. Season with salt and keep aside.
8. Preheat the Airfryer to 400 degrees F.
9. Put half of oil, half of tortilla slices and salt in a bowl and toss to coat well.
10. Place the tortilla slices in an Airfryer basket and cook for about 10 minutes.
11. Repeat with the remaining tortillas and transfer the tortillas into the serving bowl.
12. Stir in cheese, sauce and sour cream and top with the red onion and chicken.

Nutrition Calories: 472 Carbs: 52.9g Fats: 15.4g Proteins: 35.9g Sodium: 490mg Sugar: 15.1g

Honey Glazed Chicken Drumsticks

Serves: 8/Prep Time: 22 mins

Ingredients
- 2 tablespoons honey
- 2 tablespoons fresh thyme, minced
- 8 chicken drumsticks
- ½ cup Dijon mustard
- 4 tablespoons olive oil
- 1 tablespoon fresh rosemary, minced
- Salt and freshly ground black pepper, to taste

Directions
1. Put all the ingredients in a bowl except the drumsticks and mix well.
2. Add drumsticks and coat generously with the mixture.
3. Cover and refrigerate to marinate for overnight.
4. Preheat the Airfryer at 325 degrees F and place the drumsticks in air fryer basket.
5. Cook for about 12 minutes and reset the air fryer to 355 degrees F.
6. Cook for about 10 minutes and serve.

Nutrition Calories: 301 Carbs: 6g Fats: 19.7g Proteins: 4.5g Sodium: 316mg Sugar: 4.5g

Chicken Thighs with Chili Sauce

Serves: 4/Prep Time: 15 mins

Ingredients

For Chicken:
- 2 garlic cloves, minced
- 1 tablespoon rice vinegar
- Freshly ground black pepper, to taste
- 2 scallions, finely chopped
- 1 tablespoon soy sauce
- 1 teaspoon sugar
- 4 chicken thighs, deboned
- Potato flour, as required

For Chili Sauce:
- 2 shallots, sliced thinly
- 4 bird's eye chilies, chopped
- 3 tablespoons Thai chili sauce
- 2 tablespoons fresh lime juice
- 2 tablespoons sugar
- Salt, to taste

Directions

1. For chicken: Mix together all the ingredients in a bowl except chicken and potato flour.
2. Add chicken thighs and coat generously with marinade.
3. Remove chicken thighs from marinade and coat with corn flour.
4. Preheat the Airfryer to 395 degrees F and arrange the chicken thighs in the Airfryer pan, with skin side down.
5. Cook for about 10 minutes and reset the Airfryer to 355 degrees F.
6. Cook for about 10 minutes and meanwhile, mix together all ingredients in a bowl for chili sauce.
7. Remove chicken thighs from the Airfryer and top with the sauce immediately to serve.

Nutrition Calories: 241 Carbs: 16.7g Fats: 6.9g Proteins: 26.6g Sodium: 745mg Sugar: 9.5g

Asian Style Chicken

Serves: 4/Prep Time: 35 mins
Ingredients
- 2 teaspoons ginger,minced
- 1 tablespoon olive oil
- 6 tablespoons brown sugar
- 1½ pounds chickenpieces
- 2 tablespoons soy sauce
- 2 tablespoons fresh rosemary,chopped
- 2 tablespoons oyster sauce
- 2 lemons, cut into wedges

Directions
1. Mix together chicken, soy sauce, ginger and olive oil in a bowl.
2. Cover and refrigerate for about 30 minutes.
3. Preheat the Airfryer to 385 degrees F and place the chicken in an Airfryer pan.
4. Cook for about 6 minutes and meanwhile, mix together the remaining ingredients in a small bowl.
5. Dish out chicken from the Airfryer and drizzle the sauce mixture over it.

Nutrition Calories: 427 Carbs: 18.5g Fats: 16.5g Proteins: 50.2g Sodium: 657mg Sugar: 14g

Chicken Thighs with Apple

Serves: 4/Prep Time: 20 mins
Ingredients
- 2 shallots, thinly sliced
- 2 tablespoons fresh ginger, finely grated
- 2 teaspoons fresh thyme, minced
- 1 cup apple cider
- 4 tablespoons maple syrup
- Salt and freshly ground black pepper, to taste
- 4 skinless, boneless chicken thighs, cut into chunks
- 2 large apples, cored and cubed

Directions
1. Mix together all the ingredients in a large bowl except chicken and apple.
2. Add chicken pieces and coat generously with marinade.
3. Refrigerate to marinate for about 8 hours.
4. Preheat the Airfryer to 390 degrees F and place the chicken pieces and cubed apple in Airfryer basket.
5. Cook for about 20 minutes, flipping once in the middle way.

Nutrition Calories: 294 Carbs: 39.1g Fats: 4.5g Proteins: 25.8g Sodium: 46mg Sugar: 30.4g

Air Fryer Meat Recipes

Honey Mustard Cheesy Meatballs

Serves: 8/Prep Time: 15 mins

Ingredients

- 2 onions, chopped
- 1 pound ground beef
- 2 teaspoons garlic paste
- 4 tablespoons fresh basil, chopped
- 2 teaspoons honey
- Salt and freshly ground black pepper, to taste
- 2 teaspoons mustard
- 2 tablespoons cheddar cheese, grated

Directions

1. Preheat the Airfryer to 385 degrees F.
2. Put all the ingredients in a bowl and mix until well combined.
3. Make equal-sized balls from the mixture and arrange the balls in an Airfryer basket.
4. Cook for about 15 minutes and serve with fresh greens.

Nutrition Calories: 134 Carbs: 4.6g Fats: 4.4g Proteins: 18.2g Sodium: 50mg Sugar: 2.7

Spicy Lamb Kebabs

Serves: 6/Prep Time: 30 mins

Ingredients

- 4 eggs, beaten
- 1 cup pistachios, chopped
- 2 teaspoons chiliflakes
- 1 pound ground lamb
- 4 garlic cloves, minced
- 2 tablespoons fresh lemon juice
- 4 tablespoons plain flour
- 2 teaspoons cumin seeds
- 1 teaspoon fennel seeds
- 2 teaspoons dried mint
- 2 teaspoons salt
- Olive oil
- 1 teaspoon coriander seeds
- 4 tablespoons chopped flat-leaf parsley
- 1 teaspoon freshly ground black pepper

Directions

1. Mix together lamb, pistachios, eggs, lemon juice, chili flakes, flour, cumin seeds, fennel seeds, coriander seeds, mint, parsley, salt and pepper in a bowl.
2. Mold handfuls of the lamb mixture to form sausages around skewers.
3. Grease lamb skewers with olive oil.
4. Preheat the air fryer to 355 degrees F and place the lamb skewer in airfryer basket.
5. Cook for about 8 minutes on each side and dish out.

Nutrition Calories: 284 Carbs: 8.4g Fats: 15.8g Proteins: 27.9g Sodium: 932mg Sugar: 1.1g

Simple Beef Burgers

Serves: 6/Prep Time: 25 mins

Ingredients

- 2 pounds ground beef
- 12 cheddar cheese slices
- 6 tablespoons tomato ketchup
- Salt and freshly ground black pepper, to taste
- 12 dinner rolls

Directions

1. Preheat the Airfryer to 390 degrees F and grease an Airfryer pan.
2. Mix together beef, salt and black pepper in a bowl and make small patties from mixture.
3. Place half of patties onto the prepared pan and cook for about 12 minutes.
4. Top each patty with 1 cheese slice and arrange patties between rolls.
5. Top with ketchup and repeat with the remaining batch.

Nutrition Calories: 537 Carbs: 7.6g Fats: 28.3g Proteins: 60.6g Sodium: 636mg Sugar: 4.2g

Lamb with Potatoes

Serves: 2/Prep Time: 40 mins
Ingredients
- 1 garlic clove, crushed
- ½ pound lamb meat
- ½ tablespoon dried rosemary, crushed
- 2 small potatoes, peeled and halved
- 1 teaspoon olive oil
- ½ small onion, peeled and halved
- ¼ cup frozen sweet potato fries

Directions
1. Preheat the Airfryer to 355 degrees F and rub the lamb evenly with garlic.
2. Sprinkle with rosemary and arrange a divider in Airfryer.
3. Place the lamb on one side of Airfryer divider and cook for about 20 minutes.
4. Meanwhile, place the potatoes in a microwave safe bowl and microwave for about 4 minutes.
5. Drain the water from the potatoes and dish out in a large bowl along with onions and oil.
6. Toss to coat well and transfer in Airfryer divider after 20 minutes.
7. Set the Airfryer to 390 degrees F and change the side of lamb ramp.
8. Top with potato and onion halves.
9. Place the sweet potato fries in another part of Airfryer divider.
10. Cook for about 15 minutes, flipping the vegetables once after 10 minutes.

Nutrition Calories: 399 Carbs: 32.3g Fats: 18.5g Proteins: 24.5g Sodium: 104mg Sugar: 3.8g

Herbed Pork Burgers

Serves: 8/Prep Time: 45 mins
Ingredients
- 2 small onions, chopped
- 2 teaspoons mustard
- 21-ounce ground pork
- 2 teaspoons garlic puree
- 2 teaspoons tomato puree
- 2 teaspoons fresh basil, chopped
- Salt and freshly ground black pepper, to taste
- 8 burger buns
- 2 teaspoons dried mixed herbs, crushed
- ½ cup cheddar cheese, grated

Directions
1. Mix together all the ingredients in a bowl except cheese and buns.
2. Make 8 medium sized patties from the mixture.
3. Preheat the Airfryer to 395 degrees F and grease the Airfryer pan with olive oil.
4. Place patties onto the prepared pan and cook for about 45 minutes, flipping once after 25 minutes.
5. Arrange the patties in buns with cheese and serve immediately.

Nutrition: Calories: 289 Carbs: 29.2g Fats: 6.5g Proteins: 28.7g Sodium: 384mg Sugar: 4.9g

Garlicky Lamb Chops

Serves: 8/Prep Time: 45 mins
Ingredients
- 2 bulbs garlic
- 2 tablespoons fresh thyme, chopped
- ½ cup olive oil, divided
- 2 tablespoons fresh oregano, chopped

- Salt and freshly ground black pepper, to taste
- 16 (4-ounce) lamb chops

Directions
1. Preheat the Airfryer to 385 degrees F and coat the garlic bulbs with olive oil.
2. Place the garlic bulb in an Airfryer basket and cook for about 12 minutes.
3. Mix together remaining oil, herbs, salt and black pepper in a large bowl.
4. Coat the chops with about 2 tablespoons of the herb mixture.
5. Place 4 chops in Airfryer basket with 1 garlic bulb.
6. Cook for about 5 minutes and repeat with the remaining lamb chops.
7. Squeeze the garlic bulb in remaining herb mixture and mix until well combined.
8. Serve lamb chops with herb mixture.

Nutrition: Calories: 433 Carbs: 1.9g Fats: 25.2g Proteins: 47.9g Sodium: 130mg Sugar: 0.1g

Chinese Style Pork Meatballs

Serves: 3/Prep Time: 15 mins
Ingredients
- 1 egg, beaten
- 1 teaspoon oyster sauce
- 6-ounce ground pork
- ½ tablespoon light soy sauce
- ½ teaspoon sesame oil
- ¼ teaspoon five spice powder
- ½ tablespoon olive oil
- ¼ teaspoon brown sugar
- ¼ cup cornstarch

Directions
1. Mix together all the ingredients in a large bowl except cornstarch and oil.
2. Make equal sized small balls from the mixture.
3. Place the cornstarch in a shallow dish and roll the meatballs evenly into cornstarch mixture.
4. Place the meatballs in a large tray and keep aside for about 15 minutes.
5. Preheat the Airfryer to 390 degrees F and line the Airfryer basket with foil paper.
6. Arrange the balls into prepared basket and cook for about 10 minutes.
7. Drizzle the meatballs with oil and flip the side.
8. Cook for about 10 more minutes and dish out.

Nutrition Calories: 171 Carbs: 10.8g Fats: 6.6g Proteins: 16.9g Sodium: 254mg Sugar: 0.7g

Lamb Chops with Veggies

Serves: 8/Prep Time: 46 mins
Ingredients
- 4 tablespoons fresh mint leaves, minced
- 6 tablespoons olive oil
- 4 tablespoons fresh rosemary, minced
- 2 garlic cloves, minced
- Salt and freshly ground black pepper, to taste
- 2 purple carrots, peeled and cubed
- 2 parsnips, peeled and cubed
- 8 (6-ounce) lamb chops
- 2 yellow carrots, peeled and cubed
- 2 fennel bulbs, cubed

Directions
1. Mix together herbs, garlic and oil in a large bowl and add chops.
2. Coat generously with mixture and refrigerate to marinate for about 3 hours.
3. Soak the vegetables for about 15 minutes in a large pan of water.
4. Drain the vegetables and preheat the Airfryer to 385 degrees F.
5. Place half of the chops in an Airfryer basket and cook for about 2 minutes.

6. Remove the chops from the Airfryer and place half of the vegetables in the Airfryer basket.
7. Top with the chops and cook for about 6 minutes.
8. Repeat with the remaining lamb chops and serve.

Nutrition Calories: 488 Carbs: 17.2g Fats: 24.1g Proteins: 50.2g Sodium: 267mg Sugar: 3.7g

Simple Steak

Serves: 4/Prep Time: 15 mins
Ingredients
- 1 pound quality cut steaks
- Salt and freshly ground black pepper, to taste

Directions
1. Preheat the Airfryer to 385 degrees F and rub the steaks evenly with salt and pepper.
2. Place the steak in air fryer basket and cook for about 15 minutes until crispy.

Nutrition Calories: 301 Carbs: 0g Fats: 25.1g Proteins: 19.1g Sodium: 65mg Sugar: 0g

Almonds Crusted Rack of Lamb

Serves: 3/Prep Time: 50 mins
Ingredients
- 1 garlic clove, minced
- 1 pound rack of lamb
- ½ tablespoon olive oil
- Salt and freshly ground black pepper, to taste
- 1 egg
- 3-ounce almonds, finely chopped
- 1 tablespoon breadcrumbs
- ½ tablespoon fresh rosemary, chopped

Directions
1. Mix together oil, garlic, salt and black pepper in a bowl.
2. Coat the rack of lamb evenly with oil mixture.
3. Beat the egg in a shallow dish and mix together breadcrumbs, almonds and rosemary in another shallow dish.
4. Dip the rack of lamb in egg and coat with almond mixture.
5. Preheat the Airfryer to 230 degrees F and place the rack of lamb in an Airfryer basket.
6. Cook for about 30 minutes and reset the Airfryer to 390 degrees F.
7. Cook for about 5 more minutes and dish out.

Nutrition: Calories: 471 Carbs: 8.5g Fats: 31.6g Proteins: 39g Sodium: 145mg Sugar: 1.5g

Rib Eye Steak

Serves: 3/Prep Time: 15 mins
Ingredients
- 1 pound rib eye steak
- 1 tablespoon steak rub
- 1 tablespoon olive oil

Directions
1. Drizzle the steak with olive oil and rub generously with steak rub.
2. Preheat the Airfryer to 400 degrees and place the steak in air fryer basket.
3. Cook for about 15 minutes until crispy.

Nutrition Calories: 462 Carbs: 1g Fats: 38.1g Proteins: 26.8g Sodium: 307mg Sugar: 0g

Spicy Skirt Steak

Serves: 8/Prep Time: 20 mins

Ingredients

- 2 cups fresh parsley leaves, finely chopped
- 6 tablespoons fresh mint leaves, finely chopped
- 6 garlic cloves, minced
- 6 tablespoons fresh oregano, finely chopped
- 2 tablespoons ground cumin
- 4 teaspoons smoked paprika
- 2 teaspoons red pepper flakes, crushed
- 1½ cups olive oil
- 6 tablespoons red wine vinegar
- 2 teaspoons cayenne pepper
- Salt and freshly ground black pepper, to taste
- 4 (8-ounce) skirt steaks

Directions

1. Mix together all the ingredients in a bowl except the steaks.
2. Add steaks and ¼ cup of the herb mixture in a resealable bag and shake to coat well.
3. Refrigerate for about 24 hours and reserve the remaining herb mixture.
4. Remove steaks from the refrigerator and keep at room temperature for about 30 minutes.
5. Preheat the Airfryer to 390 degrees F and place half of the steaks in an Airfryer basket.
6. Cook for about 10 minutes and repeat with the remaining steaks.
7. Top with remaining herb mixture to serve.

Nutrition Calories: 445 Carbs: 5.8g Fats: 43.1g Proteins: 12.9g Sodium: 46mg Sugar: 0.5g

Leg of Lamb

Serves: 6/Prep Time: 1 hour 15 mins

Ingredients

- 2 tablespoons olive oil
- 2 pounds leg of lamb
- Salt and freshly ground black pepper, to taste
- 3 fresh thyme sprigs
- 3 fresh rosemary sprigs

Directions

1. Preheat the Airfryer to 310 degrees F.
2. Coat the leg of lamb with olive oil and season with salt and black pepper.
3. Cover the leg of lamb with herb sprigs and place the chops in an Airfryer basket.
4. Cook for about 1 hour 15 minutes and dish out.

Nutrition Calories: 325 Carbs: 0.7g Fats: 15.9g Proteins: 42.5g Sodium: 115mg Sugar: 0g

Barbecue Flavored Pork Ribs

Serves: 6/Prep Time: 15 mins

Ingredients

- 1 cup BBQ sauce
- 3 tablespoons tomato ketchup
- ¾ teaspoon garlic powder
- ½ cup honey, divided
- 1½ tablespoons Worcestershire sauce
- 1½ tablespoons soy sauce
- Freshly ground white pepper, to taste
- 2 pounds pork ribs

Directions

1. Mix together half of honey and remaining ingredients except pork ribs in a large bowl.
2. Refrigerate to marinate for about 30 minutes.
3. Preheat the Airfryer to 360 degrees F and place the ribs in an Airfryer basket.
4. Cook for about 15 minutes and remove the ribs from Airfryer.
5. Coat with remaining honey and serve hot.

Nutrition Calories: 576 Carbs: 41.6g Fats: 26.9g Proteins: 40.6g Sodium: 906mg Sugar: 36.7g

Pork Tenderloin with Veggies

Serves: 4/Prep Time: 30 mins

Ingredients

- 12 bacon slices
- 2 tablespoons olive oil
- 8 potatoes
- 1½ pounds frozen green beans
- 4 pork tenderloins

Directions

1. Preheat the Airfryer to 395 degrees F.
2. Pierce the potatoes with a fork and place in the Airfryer.
3. Cook for about 15 minutes and wrap the green beans with bacon slices.
4. Coat the pork tenderloin with some olive oil and keep aside for about 15 minutes.
5. Add pork tenderloins in Airfryer with potatoes and cook for about 5 minutes.
6. Remove the pork tenderloin and place the bean rolls in the basket.
7. Top with the pork tenderloin and cook for about 7 minutes.

Nutrition Calories: 638 Carbs: 79.1g Fats: 19g Proteins: 39.4g Sodium: 263mg Sugar: 7.3g

Air Fryer Seafood Recipes

Buttered Scallops

Serves: 4/Prep Time: 15 mins

Ingredients

- 2 tablespoons butter, melted
- 1½ pounds sea scallops
- 1 tablespoon fresh thyme, minced
- Salt and freshly ground black pepper, to taste

Directions

1. Preheat the Airfryer to 385 degrees F and grease Airfryer basket.
2. Put all the ingredients in a large bowl and toss to coat well.
3. Arrange half of the scallops in an Airfryer basket and cook for about 5 minutes.
4. Repeat with the remaining scallops and serve.

Nutrition Calories: 202 Carbs: 4.4g Fats: 7.1g Proteins: 28.7g Sodium: 315mg Sugar: 0g

Ham Wrapped Prawns

Serves: 2/Prep Time: 20 mins

Ingredients

- 1 tablespoon olive oil
- Salt and freshly ground black pepper, to taste
- 1 garlic clove, minced
- ½ tablespoon paprika
- 4 king prawns, peeled, deveined and chopped
- 2 ham slices, halved

Directions

1. Preheat the air fryer to 430 degrees F and place the bell pepper in a fryer basket
2. Cook for about 10 minutes and transfer the bell pepper into a bowl covering with a foil paper.
3. Keep aside for about 15 minutes and add the bell pepper along with garlic, paprika and oil in a blender.
4. Pulse till a puree forms and keep aside.
5. Wrap each prawn with a slice of ham and arrange in the fryer basket.
6. Cook for about 4 minutes until golden brown and serve with bell pepper dip.

Nutrition: Calories: 553 Carbs: 2.5g Fats: 33.6g Proteins: 5g Sodium: 366mg Sugar: 7.2g

Breaded Shrimp with Sauce

Serves: 2/Prep Time: 45 mins
Ingredients
For Shrimp:
- ¼ cup panko breadcrumbs
- ¼ teaspoon cayenne pepper
- 4 large shrimps, peeled and deveined

- 4 ounces coconut milk
- Salt and freshly ground black pepper, to taste

For Sauce:
- ½ teaspoon mustard
- ¼ cup orange marmalade

- ¼ teaspoon hot sauce
- ½ tablespoon honey

Directions
1. Preheat the air fryer to 345 degrees F.
2. Mix together coconut milk, salt and black pepper in a shallow dish.
3. Combine breadcrumbs, cayenne pepper, salt and black pepper in another shallow dish.
4. Coat the shrimp in coconut milk mixture and then dredge into breadcrumbs mixture.
5. Place the shrimp in the Airfryer and cook for about 20 minutes until desired doneness.
6. Meanwhile, mix together all the sauce ingredients for sauce in a bowl.
7. Serve shrimp with sauce.

Nutrition Calories: 298 Carbs: 42.1g Fats: 14.2g Proteins: 5.2g Sodium: 142mg Sugar: 30.5g

Nacho Chips Crusted Prawns

Serves: 6/Prep Time: 20 mins
Ingredients
- 1 large egg
- 18 prawns, peeled and deveined

- ounce Nacho flavored chips, crushed finely

Directions
1. Beat the egg in a bowl and place nacho chips in another bowl.
2. Dip each prawn into the beaten egg and coat with the crushed nacho chips.
3. Preheat the air fryer to 350 degrees F and place the prawns in the Airfryer.
4. Cook for about 8 minutes and dish out.

Nutrition Calories: 333 Carbs: 30.2g Fats: 14.3g Proteins: 19.9g Sodium: 463mg Sugar: 1.9g

Spicy Shrimp

Serves: 4/Prep Time: 15 mins
Ingredients
- 2 tablespoons olive oil
- 1 pound tiger shrimp
- 1 teaspoon old bay seasoning

- ½ teaspoon cayenne pepper
- ½ teaspoon smoked paprika
- Salt, to taste

Directions
1. Preheat the Airfryer to 390 degrees F and grease an Airfryer basket.
2. Put all the ingredients in a large bowl and mix until well combined.
3. Place the shrimp in an Airfryer basket and cook for about 5 minutes.

Nutrition Calories: 174 Carbs: 0.3g Fats: 8.3g Proteins: 23.8g Sodium: 414mg Sugar: 0.1g

Lemony Tuna

Serves: 8/Prep Time: 20 mins
Ingredients

- 4 teaspoons Dijon mustard
- 4 tablespoons fresh parsley, chopped
- 4 (6-ounce) cans water packed plain tuna
- 1 cup breadcrumbs
- 2 tablespoons fresh lime juice
- 2 eggs
- 6 tablespoons canola oil
- Dash of hot sauce
- Salt and freshly ground black pepper, to taste

Directions
1. Mix together tuna fish, crumbs, mustard, parsley, hot sauce and citrus juice in a bowl.
2. Add oil, eggs and salt and make the patties from tuna mixture.
3. Refrigerate the tuna patties for about 3 hours and transfer to Airfryer basket.
4. Preheat the air fryer to 360 degrees F and place Airfryer basket.
5. Cook for about 12 minutes and serve.

Nutrition: Calories: 388 Carbs: 31.7g Fats: 21.8g Proteins: 14.2g Sodium: 680mg Sugar: 1.2g

Bacon Wrapped Shrimp

Serves: 8/Prep Time: 20 mins
Ingredients
- 2 pounds bacon
- 2½ pounds tiger shrimp, peeled and deveined

Directions
1. Wrap each shrimp with a slice of bacon and refrigerate for about 20 minutes.
2. Preheat the Airfryer to 385 degrees F and arrange half of the shrimps in Airfryer basket.
3. Cook for about 7 minutes and repeat with the remaining shrimps.

Nutrition Calories: 492 Carbs: 7.2g Fats: 35g Proteins: 41.8g Sodium: 1979mg Sugar: 0g

Lemony & Spicy Coconut Crusted Prawns

Serves: 8/Prep Time: 20 mins
Ingredients
- 1 cup flour
- 1 cup breadcrumbs
- Salt and freshly ground black pepper, to taste
- 2 pounds prawns, peeled and de-veined
- 4 egg whites
- 1 cup unsweetened coconut, shredded
- ½ teaspoon lemon zest
- ½ teaspoon cayenne pepper
- Vegetable oil, as required
- ½ teaspoon red pepper flakes, crushed

Directions
1. Mix together the flour, salt and pepper in a shallow dish.
2. Beat the eggs in another shallow dish.
3. Combine the breadcrumbs, lime zest, coconut, salt and cayenne pepper in a third shallow dish.
4. Preheat the Airfryer to 395 degrees F.
5. Dredge each shrimp in the flour mixture, then dip in the egg and roll evenly into the breadcrumbs mixture.
6. Place half the shrimps in the Airfryer basket and drizzle with vegetable oil.
7. Cook for about 7 minutes and repeat with the remaining mixture.

Nutrition: Calories: 305 Carbs: 25.1g Fats: 7.9g Proteins: 31.4g Sodium: 394mg Sugar: 1.6g

Tuna Stuffed Potatoes

Serves: 2/Prep Time: 45 mins
Ingredients
- ¼ tablespoon olive oil
- 2 starchy potatoes, soaked for 30 minutes
- ½ (6-ounce) can tuna, drained
- 1 tablespoon plain Greek yogurt
- Salt and freshly ground black pepper, to taste
- ½ tablespoon capers
- ½ teaspoon red chili powder
- ½ scallion, chopped and divided

Directions
1. Preheat the air fryer to 355 degrees F and place the potatoes in a fryer basket.
2. Cook for about 30 minutes and remove onto a smooth surface.
3. Meanwhile, add yogurt, tuna, red chili powder, half of scallion, salt and black pepper in a bowl and mash the mixture completely with a potato masher.
4. Cut each potato from top side lengthwise and press the open side of potato halves slightly.
5. Stuff the potato evenly with tuna mixture and sprinkle with the capers and remaining scallion.
6. Dish out and serve immediately.

Nutrition: Calories: 222 Carbs: 28.1g Fats: 5.7g Proteins: 15.4g Sodium: 105mg Sugar: 2.1g

Cod Burgers with Salsa

Serves: 3/Prep Time: 20 mins
Ingredients
For Mango Salsa:
- 1½ cups mango, peeled, pitted and cubed
- ½ tablespoon fresh parsley, chopped
- ½ teaspoon fresh lime zest, finely grated
- ¼ teaspoon red chili paste
- ½ tablespoon fresh lime juice

For Cod Cakes:
- ½ teaspoon fresh lime zest, finely grated
- Salt, to taste
- ¼ cup coconut, grated and divided
- ½ pound cod fillets
- 1 egg
- ½ teaspoon red chili paste
- ½ tablespoon fresh lime juice
- ½ scallion, finely chopped
- 1 tablespoon fresh parsley, chopped

Directions
1. For salsa: Mix together all ingredients in a bowl and refrigerate until serving.
2. For cod cakes: Put cod filets, egg, lime zest, chili paste, lime juice and salt in a food processor and pulse until smooth.
3. Transfer the cod mixture into a bowl and mix together scallion, parsley and 1 tablespoon coconut.
4. Make equal sized round cakes from the mixture and place the remaining coconut in a shallow dish.
5. Coat the cod cakes evenly in coconut and preheat the air fryer to 375 degrees F.
6. Arrange half cakes in an Airfryer basket and cook for about 7 minutes.
7. Repeat with the remaining cod cakes and serve with mango salsa.

Nutrition Calories: 164 Carbs: 15.1g Fats: 5g Proteins: 16.5g Sodium: 91mg Sugar: 12.5g

Cajun Spiced Salmon

Serves: 4/Prep Time: 15 mins
Ingredients

- 4 tablespoons Cajun seasoning
- 4 salmon steaks

Directions
1. Rub the salmon evenly with the Cajun seasoning and keep aside for about 10 minutes.
2. Preheat the Airfryer to 385 degrees F and arrange the salmon steaks on the grill pan.
3. Cook for about 8 minutes, flipping once in the middle way.

Nutrition Calories: 225 Carbs: 0g Fats: 10.5g Proteins: 33.1g Sodium: 225mg Sugar: 0g

Tangy Salmon

Serves: 4/Prep Time: 15 mins
Ingredients
- 2 tablespoons Cajun seasoning
- 4 (7-ounce) (¾-inch thick) salmon fillets
- 2 tablespoons fresh lemon juice

Directions
1. Preheat the air fryer to 360 degrees F and season evenly with Cajun seasoning.
2. Place the fish in an Airfryer, grill pan, skin-side up and cook for about 7 minutes.
3. Drizzle with lemon juice and serve

Nutrition Calories: 264 Carbs: 0.2g Fats: 12.3g Proteins: 38.6g Sodium: 164mg Sugar: 0.2g

Haddock with Cheese Sauce

Serves: 4/Prep Time: 15 mins
Ingredients
- 2 tablespoons olive oil
- 4 (6-ounce) haddock fillets
- Salt and freshly ground black pepper, to taste
- 6 tablespoons fresh basil, chopped
- 4 tablespoons pine nuts
- 2 tablespoons Parmesan cheese, grated

Directions
1. Preheat the Airfryer at 360 degrees F.
2. Coat the haddock fillets evenly with oil and season with salt and black pepper.
3. Place the fish fillets in an Airfryer basket and cook for about 8 minutes.
4. Meanwhile, add remaining ingredients in a food processor and pulse until smooth.
5. Transfer the fish fillets in serving plates and top with cheese sauce to serve.

Nutrition Calories: 354 Carbs: 1.7g Fats: 17.5g Proteins: 47g Sodium: 278mg Sugar: 0.3g

Sesame Seeds Coated Fish

Serves: 14/Prep Time: 20 mins
Ingredients
- 3 eggs
- ¾ cup breadcrumbs
- Pinch of black pepper
- 4 tablespoons plain flour
- ¾ cup sesame seeds, toasted
- ¼ teaspoon dried rosemary, crushed
- Pinch of salt
- 4 tablespoons olive oil
- 7 frozen fish fillets (white fish of your choice)

Directions
1. Place flour in a shallow dish and beat the eggs in a second shallow dish.
2. Mix together the remaining ingredients except fish fillets in a third shallow dish.
3. Coat the fillets with flour and dip the fillets in egg.
4. Dredge the fillets generously with sesame seeds mixture.
5. Preheat the Airfryer to 390 degrees F and line an Airfryer basket with a piece of foil.

6. Arrange the fillets into prepared basket and cook for about 14 minutes, flipping once in the middle way.

Nutrition: Calories: 223 Carbs: 19.8g Fats: 12.1g Proteins: 9.1g Sodium: 283mg Sugar: 1g

Crumbed Cod

Serves: 4/Prep Time: 20 mins
Ingredients

- 1 cup flour
- 4 garlic cloves, minced
- 4 (4-ounce) skinless cod fish fillets, cut into rectangular pieces
- 6 eggs
- 2 green chilies, finely chopped
- 6 scallions, finely chopped
- Salt and freshly ground black pepper, to taste
- 2 teaspoons soy sauce

Directions
1. Place the flour in a shallow dish and mix together remaining ingredients except cod in another shallow dish.
2. Coat each cod fillet into the flour and then dip in egg mixture.
3. Preheat the Airfryer to 375 degrees F and place cod fillets in an Airfryer basket.
4. Cook for about 7 minutes and dish out.

Nutrition Calories: 462 Carbs: 51.3g Fats: 16.9g Proteins: 24.4g Sodium: 646mg Sugar: 3.3g

Air Fryer Snacks Recipes

Apple Chips

Serves: 4/Prep Time: 15 mins
Ingredients

- 2 tablespoons sugar
- 2 apples, peeled, cored and thinly sliced
- 1 teaspoon ground cinnamon
- ½ teaspoon salt
- ½ teaspoon ground ginger

Directions
1. Preheat the Airfryer to 390 degrees F.
2. Put all the ingredients in a bowl and toss to coat well.
3. Place the apple slices in an Airfryer basket.
4. Cook for about 8 minutes, flipping once in the middle way.

Nutrition Calories: 83 Carbs: 22g Fats: 0.2g Proteins: 0.3g Sodium: 292mg Sugar: 17.6g

Roasted Cashews

Serves: 4/Prep Time: 15 mins
Ingredients

- ½ teaspoon butter, melted
- 1 cup raw cashew nuts
- Salt and freshly ground black pepper, to taste

Directions
1. Preheat the Airfryer to 360 degrees F.
2. Put all the ingredients in a bowl and toss to coat well.
3. Place the cashews in an Airfryer basket and cook for about 5 minutes.

Nutrition Calories: 201 Carbs: 11.2g Fats: 16.4g Proteins: 5.3g Sodium: 9mg Sugar: 1.7g

Buttered Corn

Serves: 4/Prep Time: 30 mins

Ingredients

- 4 corns on the cob
- 4 tablespoons butter, softened and divided
- Salt and freshly ground pepper, to taste

Directions

1. Preheat the Airfryer to 325 degrees F.
2. Season the cobs evenly with salt and black pepper.
3. Rub with 1 tablespoon butter and wrap the cobs in foil paper.
4. Place in the Airfryer basket and cook for about 20 minutes.
5. Top with remaining butter and serve.

Nutrition Calories: 257 Carbs: 31.9g Fats: 14.9g Proteins: 4.6g Sodium: 111mg Sugar: 0g

Polenta Sticks

Serves: 8/Prep Time: 15 mins

Ingredients

- 5 cups cooked polenta
- 2 tablespoons oil
- Salt, to taste
- ½ cup Parmesan cheese

Directions

1. Preheat the air fryer at 360 degrees F and grease the baking dish with oil.
2. Place the polenta in a baking dish and refrigerate for about 1 hour.
3. Remove from the refrigerator and cut into desired sized slices.
4. Place the polenta sticks into the Airfryer and season with salt.
5. Cook for about 6 minutes and serve.

Nutrition Calories: 382 Carbs: 76.1g Fats: 4.6g Proteins: 7.8g Sodium: 20mg Sugar: 1g

Zucchini Fries

Serves: 8/Prep Time: 30 mins

Ingredients

- 2 pounds zucchinis, sliced into 2 ½-inch sticks
- 4 tablespoons olive oil
- Salt, to taste
- 1½ cups panko bread crumbs

Directions

1. Place the zucchini in a colander and season with salt.
2. Keep aside for about 10 minutes and preheat the Airfryer to 395 degrees F.
3. Pat dry the zucchini fries with the paper towels.
4. Place the bread crumbs in a shallow dish and coat zucchini fries evenly.
5. Place the zucchini in a fryer basket in batches and cook for about 10 minutes.

Nutrition Calories: 158 Carbs: 18.4g Fats: 8.3g Proteins: 4.1g Sodium: 160mg Sugar: 3.2g

Eggplant Slices

Serves: 8/Prep Time: 30 mins

Ingredients

- ½ cup olive oil
- 2 medium eggplants, peeled and cut into ½-inch round slices
- 1 cup all-purpose flour
- 2 cups Italian-style breadcrumbs
- 4 eggs, beaten
- Salt, to taste

Directions

1. Place the eggplant slices in a colander and season with salt.
2. Keep aside for about 45 minutes and drain excess water with paper towels.
3. Preheat the Airfryer to 385 degrees F.
4. Place the flour in a shallow dish and beat the eggs in a second shallow dish.
5. Mix together oil and breadcrumbs in a third shallow dish.
6. Coat the eggplant slices in flour mixture, then dip in the beaten eggs and dredge in the breadcrumbs.
7. Place half of the eggplant slices in the Airfryer and cook for about 5 minutes.

Nutrition: Calories: 335 Carbs: 38.8g Fats: 16.7g Proteins: 9.5g Sodium: 483mg Sugar: 5.7g

Broccoli Poppers

Serves: 4/Prep Time: 20 mins
Ingredients
- 1 teaspoon red chili powder
- 4 tablespoons plain yogurt
- ½ teaspoon ground cumin
- Salt, to taste
- 2 pounds broccoli, cut into small florets
- ½ teaspoon ground turmeric
- 4 tablespoons chickpea flour

Directions
1. Mix together yogurt and spices in a bowl and add broccoli.
2. Coat with the marinade and refrigerate for about 20 minutes.
3. Preheat the Airfryer to 395 degrees F and season the broccoli florets with chickpea flour.
4. Place the broccoli in the Airfryer basket and cook
5. Cook for about 10 minutes, tossing once in the middle way.

Nutrition Calories: 138 Carbs: 24.4g Fats: 1.9g Proteins: 9.8g Sodium: 96mg Sugar: 6.4g

Risotto Bites

Serves: 8/Prep Time: 30 mins
Ingredients
- ½ cup Parmesan cheese, grated
- 6 cups cooked risotto
- 2 eggs, beaten
- 1½ cups bread crumbs
- ounce mozzarella cheese, cubed

Directions
1. Mix together risotto, Parmesan cheese and egg in a bowl.
2. Make equal-sized balls from the mixture and insert a mozzarella cube in the center of each ball.
3. Smooth the risotto mixture with your fingers to cover the ball.
4. Place the bread crumbs in a shallow dish and coat the balls evenly with bread crumbs.
5. Preheat the Airfryer to 390 degrees F and place the balls in an Airfryer basket in batches.
6. Cook for about 10 minutes until golden brown.

Nutrition Calories: 487 Carbs: 82.1g Fats: 9.2g Proteins: 20.1g Sodium: 703mg Sugar: 4.7g

Salmon Croquettes

Serves: 8/Prep Time: 25 mins
Ingredients
- 1 egg, lightly beaten
- Salt and freshly ground black pepper, to taste
- ½ large can red salmon, drained
- 1 tablespoon fresh parsley, chopped

- ¼ cup vegetable oil
- ½ cup bread crumbs

Directions
1. Preheat the Airfryer to 385 degrees F.
2. Add salmon and mash completely in a bowl.
3. Add parsley, egg, salt and black pepper and mix until well combined.
4. Make equal-sized croquettes from the mixture.
5. Mix together oil and breadcrumbs in a shallow dish.
6. Coat croquettes in breadcrumbs mixture and place the croquettes in an Airfryer basket in batches.
7. Cook for about 7 minutes.

Nutrition Calories: 105 Carbs: 4.9g Fats: 8.2g Proteins: 3.1g Sodium: 82mg Sugar: 0.5g

Cod Nuggets

Serves: 8/Prep Time: 25 mins
Ingredients
- 2 cups all-purpose flour
- 4 eggs
- 1½ cups breadcrumbs
- ½ teaspoon salt
- 4 tablespoons olive oil
- 2 pounds cod, cut into 1x2½-inch strips

Directions
1. Preheat the Airfryer to 385 degrees F.
2. Place the flour in a shallow dish and beat the eggs in another shallow dish.
3. Combine breadcrumbs, salt and oil in a third shallow dish.
4. Coat the cod strips evenly in flour.
5. Dip in eggs and roll evenly into breadcrumbs mixture.
6. Arrange the croquettes in an Airfryer basket and cook for about 10 minutes.

Nutrition Calories: 404 Carbs: 38.6g Fats: 11.6g Proteins: 34.6g Sodium: 415mg Sugar: 1.5g

Air Fryer Desserts Recipes

Fudge Brownies Muffins

Serves: 6/Prep Time: 20 mins
Ingredients
- 1/8 cup walnuts, chopped
- ½ package Betty Crocker fudge brownie mix
- 1 egg
- 1 teaspoon water
- ¼ cup vegetable oil

Directions
1. Preheat the Airfryer to 300 degrees F and grease 6 muffin molds.
2. Mix together all the ingredients in a bowl and transfer the mixture into prepared muffin molds.
3. Cook for about 10 minutes and remove the muffin molds from Airfryer.
4. Keep on wire rack to cool for about 10 minutes.

Nutrition Calories: 115 Carbs: 2.2g Fats: 11.4g Proteins: 1.6g Sodium: 18mg Sugar: 1.3g

Chocolaty Squares

Serves: 4/Prep Time: 35 mins
Ingredients

- 1¼-ounce brown sugar
- 2-ounce cold butter
- 3-ounce self-rising flour
- 1/8 cup honey
- ½ tablespoon milk
- ounce chocolate, chopped

Directions
1. Preheat the Airfryer at 320 degrees F.
2. Put the butter in a large bowl and beat until soft.
3. Add brown sugar, flour and honey and beat till smooth.
4. Stir in milk and chocolate and place the mixture into a tin.
5. Arrange the tin in a baking sheet and place in an Airfryer basket.
6. Cook for about 20 minutes and remove from Airfryer.
7. Keep aside to cool slightly and cut into desired squares and serve.

Nutrition Calories: 322 Carbs: 42.2g Fats: 15.9g Proteins: 3.5g Sodium: 97mg Sugar: 24.8g

Lemon Biscuits

Serves: 5/Prep Time: 20 mins
Ingredients
- 2-ounce caster sugar
- 5-ounce self-rising flour
- 2-ounce cold butter
- ½ teaspoon fresh lemon zest, grated finely
- ½ teaspoon vanilla extract
- ½ small egg
- 1 tablespoon fresh lemon juice

Directions
1. Mix together flour and sugar in a large bowl.
2. Cut cold butter with a pastry cutter and mix until a coarse crumb forms.
3. Add lemon zest, egg and lemon juice and mix until a soft dough forms.
4. Place the dough onto a floured surface and roll the dough.
5. Cut the dough into medium-sized biscuits and arrange the biscuits in a baking sheet in a single layer.
6. Preheat the Airfryer at 360 degrees F and cook for about 5 minutes.

Nutrition: Calories: 234 Carbs: 33.2g Fats: 9.9g Proteins: 3.5g Sodium: 72mg Sugar: 11.6g

Buttered Cookies

Serves: 8/Prep Time: 25 mins
Ingredients
- 2½-ounce icing sugar
- ounce unsalted butter, softened
- 2 cups all-purpose flour
- ½ teaspoon baking powder

Directions
1. Preheat the Airfryer to 345 degrees F.
2. Add butter in a large bowl and beat until soft.
3. Add icing sugar and beat until smooth.
4. Add baking powder and flour and beat until a sticky dough forms.
5. Place the dough into a piping bag fitted with a fluted nozzle.
6. Pipe the dough onto a baking sheet in a single layer.
7. Place the baking sheet in an Airfryer basket and cook for about 10 minutes.

Nutrition Calories: 352 Carbs: 32.8g Fats: 23.3g Proteins: 3.5g Sodium: 164mg Sugar: 8.8g

Stuffed Pear Pouch

Serves: 8/Prep Time: 25 mins

Ingredients

- 4 cups vanilla custard
- 2 eggs, beaten lightly
- 4 small pears, peeled, cored and halved
- 8 puff pastry sheets
- 4 tablespoons sugar
- Pinch of ground cinnamon
- 4 tablespoons whipped cream

Directions

1. Put a spoonful of vanilla custard in the center of each pastry sheet and top with a pear half.
2. Mix together sugar and cinnamon in a bowl and sprinkle this mixture over pear halves evenly.
3. Pinch the corners to shape into a pouch and preheat the Airfryer at 335 degrees F.
4. Place the pear pouches in an Airfryer basket and cook for about 15 minutes.
5. Top with whipped cream and serve with remaining custard

Nutrition: Calories: 308 Carbs: 37.6g Fats: 15.5g Proteins: 5.9g Sodium: 139mg Sugar: 20g

Nutty Banana Split

Serves: 4/Prep Time: 20 mins

Ingredients

- ½ cup panko bread crumbs
- 1½ tablespoons coconut oil
- 2 bananas, peeled and halved lengthwise
- ¼ cup corn flour
- 1½ tablespoons sugar
- 1 tablespoon walnuts, chopped
- 1 egg
- 1/8 teaspoon ground cinnamon

Directions

1. Heat oil in a skillet on medium heat and add bread crumbs.
2. Cook for 4 minutes until golden brown and transfer into a bowl.
3. Keep aside to cool and put the flour in a shallow dish.
4. Beat egg in another shallow dish and coat banana slices evenly with flour.
5. Dip in the egg and coat with bread crumbs evenly.
6. Mix together sugar and cinnamon in a small bowl.
7. Preheat the air fryer at 285 degrees F and place banana slices in an Airfryer basket.
8. Sprinkle with cinnamon sugar and cook for about 10 minutes.
9. Sprinkle with walnuts and serve.

Nutrition: Calories: 221 Carbs: 33.7g Fats: 8.5g Proteins: 4.8g Sodium: 115mg Sugar: 12.7g

Cherry Pie

Serves: 4/Prep Time: 35 mins

Ingredients

- ½ (21-ounce) can cherry pie filling
- 1 refrigerated pre-made pie crust
- ½ tablespoon milk
- 1 egg yolk

Directions

1. Preheat the Airfryer to 325 degrees F and press pie crust into a pie pan.
2. Poke the holes all over dough with a fork.
3. Place the pie pan into Airfryer basket and cook for about 5 minutes.
4. Remove pie pan from Airfryer basket and pour cherry pie filling into pie crust.
5. Roll out the remaining pie crust and cut into ¾-inch strips.
6. Place strips in a criss-cross manner.

7. Add milk and egg in a small bowl and beat well.
8. Brush the top of pie with egg wash and place the pie pan into Airfryer basket.
9. Cook for about 15 minutes and serve.
Nutrition: Calories: 307 Carbs: 70g Fats: 1.4g Proteins: 1g Sodium: 130mg Sugar: 57.9g

Apple Crumble

Serves: 8/Prep Time: 40 mins
Ingredients
- ½ cup butter, softened
- 2 (14-ounce) cans apple pie
- 18 tablespoons self-rising flour
- ¼ teaspoon salt
- 14 tablespoons caster sugar

Directions
1. Preheat the Airfryer at 320 degrees F and lightly grease a baking dish.
2. Place the apple pie evenly in the prepared baking dish.
3. Add remaining ingredients in a bowl and mix until a crumbly mixture forms.
4. Spread the mixture over apple pie evenly and arange the baking dish in an Airfryer basket.
5. Cook for about 25 minutes and serve.
Nutrition Calories: 425 Carbs: 66.5g Fats: 16.7g Proteins: 3.4g Sodium: 401mg Sugar: 33.6g

Marshmallow Pastries

Serves: 8/Prep Time: 20 mins
Ingredients
- 4-ounce butter, melted
- 8 phyllo pastry sheets, thawed
- ½ cup chunky peanut butter
- Pinch of salt
- 8 teaspoons marshmallow fluff

Directions
1. Brush 1 filo pastry sheet with butter and place a second sheet of filo on top of first one.
2. Brush it with butter and repeat till all sheets are used.
3. Cut the phyllo layers in 8 strips and put 1 teaspoon of marshmallow fluff and 1 tablespoon of peanut butter on the underside of a filo strip.
4. Fold the tip of the sheet over the filling to form a triangle.
5. Fold repeatedly in a zigzag manner until the filling is fully covered.
6. Preheat air fryer 360 degrees F and place the pastries into cooking basket.
7. Cook for about 5 minutes and season with a pinch of salt before serving.
Nutrition: Calories: 283 Carbs: 20.2g Fats: 20.6g Proteins: 6g Sodium: 320mg Sugar: 3.4g

Fruity Tacos

Serves: 4/Prep Time: 15 mins
Ingredients
- 8 tablespoons strawberryjelly
- 4 soft shell tortillas
- ½ cup blueberries
- 4 tablespoons powdered sugar
- ½ cup raspberries

Directions
1. Preheat the air fryer at 300 degrees F.
2. Spread strawberryjelly over each tortilla and top with blueberries and raspberries.
3. Sprinkle with powdered sugar and place the tortillas in an Airfryer basket.
4. Cook for about 5 minutes until crispy.

Nutrition Calories: 310 Carbs: 64.4g Fats: 4.7g Proteins: 3.3g Sodium: 370mg Sugar: 35.3g

21-Day Keto Meal Prep Recipes

Day 1

Breakfast: Keto Bacon Eggs
Serves: 15 /Prep Time: 5 minutes

Ingredients:

- 12 eggs
- salt and pepper, to taste
- 4 oz. cooked bacon

Directions

1. Adjust your oven to 400 degrees F (200°C).
2. Line a muffin tray with cupcake liners.
3. Crack one egg into each liner and top it with bacon.
4. Drizzle some salt and pepper on top.
5. Bake for 15 minutes.
6. Serve warm.

Nutrition Calories: 211 Carbs: 0.5g Fats: 18.5g Proteins: 11.5g Sodium: 280g Sugar: 0.3g

Lunch: Chicken Enchilada Bowl
Prep Time: 10 mins/Serves: 4

Ingredients:

- 2-3 chicken breasts
- 3/4 cups red enchilada sauce
- 1/4 cup water
- 1/4 cup onion
- 1 4 oz. can green chile
- 1 (12oz) steam bag cauliflower rice
- Preferred toppings- avocado, jalapeno, cheese, and Roma tomatoes
- Seasoning, to taste

Directions

1. Heat a greased skillet and sear chicken breasts until golden brown from both the sides.
2. Stir in enchilada sauce, onions, chile and water. Reduce the heat and cover the lid.
3. Cook until chicken is completely cooked.
4. Remove the chicken and shred it with fork.
5. Return the chicken to the skillet and cook for 10 minutes.
6. Serve on top of cauliflower rice along with desired toppings.

Nutrition *Calories: 182; Carbs: 11.1g; Fats: 1.4g; Proteins: 22.2g; Sodium: 560mg; Sugar: 2.1g*

Dinner: Zoodles with Avocado Sauce
Serves: 15 /Prep Time: 5 minutes

Ingredients

- 3 cups yellow and red cherry tomatoes

avocado sauce:

- 1 avocado
- 1/4 cup olive oil
- 1/2 teaspoon salt
- 1/2 cup fresh flat leaf parsley

Directions

1. For sauce add everything to a blender
2. Take a skillet and heat a drizzle of oil
3. Add tomatoes and sauté until soft. K
4. Now add zucchini to the same skille
5. Toss sautéed zucchini with tomatoe
6. Top this mixture with cheese.
7. Serve.

Nutrition *Calories: 109 Carbs: 6.2g Fats: 9.6g Proteins: 0.9g 1.8g*

Day 2

Breakfast: Breakfast Biscuits with Sausage and Cheese
Serves: 6 /Prep Time: 8 minutes

Ingredients:
- 2 ounces cream cheese
- 2 cups mozzarella, shredded
- 2 eggs, beaten
- 1 cup almond flour
- pinch salt & pepper
- 2 ounces Colby jack cheese, thin cubes
- 6 breakfast sausage patties, pre-cooked

Directions

1. Add cream cheese and mozzarella to a bowl and microwave for 30 seconds. Mix well.
2. Beat egg with almond flour in the mixer then add cream cheese mixture. Blend well.
3. Knead the dough on a lightly floured surface. Wrap it a plastic sheet then refrigerate until firm.
4. Cut the dough ball into six 3inch balls.
5. Flatten each dough ball and place the sausage on each.
6. Top the sausages with cheese then wrap the dough around the sausage.
7. Place stuffed dough in a greased baking tray.
8. Bake for 15 minutes until golden brown.
9. Top with mozzarella and serve warm.

Nutrition *Calories: 489 Carbs: 5g Fats: 43.6g Proteins: 0.9g Sodium: 662mg Sugar: 0.1g*

Lunch: Zucchini Noodles with Spicy Pepita Gremolata
Serves: 4/Prep Time: 8 minutes

Ingredients

Gremolata
- 1/4 cup pepitas
- zest of one lem
- 1/3 cup
- chopped
- Noodle
- 2 larg
- 2-3

Direction
1.
2.
3

- roughly chopped
- ~~on~~
- ~~alian~~ flat-leaf parsley,

- ~~e~~ zucchinis, peeled
- ~~T~~ olive oil

- 1 tsp fresh garlic, finely minced
- a dash of cayenne pepper, to taste
- a big pinch of salt

- salt, to taste

~~ns~~

For gremolata mix everything in a bowl and set it aside.
Process zucchinis through a spiralizer to get its noodles.
Take a wok and heat a drizzle of oil in it on medium heat.
4. Add zucchini noodles and sauté for 7 minutes. (in batches if needed)
5. Sprinkle salt over these noodles and sauté.
6. Top the noodles with gremolata.
7. Serve.

Nutrition Calories: 109 Carbs: 6.2g Fats: 9.6g Proteins: 0.9g Sodium: 227mg Sugar: 1.8g

Dinner: Bacon, Chicken & Tomato Stuffed Avocado
Serves: 3/Prep Time: 10mins

Ingredients:

- 2 Chicken Breasts grilled
- 3 pieces bacon cooked and chopped
- 2 Avocado, pitted, peeled and sliced

- 1/3 cup Grape Tomatoes chopped
- 1/3 cup mayo paleo
- Additional seasonings to taste

Directions

1. Season chicken with salt and pepper. Grill over medium heat until tender.
2. Add bacon strips to the grill and cook until crispy.
3. Cut the chicken into cubes and transfer it to a bowl.
4. Add bacon, onions, and tomatoes.
5. Stir in mayo along with seasoning.
6. Top the mixture with avocado slices.
7. Serve.

Nutrition Calories: 487; Carbs: 10.6g; Fats: 37.4g; Proteins: 28.1g; Sodium: 501mg; Sugar: 1.2g

Day 3

Breakfast: Greek Egg Bake
Serves: 10/Prep Time: 5 minutes

Ingredients:

- 12 Eggs

- 1 cup Chopped Kale

- 1/4 cup Sun-dried tomatoes
- 1/2 cup Feta
- 1/2 teaspoon Oregano
- Salt & pepper, to taste

Directions

1. Adjust your oven to 350 degrees F.
2. Whisk eggs in a glass bowl then stir in all the remaining ingredients.
3. Line a baking pan with a parchment paper.
4. Grease the pan with non-stick cooking spray.
5. Bake for 25 minutes in the oven
6. Slice and serve.

Nutrition Calories: 139; Carbs: 2.3g; Fats: 10.1g; Proteins: 10.9g; Sodium: 238mg; Sugar: 1.5g

Lunch: South Western Chicken
Serves: 1/Prep Time: 10 mins

Ingredients:

- 1 boneless Chicken Breasts (boneless)
- 2 teaspoon Olive Oil (extra virgin optional)
- 1 whole Lemon - zested and juices
- 1/2 teaspoon Red chili powder
- 1/2 teaspoon Cumin
- 1 teaspoon Oregano dried
- 3 cloves Garlic minced
- 1 teaspoon Onion powder
- 1/2 teaspoon Salt
- 1/2 teaspoon Black pepper freshly ground

Directions

1. Mix everything in a large bowl.
2. Cover the bowl and marinate for 1 hour in the refrigerator.
3. Meanwhile, Adjust a grill pan over low heat for 4 minutes.
4. Add a tsp olive oil and add the marinated chicken.
5. Cook for 7 minutes per side on medium heat.
6. Serve warm.

Nutrition *Calories: 355; Carbs: 11.8g; Fats: 15g; Proteins: 44.2g; Sodium: 971mg; Sugar: 2.5g*

Dinner: Thai Quinoa Salad
Serves: 1 /Prep Time: 15 minutes

Ingredients

For the Salad

- ½ cup cooked quinoa
- 3 tbsp grated carrot
- 2 tbsp red pepper, finely chopped
- 3 tbsp cucumber, finely chopped
- ½ cup edamame (thawed)
- 2 scallions, finely chopped
- ¼ cup red cabbage, finely sliced
- 1 tbsp cilantro, finely chopped
- 2 tbsp roasted peanuts, chopped
- to taste salt

Thai Peanut Dressing:

- 1 tbsp creamy natural peanut butter

- 2 tsp low sodium soy sauce
- 1 tsp rice vinegar
- ½ tsp sesame oil
- 1 tsp sriracha sauce (optional)
- 1 garlic clove, finely minced
- ½ tsp grated ginger
- 1 tsp lemon juice
- ½ tsp agave nectar (or honey)

Directions:
1. For salad dressing mix everything in a small bowl.
2. Toss the salad ingredients in a large bowl.
3. Pour in the prepared dressing and mix well.
4. Serve

Nutrition *Calories: 109 Carbs: 6.2g Fats: 9.6g Proteins: 0.9g Sodium: 227mg Sugar: 1.8g*

Day 4

Breakfast: Turmeric Scrambled Egg
Serves: 2 /Prep Time: 5 minutes

Ingredients
- 4 large eggs
- 2 tablespoons coconut milk
- 2 teaspoons dried turmeric
- ½ teaspoon. dried parsley
- salt & black pepper to taste
- steamed veggie of choice
- pre-cooked sausage of choice

Directions
1. Grease a small frying pan with nonstick cooking spray and place it on medium heat.
2. Whisk eggs with milk, parsley, salt, pepper and turmeric in a bowl.
3. Pour this eggs mixture into the greased pan and cook for 3 minutes with constant stirring.
4. Flip and cook for another 3 minutes.
5. Transfer the scramble to the meal prep containers.
6. Serve with sautéed vegetables and sausage.

Nutrition *Calories: 231; Carbs: 3.1g; Fats: 17.6g; Proteins: 15.7g; Sodium: 244mg; Sugar: 1.3g*

Lunch: Lasagna Stuffed Portobello Mushrooms
Serves: 4/Prep Time: 5 minutes

Ingredients
- 4 large portobello mushrooms
- 1-2 tablespoons olive oil
- 1 cup marinara sauce
- 1 1/2 cups light ricotta
- 1/4 teaspoon salt
- 1 egg
- 1 1/2 cup chopped spinach
- 1/2 cup basil chopped
- 1 cup shredded mozzarella

Directions

1. Adjust your oven to 400 degrees F. Layer a baking sheet with parchment paper.

2. Clean the mushrooms by removing the gills and stem then wash them.

3. Layer the mushrooms with olive oil inside out.

4. Add ¼ cup marinara sauce into each mushroom cap.

5. Add ricotta, spinach, basil, egg, and salt to a bowl and toss well.

6. Divide this mixture into the four mushrooms.

7. Top each mushroom cup with ¼ cup mozzarella.

8. Place the stuffed mushrooms in the baking sheet.

9. Bake for 20 minutes.

10. Serve.

Nutrition *Calories: 261 Carbs: 11g Fats: 16g Proteins: 21g Sodium: 457mg Sugar: 5g*

Dinner: Chicken Pesto
Serves: 1/Prep Time: 10 minutes

Ingredients:

- 1 chicken breasts (boneless)
- 3 tablespoons olive oil extra virgin
- ¼ cup almonds, chopped
- 2 garlic cloves, minced
- 1 cup basil leaves
- 1/2 cup coriander leaves
- 1/2 teaspoon salt each
- 1/2 teaspoon black pepper freshly crushed

Directions

1. Add everything to a food processor except chicken.
2. Mix the marinade with chicken in a bowl.
3. Cover the bowl and marinate for 1 hour in the refrigerator.
4. Meanwhile, Adjust a grill pan over low heat for 4 minutes.
5. Add a tsp olive oil and add the marinated chicken.
6. Cook for 7 minutes per side on medium heat.
7. Serve warm.

Nutrition *Calories: 455; Carbs: 10.8g; Fats: 34.4g; Proteins: 10.9g; Sodium: 227mg; Sugar: 1.8g*

Day 5

Breakfast: Cauliflower Cheddar Pancakes
Serves: 4/Prep Time: 10 minutes

Ingredients

- 1 small head grated cauliflower
- 1 large Egg
- 3/4 cup Shredded Cheddar Cheese
- 1/4 teaspoon Cayenne Pepper
- 1/4 teaspoon garlic powder
- 1/2 teaspoon Pink Salt
- 1/8 teaspoon black pepper

Directions

1. Add grated cauliflower to a bowl and microwave for 3 minutes.
2. Transfer the cauliflower to the cheesecloth and drain excess water.
3. Mix the drained cauliflower with all the remaining ingredients in a bowl.

4. Divide the batter into six squares arrange on a greased baking tray.
5. Bake for 15 to 20 minutes at 400 degrees F.
6. Serve warm.

Nutrition Calories: 111; Carbs: 1.9g; Fats: 8.3g; Proteins: 7.4g; Sodium: 896mg; Sugar: 0.8g

Lunch: Chicken Vegetable Stew
Serves: 10/Prep Time: 10 minutes

Ingredients:

- 3.5 pounds chicken thighs, bone & skin on
- 1 large yellow onion, chopped
- 4 medium-size carrots, diced
- 4 stalks celery, diced
- 10 ounces cremini mushrooms, sliced
- ½ teaspoon dried thyme

- 3 cloves garlic, minced
- ½ cup frozen peas
- 1-2 cups low sodium chicken broth
- 2 tablespoons Xanthan gum
- Olive oil
- Kosher salt
- Fresh cracked pepper

Directions

1. Adjust your oven to 400 degrees F.
2. Rub the chicken with pepper and salt then place it on a baking sheet.
3. Bake for 1 hour then allow it to cool for 10 minutes.
4. Pull the meat then cut it into small pieces.
5. Heat oil in a saucepan over medium heat and add celery, carrots, onion, mushrooms, thyme, salt, and pepper.
6. Sauté for 12 minutes then add garlic to cook for another 7 minutes.
7. Add chicken shred, peas and stock to the pan and cook for 10 minutes.
8. Mix xanthan gum with water in a small bowl and pour the mixture into the pan.
9. Stir cook for 10 minutes.
10. Serve warm.

Nutrition *Calories: 364 Carbs: 10.8g Fats: 13.6g Proteins: 47.9g Sodium: 227mg Sugar: 2.8g*

Dinner: Enchilada Stuffed Eggplants
Serves: 4/Prep Time: 5 minutes

Ingredients

- 2 medium eggplants
- 1/2 cup enchilada sauce
- 1/4 tsp salt
- 1/4 teaspoon chili powder

- 1/8 teaspoon ground cumin
- 1.5 cups shredded cheese
- Serve with avocado salsa and/or sour cream

Directions

1. Adjust your oven to 400 degrees F.
2. Prepare eggplant by scrubbing them gently and poke some holes using a fork.
3. Place these prepared potatoes in the baking sheet.
4. Bake them for 50 mins until they are soft.
5. Slice each eggplant into half lengthwise.
6. Scoop out the flesh from the center while leaving some with the skins.

7.   Mash this scooped out flesh in a bowl and add cumin, chili powder, salt, enchilada sauce, corn, beans, and ¾ cup cheese.
8.   Mix well then divide the mixture into the eggplant skins.
9.   Top each with the remaining cheese.
10.   Bake the eggplant for 15 minutes.
11.   Serve warm.

Nutrition *Calories: 359 Carbs: 11 g Fats: 9.6g Proteins: 0.9g Sodium: 227mg Sugar: 1.8g*

Day 6

Breakfast: Strawberry Pancake Bites
Serves: 8/Prep Time: 10 minutes

Ingredients:

- 4 large eggs
- 1/4 cup Swerve Sweetener
- 1/2 teaspoon vanilla extract
- 1/2 cup coconut flour
- 1/4 cup butter melted

- 1 teaspoon baking powder
- 1/2 teaspoon salt
- 1/4 teaspoon cinnamon
- 1/3 to 1/2 cup water
- 1/2 cup strawberry, chopped

Directions
1.   Adjust your oven to 325 degrees F and grease a muffin tray.
2.   Blend eggs with vanilla extract, the sweetener in a blender.
3.   Stir in melted butter, coconut flour, salt, cinnamon, and baking powder. Blend well until smooth.
4.   Add 1/3 cup water to the mixture and blend again.
5.   Divide the batter into each muffin cups and top it with few blueberries.
6.   Press the blueberries gently and bake for 20 to 25 minutes.
7.   Serve warm.

Nutrition *Calories: 121 Carbs: 13.8g Fats: 9g Proteins: 4.3g Sodium: 184mg Sugar: 8.2g*

Lunch: Broccoli Quinoa Casserole
Serves: 5/Prep Time: 10 minutes

Ingredients:

- 2 1/2 cup uncooked quinoa
- 4 1/2 cup low-sodium vegetable stock, or water
- 2 tbsp pesto sauce
- 1/2 tsp Celtic salt
- 2 tsp arrowroot powder, or cornstarch

- 2 cups fresh organic spinach
- 12 oz skim mozzarella cheese, I used 16oz
- 1/3 cup parmesan cheese
- 12 oz fresh broccoli florets
- 3 green onions, chopped

Directions

1.   Adjust the oven to 400 degrees F.
2.   Spread green onions and quinoa in a 9x13 baking sheet.
3.   Add broccoli to a glass bowl and heat it for 5 minutes on high temperature.
4.   Now whisk vegetable stock with salt, arrowroot, and pesto in a saucepan.

5. Heat the stock mixture until it boils.
6. Pour the stock over quinoa in the baking pan.
7. Top it with spinach, ¾ mozzarella cheese, and parmesan.
8. Bake it for 35 minutes.
9. Add in broccoli and top the casserole with remaining cheese.
10. Bake for another 5 minutes.
11. Serve warm.

Nutrition *Calories: 109 Carbs: 6.2g Fats: 9.6g Proteins: 0.9g Sodium: 227mg Sugar: 1.8g*

Dinner: Meal Prep Chicken Fajitas
Serves: 4/Prep Time: 10 minutes

Ingredients:

Rub:

- 1 tablespoon erythritol
- 3/4 teaspoon salt
- 1 tablespoon chili powder
- 1.5 teaspoon cumin
- 1.5 teaspoon paprika
- 1/2 teaspoon garlic powder
- 1/2 teaspoon onion powder
- 1/8-1/4 teaspoon cayenne optional

Fajitas

- 2 large chicken breasts sliced into 1/2-inch-thick strips
- 6 cups mixed veggies sliced into strips
- -bell peppers
- -zucchini
- -red onion
- -mushrooms
- juice from 1 lime
- 1 tablespoon olive oil

To Serve

- Tortillas or tortilla bowls
- Salsa & Greek yogurt
- Fresh avocado

Directions

1. Adjust oven to 425 degrees F.
2. Mix chicken with all the vegetables, lime juice and olive oil in a bowl.
3. Gradually add the rub with continuous mixing.
4. Spread the chicken and vegetables on two large sheet pans.
5. Roast for 10 minutes then flip. Roast for another 10 minutes.
6. Transfer the roasted chicken and veggies to the meal prep containers.
7. Store up to 4 days in the refrigerator.
8. Reheat and serve with salsa.

Nutrition *Calories: 202 Carbs: 11.5g Fats: 9.6g Proteins: 22g Sodium: 526mg Sugar: 1.5g*

Day 7

Breakfast: Low Carb Bagels
Serves: 14/Prep Time: 5 minutes

Ingredients:
- 2 cups almond flour
- 1 tablespoon baking powder
- 1 teaspoon garlic powder
- 1 teaspoon onion powder
- 1 teaspoon dried Italian seasoning
- 3 large eggs, divided
- 3 cups shredded low moisture mozzarella cheese
- 5 tablespoons cream cheese
- 3 tablespoons Everything Bagel Seasoning

Directions
1. Adjust the oven to 425 degrees F.
2. Layer a rimmed baking sheet with wax paper.
3. Mix almond flour with garlic powder, baking powder, onion powder and Italian seasoning in a mixing bowl.
4. Whisk 1 egg in a bowl and set it aside.
5. Add cream cheese with mozzarella to a bowl and heat for 1.5 minutes in the microwave.
6. Whisk 2 eggs with the almond flour mixture in a mixing bowl.
7. Stir in cream cheese mixture and mix well.
8. Divide the dough into 6 pieces and shape them into smooth balls.
9. Press your finger through the center of each ball to make a ring. Stretch the ring into a bagel.
10. Place all the bagels on the baking sheet.
11. Brush each bagel with egg wash and Everything bagel seasoning.
12. Bake for 14 minutes until golden brown.

Nutrition *Calories: 207 Carbs: 5.4g Fats: 15g Proteins: 11.1g Sodium: 252mg Sugar: 0.2g*

Lunch: Fiesta Lime Chicken Chowder
Serves: 4/Prep Time: 10 minutes

Ingredients:
- 1 pound of chicken thighs, skinless and boneless
- 8 oz. cream cheese
- 1 cup of chicken broth
- 1 can of diced tomatoes
- 1 small onion, diced
- 1 jalapeno, diced
- 1 lime, juiced
- 2 tablespoons of cilantro, chopped
- 1 clove of garlic, chopped
- a few dashes of liquid smoke
- 1 teaspoon of salt
- 1 tablespoon of pepper
- Garnish with shredded cheddar cheese
- lime wedge
- fresh cilantro

Directions
5. Add all the ingredients to a slow cooker.
6. Cover the lid and cook on low for 6 hours.
7. Use two forks to shred the chicken.
8. Garnish with cheddar cheese, lime wedges, and cilantro.
9. Serve.

Nutrition *Calories: 449; Carbs: 8.4g; Fats: 28.7g; Proteins: 39.3g; Sodium: 1044mg; Sugar: 2.6g*

Dinner: Butter Chicken
Serves: 6/Prep Time: 10 minutes

Ingredients

- 1-pound boneless skinless chicken breast cut into bite-size chunks
- 1/2 onion finely minced
- 2 tablespoons butter
- 3 cloves garlic minced or grated
- 1 tablespoon freshly grated ginger
- 2 teaspoons curry powder
- 1-2 teaspoons Thai red curry paste
- 2 tablespoons garam masala
- 1/2-1 teaspoon turmeric
- 1 teaspoon cayenne pepper
- 1/4 teaspoon salt
- 1 (6 ounces) can tomato paste
- 1 (14 ounces) can coconut milk
- 1/2 cup Greek yogurt
- 1/4 cup half and half cream
- cooked white rice for serving
- Fresh homemade naan for scooping

Directions

12. Mix coconut milk, cream and Greek yogurt in a glass bowl.
13. Add garlic, ginger, all the spices, and tomato paste. Mix until well combined.
14. Layer the bowl of the crockpot with olive oil.
15. Add onion, chicken, and coconut milk mixture to the crockpot.
16. Top the mixture with butter and seal the lid.
17. Cook on the high-temperature setting for 4 hours.
18. Adjust seasoning with salt and pepper.
19. Serve warm.

Nutrition *Calories: 109 Carbs: 6.2g Fats: 9.6g Proteins: 0.9g Sodium: 227mg Sugar: 1.8g*

Day 8

Breakfast: Bacon and Mushroom Casserole
Serves: 8/Prep Time: 10 minutes

Ingredients:

- 6 oz. mushrooms, trimmed and quartered
- 10 oz. bacon, diced
- 2 oz. butter
- 8 eggs
- 1 cup heavy whipping cream
- 5 oz. shredded cheddar cheese
- 1 teaspoon onion powder
- salt and pepper

Directions

1. Adjust your oven to 400 degrees F (200°C).
2. Heat butter in a skillet over medium-high heat and add bacon and mushrooms to sauté until golden brown.
3. Season the mixture with salt and pepper. Add it to a greased baking dish.
4. Mix all the remaining ingredients in a bowl along with salt and pepper.
5. Pour this mixture over the mushrooms and bake for 30 to 40 minutes.
6. Add remaining ingredients to a medium bowl and whisk to combine.
7. Serve warm.

Nutrition *Calories: 434 Carbs: 2.5g Fats: 36.4g Proteins: 24.9g Sodium: 1038mg Sugar: 0.9g*

Lunch: Mixed Cauliflower Rice
Serves: 8/Prep Time: 10 minutes

Ingredients

- 2 Eggs
- Salt and Pepper to taste
- 1 tbsp. Vegetable Oil Divided
- 1/2 Yellow Onion Diced
- 1 cup Frozen Peas and Carrots

Sauce:

- 4 tbsp. Soy Sauce Low Sodium
- 3 Garlic Cloves Minced

- 1/2 Cup Frozen Corn
- 5 cups Fresh Minced/Crumbled Cauliflower
- 1 tsp. Sesame Oil
- 2 Green Onions Chopped

- 2 tsp. Sesame Oil

Directions

20. Whisk eggs in a bowl and add pepper and salt.
21. Mix soy sauce with 1 tsp. sesame oil and garlic in a bowl.
22. Use a large skillet and add ½ tbsp oil.
23. After heating the oil add onion and all the frozen vegetables.
24. Sauté them for 5 minutes while adding salt and pepper to taste.
25. Stir in remaining vegetable oil, cauliflower rice, and soy sauce mixture.
26. Sauté for 6 minutes.
27. Keep this mixture on one side of the pan and reduce the heat.
28. Pour 1 tsp sesame oil to empty side and pour the whisked egg into it.
29. Cook the egg scramble for 2-3 minutes.
30. Sauté with the cauliflower mixture.
31. Garnish with green onions and serve.

Nutrition *Calories: 109 Carbs: 6.2g Fats: 9.6g Proteins: 0.9g Sodium: 227mg Sugar: 1.8g*

Dinner: Turkey Zucchini Noodles in Romesco Sauce
Serves: 4/Prep Time: 10 minutes

Ingredients:

Romesco Sauce:

- 1 jar roasted red peppers drained
- 1/2 cup cherry tomatoes
- 1 clove garlic
- 1/4 cup almonds

Ground Turkey Pasta:

- 1 lb. lean ground turkey
- 2 large zucchini spiralized (approx. 4-6 cups)

- 2 tablespoons red wine vinegar
- 1/4 cup olive oil
- 1/2 teaspoon salt
- 1/4 teaspoon smoked paprika

- Parmesan cheese to taste

Directions

1. Add all the ingredients for Romesco sauce to a blender and blend until smooth.
2. Heat a skillet and add ground turkey to sauté until it is no longer pink.
3. Stir in spiralized zucchini and cook for 3 minutes.
4. Add Romesco sauce and toss everything together.

5.   Serve.

Nutrition Calories: 225 Carbs: 11.3g Fats: 17.7g Proteins: 7.9g Sodium: 386mg Sugar: 2.3g

Day 9

Breakfast: Turkey Edamame Bowl
Serves: 4/Prep Time: 10 mins

Ingredients:

- 1 cup turkey, thinly sliced
- 3/4 cups red enchilada sauce
- 1/4 cup water
- 1/4 cup onion
- 1 4 oz. can green chile
- 1 12oz steamed edamame
- Preferred toppings- avocado, jalapeno, cheese, and Roma tomatoes
- Seasoning, to taste

Directions

1. Heat a greased skillet and sauté turkey until golden brown.
2. Stir in enchilada sauce, onions, chile and water. Reduce the heat and cover the lid.
3. Cook until turkey is completely cooked.
4. Remove the turkey and shred it with a fork.
5. Return the chicken to the skillet and cook for 10 minutes.
6. Serve on top of edamame along with desired toppings.

Nutrition *Calories: 182; Carbs: 11.1g; Fats: 4.6g; Proteins: 22.2g; Sodium: 560mg; Sugar: 2.1g*

Lunch: Caribbean Shrimp
Serves: 4/Prep Time: 10mins

Ingredients:

- 10 oz. large shrimp, peeled and deveined
- 2 tablespoons olive oil
- 2 tablespoons red wine vinegar
- 2 tablespoons freshly squeezed lemon juice
- 1 tablespoon erythritol
- 1 tablespoon coconut aminos
- 2 tablespoons green onions, chopped
- 1 tablespoon jalapeño, seeded and finely chopped
- Lime wedges, if desired

Directions

1. Gently mix all the ingredients for shrimps in a bowl.
2. Cover and marinate for 30 minutes in the refrigerator.
3. Adjust the grill over medium heat.
4. Thread the marinated shrimp onto the skewers.
5. Place the skewers on the grill . Cook, it covered for 6 minutes over indirect heat.
6. Pour the remaining marinade into a saucepan and boil.
7. Decrease the heat to low then let it simmer for 10 minutes.
8. Pour the sauce over the shrimps and serve.

Nutrition *Calories: 132; Carbs: 8.2g; Fats: 9.6g; Proteins: 13.9g; Sodium: 94mg; Sugar: 1.9g*

Dinner: Broccoli Stir Fry Recipe
Serves: 4/Prep Time: 10mins

Ingredients
- 1 tbsp. Vegetable Oil
- 1/2 Red Onion thinly sliced
- 1 Orange Bell Pepper thinly sliced
- 12 oz Broccoli Florets Fresh
- Salt and Pepper to taste

Sauce:
- 5 Garlic Cloves minced
- 2 tsp. Sesame Oil
- 1/4 Cup Soy Sauce Low Sodium
- 1/2 cup Vegetable Broth
- 1 cup Sugar Snap Peas
- 1 Green Onion chopped
- 1 tbsp. Sesame Seeds
- Juice of half a lime
- 2 tsp. Maple Syrup
- Salt and Pepper to taste
- 2 tsp. Corn Starch

Directions
1. Add garlic, sesame oil, broth, cornstarch, maple starch and soy sauce in a bowl and mix.
2. Take a pan and add vegetable oil.
3. Add bell pepper, broccoli florets, and onions. Sauté for 7 minutes.
4. Add salt and pepper for seasoning.
5. Decrease the heat then add soy sauce mixture and sugar snap peas.
6. Stir cook for 3 minutes until it thickens.
7. Add green onion, sesame seeds, and lime juice.
8. Serve warm.

Nutrition *Calories: 109 Carbs: 6.2g Fats: 9.6g Proteins: 0.9g Sodium: 227mg Sugar: 1.8g*

Day 10

Breakfast: Chicken Avocado Bowl
Serves: 3/Prep Time: 10mins

Ingredients:

- 2 Chicken Breasts grilled
- 3 pieces bacon cooked and chopped
- 2 Avocado, pitted, peeled and diced
- 1/3 cup Grape Tomatoes chopped
- 1/3 cup mayo paleo
- Additional seasonings to taste

Directions

1. Season chicken with salt and pepper. Grill over medium heat until tender.
2. Add bacon strips to the grill and cook until crispy.
3. Cut the chicken into cubes and transfer it to a bowl.
4. Add bacon, onions, and tomatoes.
5. Stir in mayo along with seasoning.
6. Toss in avocado cubes and mix.
7. Serve.

Nutrition *Calories: 487; Carbs: 12.6g; Fats: 37.4g; Proteins: 28.1g; Sodium: 501mg; Sugar: 1.2g*

Lunch: Instant Pot Pulled Pork
Serves: 4/Prep Time: 10 minutes

Ingredients:

- 2 tablespoons olive oil
- 3-4 lbs. boneless pork shoulder cut into 3-4 pieces
- 2 cups barbecue sauce
- 1 1/2 cups beer of choice or water or chicken broth
- 2 tablespoons molasses

Directions

1. Select sauté function on the pressure cooker.
2. Add oil to the cooking pot along with pork. Cook for 3 minutes per side.
3. Transfer the seared pork to a plate.
4. Stir in 1 cup BBQ sauce, 1 cup beer and molasses to the cooking pot.
5. Return the beef to the pot.
6. Secure the lid and cook for 90 mins on high pressure.
7. Allow the pressure to release naturally for 20 minutes.
8. Shred the pork using two forks.
9. Return the shredded pork to the pot along with all the remaining ingredients.
10. Serve.

Nutrition *Calories: 392; Carbs: 7.2g; Fats: 40.4g; Proteins: 21g; Sodium: 423mg; Sugar: 3g*

Dinner: Stuffed Salmon Rolls with Lemon Sauce
Serves: 4/Prep Time: 10 minutes

Ingredients:

- 4 (5 ounces) salmon fillets, skins removed
- salt and pepper to taste
- 1 (12 ounces) container ricotta
- 1/2 cup Parmigiano Reggiano (parmesan), grated
- 2 tablespoons basil, chopped
- 2 teaspoons lemon zest
- 1/2-pound asparagus, trimmed
- 1 tablespoon butter
- 1/2 cup chicken broth
- 2 tablespoons lemon juice
- 2 teaspoons xanthan gum

Directions

1. Season the fillets with salt and pepper.
2. Spread them on a surface with their skin side up.
3. Top each fillet with ricotta, parmesan, lemon zest, basil, salt, pepper, and asparagus.
4. Roll each fillet and place on a baking sheet with its seam side down.
5. Bake for 15 to 20 minutes at 425 F in a preheated oven.
6. Heat butter on medium flame in a small saucepan.
7. Pour in broth mixture, lemon juice, and xanthan gum to the pan and stir cook for 5 minutes.
8. Pour this sauce over the baked rolls and serve with basil and lemon zest on top.
9. Serve the salmon rolls topped with the lemon sauce and optionally garnish with more basil and lemon zest.

Nutrition *Calories: 394 Carbs: 8.3g Fats: 21.7g Proteins: 43.2g Sodium: 384mg Sugar: 1.6g*

Day 11

Breakfast: Teriyaki Beef Zoodles
Serves: 4/Prep Time: 10 minutes

Ingredients:

- 1/4 cup coconut aminos
- 2-3 tablespoons erythritol
- 3 tablespoons rice vinegar
- 2 garlic cloves minced

For the zoodles

- 8 ounces flank steak sliced against the grain into 1/4-inch thick slices
- 1 teaspoon sesame oil
- Salt and black pepper to taste

- 1/2 teaspoon grated ginger
- 1 tablespoon xanthan gum
- 2 tablespoons water

- 5-6 medium zucchini cut into noodles
- 3 tablespoons olive oil divided
- Salt and black pepper, to taste
- Red chili flakes to taste

Directions

1. Mix all the ingredients for sauce in a container without water.
2. Rub the steak with salt, pepper, sesame oil, and 2 tablespoons sauce.
3. Let it marinate at room temperature.
4. Heat 2 tablespoons in a large flat pan over medium flame.
5. Add beef to cook for 1 minute per side.
6. Transfer the beef to a plate.
7. Heat remaining oil in a skillet and stir in beef along with the sauce.
8. Cook until the sauce thickens and add the water.
9. Stir in zucchini noodles to the pan and cook for 2 minutes.
10. Garnish with green onions and sesame seeds.
11. Serve.

Nutrition *Calories: 406 Carbs: 10g Fats: 40.4g Proteins: 2.2g Sodium: 406mg Sugar: 4.8g*

Lunch: Tuscan Baked Salmon and Veggies
Serves: 4/Prep Time: 10 mins

Ingredients:

For the Topping and Salmon:

- 1/4 cup tomato paste
- 2 tablespoons olive oil
- 1 teaspoon mustard
- 1 tablespoon dried Italian herb

For the Vegetables:

- 2 large red peppers , sliced
- 1-2 large zucchini sliced

- 1 teaspoon ground paprika
- 1/ teaspoon salt
- Pepper to taste
- 1 1/2-pound salmon fillet skin on

- 1 tablespoon dried Italian herb
- 1 tablespoon olive oil

- Salt and pepper to taste
- 1/2-pound cherry tomatoes

Directions

1. Adjust the oven to 400 degrees F. Line a baking tray with a parchment sheet.
2. Mix all topping ingredients in a bowl.
3. Spread the salmon fillet on the baking sheet and top it with the topping evenly.
4. Toss peppers with zucchini, herbs, 1 tablespoon olive oil, salt, and pepper in a large bowl.
5. Place this mixture around the salmon fillets along with cherry tomatoes.
6. Bake for 15 to 20 minutes.
7. Serve.

Nutrition *Calories: 336 Carbs: 10.6g Fats: 18.3g Proteins: 35.9g Sodium: 104mg Sugar: 6.1g*

Dinner: Parmesan-Dijon Crusted Pork Chops
Serves: 2/Prep Time: 10 minutes

Ingredients:

- 4 boneless pork loin chops
- 1/4 teaspoon sea salt
- 1/4 teaspoon black pepper
- 1/4 cup Dijon mustard
- 2 tablespoons spicy brown mustard
- 2 tablespoons olive oil
- 1/2 teaspoon garlic powder
- 1/2 teaspoon dried thyme
- 1/4 teaspoon onion powder
- 1/4 teaspoon dried oregano
- 1/4 teaspoon dried basil
- 1/4 teaspoon Italian seasoning
- 1 cup grated Parmesan cheese

Directions
1. Adjust the oven to 400 degrees F.
2. Keep a wire rack on a baking sheet.
3. Place the pork chops on the wire rack and bake until crispy.
4. Season the chops with salt and pepper.
5. Mix spicy mustard, olive oil, thyme, garlic powder, onion powder, basil, oregano and Italian seasoning in a mixing bowl.
6. Dip the chops in the mustard the mixture and mix well to coat.
7. Coat the chops with a thin layer of Parmesan cheese.
8. Place the pork chops over the wire rack in the baking sheet.
9. Bake for 20 minutes.
10. Broil it for 4 minutes until golden brown.

Nutrition *Calories: 349 Carbs: 23.1g Fats: 6.6g Proteins: 11g Sodium: 237mg Sugar: 1.4g*

Day 12

Breakfast: Butter Pecan Fat Bombs
Prep Time: 10mins /Serves: 12

Ingredients:

- 1/2 cup pecans
- 1/4 cup coconut butter
- 1/4 cup ghee or butter
- 1/4 cup coconut oil

- 1/2 teaspoon vanilla extract
- 1/8 teaspoon sea salt

Directions

1. Heat a frying pan over medium heat.
2. Add pecans to the pan and toast until dark brown.
3. Coarsely chop the roasted pecan. Set them aside.
4. Mix coconut butter with ghee and coconut oil in a saucepan. Let it simmer over low heat.
5. Stir in sea salt and vanilla extract. Mix well.
6. Transfer the chopped pecan into the silicon mold having 12 mini cubes.
7. Pour the butter mixture over the pecans
8. Refrigerate for 30 mins.
9. Serve.

Nutrition *Calories: 145; Carbs: 2g; Fats: 16g; Proteins: 1g; Sodium: 111mg; Sugar: 1g*

Lunch: Creamy Mustard Pork Loin
Serves: 4/Prep Time: 10 minutes

Ingredients:

Pork Loins

- 4 4 oz. pork loins
- 1 tablespoon pink Himalayan sea salt
- 1 teaspoon black pepper
- 1 teaspoon paprika
- 1 teaspoon thyme

Mustard Sauce

- 1/2 cup chicken broth
- 1/4 cup heavy cream
- 1 teaspoon apple cider vinegar
- 1/2 lemon
- 1 tablespoon mustard
- Suggested Side
- 2 cups green beans

Directions

1. Pat dry the pork loins with salt, pepper, paprika, and thyme.
2. Heat a large pan and brown the pork in it for 3 minutes per side. Set them aside.
3. Add apple cider vinegar, chicken broth and ¼ cup heavy cream to a skillet.
4. Bring the mixture to a simmer.
5. Add lemon juice and mustard. Mix well.
6. Return the pork to the sauce and combine well.
7. Let it cook for 10 minutes.
8. Serve with sautéed green beans.

Nutrition *Calories: 269 Carbs: 8.6g Fats: 11.9g Proteins: 15g Sodium: 437mg Sugar: 1.2g*

Dinner: Avocado Tuna Salad
Serves: 10/Prep Time: 10mins

Ingredients:

- 15 oz. tuna in oil, drained
- 1 English cucumber, sliced

- 2 large avocados peeled, sliced
- 1 small/medium red onion thinly sliced
- 1/4 cup cilantro
- 2 tablespoons lemon juice freshly squeezed
- 2 tablespoons extra virgin olive oil
- 1 teaspoon sea salt or to taste
- 1/8 teaspoon black pepper

Directions

1. Add all the vegetables and drained tune to a large bowl.
2. Mix all the remaining ingredients in a bowl to prepare the dressing.
3. Pour the dressing over the vegetables.
4. Toss well and serve.

Nutrition *Calories: 304; Carbs: 9g; Fats: 20g; Proteins: 22g; Sodium: 645mg; Sugar: 2g*

Day 13

Breakfast: **Avocado Brownies**
Serves: 12/Prep Time: 10 minutes

Ingredients:

- 2 avocados, pitted and peeled
- 1/2 teaspoon vanilla
- 4 tablespoons cocoa powder
- 1 teaspoon stevia powder

Dry Ingredients

- 1/3 blanched almond flour
- 1/4 teaspoon baking soda
- 1 teaspoon baking powder

- 3 tablespoons refined coconut oil
- 2 eggs
- 1/2 cup lily's dark chocolate melted

- 1/4 teaspoon salt
- 1/4 cup erythritol

Directions

1. Adjust the oven to 350 degrees F.
2. Blend the avocado flesh in a blender until smooth.
3. Add all the remaining ingredients to the food processor.
4. Blend well until smooth.
5. Line a baking dish with wax paper and pour the batter into the dish.
6. Bake for 35 minutes. Allow it to cool for 10 minutes.
7. Slice the cake into 12 pieces.
8. Serve.

Nutrition *Calories: 158 Carbs: 9.1g Fats: 14.2g Proteins: 3.8g Sodium: 243mg Sugar: 1.1g*

Lunch: **Sesame Salmon with Bok Choy**
Serves: 4/Prep Time: 10 minutes

Ingredients:
Main Dish

- 4 each 4-6 oz. salmon fillet

- 2 each Portobello mushroom caps, sliced
- 4 each baby bok choy, trimmed and halved

Marinade

- 1 tablespoon olive oil
- 1 teaspoon sesame oil
- 1 tablespoon Coconut Aminos
- 1/2-inch Ginger grated (approx. 1 teaspoon.)

- 1 tablespoon toasted sesame seeds
- 1 green onion, chopped

- 1/2 lemon juice
- 1/2 teaspoon Salt
- 1/2 teaspoon black pepper

Directions
1. Mix all the marinade ingredients in a container.
2. Pour half of this marinade over the salmon and mix well to coat.
3. Cover the fish and marinate for 1 hour in the refrigerator.
4. Adjust the oven to 400 degrees F.
5. Mix the remaining half of the marinade with all the vegetables in a bowl.
6. Spread the veggies mixture over the baking sheet lined with parchment paper.
7. Place the marinated fillets on the baking sheet as well and bake for 20 minutes.
8. Garnish with green onions and sesame seeds
9. Serve.

Nutrition *Calories: 294 Carbs: 1.1g Fats: 16.4g Proteins: 35g Sodium: 343mg Sugar: 0.1g*

Dinner: Spiced lamb shoulder chops
Serves: 4/Prep Time: 10 minutes

Ingredients:
For the lamb

- 5-10 lamb shoulder chops
- 1.5 teaspoons smoked paprika
- 1.5 teaspoons ground cumin
- ½ teaspoon dried oregano

For the yogurt dipping sauce:

- ½ cup whole fat Greek-style yogurt
- Zest & juice of half a lemon
- 2 teaspoons freshly chopped dill

For the green beans

- 1-pound green beans
- 2 tablespoons sunflower seeds & pumpkin seeds
- ¼ cup pitted Kalamata olives, sliced
- 1 small red-hot chili or jalapeno pepper, thinly sliced

- ½ teaspoon cayenne pepper
- ¼ teaspoon ground cinnamon
- Olive oil
- Kosher salt

- 1 teaspoon extra virgin olive oil
- ¼ teaspoon kosher salt
- Couple cracks of fresh black pepper

- ½ cup orange peppers, diced
- ½ cup cherry tomatoes quartered lengthwise
- ¼ cup crumbled feta cheese
- Kosher salt
- Fresh cracked black pepper

Directions
1. Season the lamb chops with all the ingredients for lamb in a bowl.
2. Let it marinate for 20 minutes at room temperature.

3. Add 2 teaspoons salt to a pot filled with water. Bring the water to a boil.
4. Add green beans to boiling water and let them soak for about 2 ½ minutes.
5. Immediately transfer the beans to an ice bath and strain. Let it set aside.
6. Mix pumpkin and sunflower seeds in a bowl along with all the remaining ingredients for green beans.
7. Heat oil in a skillet and brown the chops for 6 minutes per side.
8. Allow them rest for 5 to 7 minutes.
9. Mix all the ingredients for yogurt sauce in a bowl.
10. Serve the lamb with green beans and yogurt sauce.

Nutrition *Calories: 376 Carbs: 12.1g Fats: 21.9g Proteins: 33.2g Sodium: 227mg Sugar: 1.2g*

Day 14

Breakfast: **Cloud Bread**
Serves: 4/Prep time: 15minutes

Ingredients

- 3 eggs
- 4¼ oz. cream cheese
- 1 pinch salt

Toppings

- 8 tbsp mayonnaise
- 5 oz. bacon
- 2 oz. lettuce

- ½ tbsp ground psyllium husk powder
- ½ tsp baking powder
- ¼ tsp cream of tartar (optional)

- 1 tomato, thinly sliced
- fresh basil (optional)

Directions

1. Adjust your oven to 300 degrees F.
2. Separate egg yolks from egg whites.
3. Whisk egg whites with salt until foamy using a hand-held blender.
4. Mix egg yolks with cream cheese, baking powder, and psyllium husk.
5. Stir in egg white foam and fold in gently.
6. Mix well and divide the dough into 8 pieces on a baking sheet, lined with parchment paper.
7. Bake for 25 minutes until golden brown.
8. Serve with your favorite toppings.

Nutrition *Calories: 109 Carbs: 6.2g Fats: 9.6g Proteins: 0.9g Sodium: 227mg Sugar: 1.8g*

Lunch: **Harissa Portobello Mushroom**
Serves: 6/Prep Time: 10mins

Ingredients:

Portobello Mushrooms

- 1-pound Portobello mushrooms stem removed and rinsed
- 1/4 cup spicy harissa

- 3 tablespoons olive oil, divided
- 1 teaspoon ground cumin

Guacamole

- 2 medium ripe avocados
- 2 tablespoons chopped tomatoes
- 2 tablespoons chopped red onion

Optional Toppings

- cashew cream
- chopped tomatoes

- 1 teaspoon onion powder
- 6 collard green leaves

- 1 1/2 lemon juice
- 1 pinch of salt
- 1 tablespoon chopped cilantro

- chopped cilantro

Directions

1. Combine harissa with cumin, 1 1/2 tablespoons olive oil and onion powder in a bowl.
2. Coat each mushroom with harissa mixture and let them marinate for 15 minutes.
3. Meanwhile, mash avocados in a bowl and add all the ingredients for guacamole to the bowl.
4. Heat remaining olive oil in a frying pan.
5. Stir in marinated mushrooms and cook for 3 minutes per side.
6. Turn off the heat and for 3 mins, let them rest.
7. Slice the mushrooms and serve with guacamole and collard green.
8. Add desired toppings.

Nutrition *Calories: 131 Carbs: 9.1g Fats: 10.4g Proteins: 2.3g Sodium: 106mg Sugar: 0.5g*

Dinner: Lemon Pepper Sheet Pan Salmon
Serves: 4/Prep Time: 10 minutes

Ingredients:

- 16 oz. salmon cut into four portions
- 12 oz. green beans, trimmed
- 1 bunch asparagus ends trimmed

Lemon Dill Yogurt

- 3/4 cup yogurt
- 1 clove garlic minced
- 1/4 teaspoon salt

- 1 lemon sliced into rounds
- 1 tablespoon olive oil
- 1 1/2 tablespoons lemon herb seasoning

- 1/2 teaspoon dill
- 1 tablespoon lemon zest

Directions

1. Adjust the oven to 425 degrees F.
2. Mix green beans with asparagus, olive oil, and 1 tablespoon lemon herb seasoning.
3. Spread this mixture over a baking sheet with lemon slices.
4. Place the salmon pieces in the asparagus mixture and drizzle the remaining herb seasoning on top.
5. Place lemon slices over the fish and bake for 15 minutes.

6. Meanwhile, mix all the ingredients for dill yogurt in a bowl.
7. Serve the roasted fish and veggies with dill yogurt.

Nutrition *Calories: 202 Carbs: 10g Fats: 6g Proteins: 25g Sodium: 141mg Sugar: 7g*

Day 15

Breakfast: Frittata with fresh spinach
Serves: 4/Prep Time: 10 minutes

Ingredients

- 5 oz. diced bacon or chorizo
- 2 tbsp butter, for frying
- 8 oz. fresh spinach
- 8 eggs
- 1 cup heavy whipping cream
- 5 oz. shredded cheese
- salt and pepper

Directions

1. Adjust the oven to 350 degrees F.
2. Grease a skillet with butter and sauté bacon on medium heat until crispy.
3. Add spinach and cook for 2 to 3 minutes until wilted.
4. Beat eggs with cream in a bowl and pour the mixture into a 9x9inch baking dish.
5. Top this mixture with spinach, bacon, and cheese.
6. Bake for 30 minutes until golden brown.
7. Slice and serve.

Nutrition *Calories: 109; Carbs: 6.2g; Fats: 9.6g; Proteins: 0.9g; Sodium: 227mg; Sugar: 1.8g*

Lunch: Shrimp Zucchini Noodles
Serves: 4/Prep Time: 10 minutes

Ingredients:

- 4 medium zucchinis, spiralized
- 1 tablespoon olive oil

Sauce

- 1/4 cup 2 tablespoons fat-free plain Greek yogurt
- 1/4 cup 2 tablespoons light mayonnaise
- 1/4 cup 2 tablespoons Thai sweet chili sauce
- 1/2 lb. Shrimps
- 1 1/2 tablespoons liquid erythritol
- 1 1/2 teaspoon Sriracha sauce
- 2 teaspoon lime juice

Directions

1. Heat a greased skillet and add shrimp to sauté until well cooked.
2. Season the shrimps with salt and pepper then set them aside.
3. Heat olive oil in a large skillet and add zucchini noodles.
4. Cook until zucchini noodles are just cooked.
5. Turn off the heat and let them rest for 10 mins.
6. Drain the excess water out of zucchini and set it aside.

7. Mix all the ingredients for sauce in a small bowl.
8. Divide the sauce into 4 meal prep containers and top it with zucchini noodles and sautéed shrimp.
9. Serve or refrigerate up to 3 days.
10. Toss well before each serving.

Nutrition *Calories: 135 Carbs: 3.1g Fats: .9g Proteins: 8.6g Sodium: 10mg Sugar: 3.4g*

Dinner: One Pot Zucchini Pasta
Serves: 4/Prep Time: 10mins

Ingredients:

- 2 pounds zucchini (approx. 4-5 large zucchini), spiralized
- 1-pint cherry tomatoes halved
- 1 large red onion, thinly sliced
- 4 garlic cloves, minced
- 1/4 cup extra-virgin olive oil
- 1/2 cup fresh basil
- salt & pepper to taste
- 1/2 teaspoon crushed red pepper
- shredded parmesan for topping

Directions

1. Heat olive oil in a saucepan over medium heat.
2. Add garlic and onion to sauté for 3 minutes.
3. Stir in zucchini noodles along with salt and pepper.
4. Cover the lid and cook for 2 mins. With occasional stirring.
5. Stir in tomatoes and cook for 4 minutes with constant stirring.
6. Add red pepper, parmesan cheese, and fresh basil.
7. Garnish with basil and serve.

Nutrition *Calories: 204; Carbs: 10.7g; Fats: 15.6g; Proteins: 6.3g; Sodium: 141mg; Sugar: 3.4g*

Day 16

Breakfast: Coconut Porridge
Serves: 4/Prep Time: 10mins

Ingredients

- 1 oz. butter or coconut oil
- 1 egg
- 1 tbsp coconut flour
- 1 pinch ground psyllium husk powder
- 4 tbsp coconut cream
- 1 pinch salt

Directions

1. Add everything to a cooking pot and cook on low heat until it reaches desired consistency.
2. Pour a splash of cream or coconut milk.
3. Top with frozen berries.
4. Serve.

Nutrition *Calories: 109; Carbs: 6.2g; Fats: 9.6g; Proteins: 0.9g; Sodium: 227mg; Sugar: 1.8g*

Lunch: Sesame Pork Tenderloin
Serves: 4/Prep Time: 10 mins

Ingredients:

- 1/2 cup hoisin sauce
- 2 teaspoons coconut aminos
- 1 teaspoon sesame oil
- Two 1- to 1 1/4-pound pork tenderloins, trimmed

- 2 pounds carrots, cut diagonally into 1/4-in. slices
- 1 tablespoon olive oil
- 3 scallions, thinly sliced
- 1 1/2 teaspoons toasted sesame seeds

Directions

1. Preheat the oven to 500 degrees F.
2. Mix coconut aminos, hoisin sauce and sesame oil in a bowl.
3. Spread the pork on a rimmed baking sheet and pour the hoisin mixture over the pork.
4. Arrange the carrots around the pork and drizzle the sesame seeds and scallions on top
5. Roast for 25 minutes then let it rest for 10 minutes.
6. Slice the pork and serve with carrots.

Nutrition *Calories: 234; Carbs: 10.1g; Fats: 23.4g; Proteins: 2.3g; Sodium: 10mg; Sugar: 12.7g*

Dinner: Zucchini Scallops Scampi
Serves: 4/Prep Time: 10 minutes

Ingredients:

- 2 tablespoons unsalted butter
- 1-pound scallops
- 3 cloves garlic, minced
- 1/2 teaspoon red pepper flakes
- 1/4 cup chicken stock
- Juice of 1 lemon

- Kosher salt and black pepper, to taste
- 1 1/2 pounds (4 medium-sized) zucchini, spiralized
- 2 tablespoons freshly grated Parmesan
- 2 tablespoons chopped fresh parsley leaves

Directions

1. Heat butter in large skillet over medium flame.
2. Stir in scallops, garlic, and red pepper flakes.
3. Cook for 2 to 3 minutes then adds chicken stock, lemon juice, salt, and pepper.
4. Bring the mixture to a simmer and add zucchini noodles.
5. Cook for 3 minutes then garnish with Parmesan and parsley.
6. Serve.

Nutrition *Calories: 154 Carbs: 3.4g Fats: 10.4g Proteins: 6.7g Sodium: 156mg Sugar: 0.9g*

Day 17

Breakfast: Keto mushroom omelet
Serves: 4/Prep Time: 10 mins

Ingredients

- 3 eggs
- 1 oz. butter, for frying
- 1 oz. shredded cheese
- 1⁄5 yellow onion
- 3 mushrooms
- salt and pepper

Directions

1. Take a bowl and beat eggs with salt and pepper in it.
2. Take a frying pan and melt butter in it.
3. Pour the egg mixture into it and cook for 2 mins until firm.
4. Top the egg with onion, mushrooms, and cheese.
5. Flip the egg and cook for 1 minute.
6. Serve.

Nutrition *Calories: 109; Carbs: 6.2g; Fats: 9.6g; Proteins: 0.9g; Sodium: 227mg; Sugar: 1.8g*

Lunch: Skinny Lemon Garlic Shrimp Caesar Salad
Serves: 2/Prep Time: 10 minutes

Ingredients:

- 1/4 cup cubed almond flour bread
- 1-pound large raw shrimp (prawns), peeled and deveined, tails intact
- Juice of 1/2 a large lemon
- 1 tablespoon minced garlic
- Pinch of salt
- Cracked pepper, to taste

- ¼ cup nonfat diced bacon
- 1 egg, soft boiled (or poached)
- 4 cups Romaine (Cos) lettuce, leaves washed and dried
- 1/2 an avocado, sliced
- 1/4 cup shaved parmesan cheese

Dressing:

- 1/4 cup plain, nonfat Greek yogurt
- 1 tablespoon whole egg mayo
- 1/2 tablespoon olive oil
- 1 garlic clove, crushed

- 1 anchovy fillet, finely chopped or minced
- 1 tablespoon lemon juice
- 1 1/2 tablespoons parmesan cheese, freshly grated
- Salt and pepper for seasoning

Directions

1. Adjust the oven to medium-high heat on grill settings.
2. Spread the bread cubes on a baking tray and drizzle olive oil on top.
3. Bake for 5 to 10 minutes until crispy.

4. Mix shrimp with lemon juice, salt, pepper and garlic in a small bowl. Set it aside.
5. Heat a lightly greased grill pan over medium heat and add shrimp.
6. Cook for 3 minutes per side then set them aside.
7. Blend yogurt with garlic, oil, mayo, lemon juice, anchovies and parmesan in a blender.
8. Season the mixture with salt and pepper.
9. Toss lettuce with shrimp, bacon, bread cubes, parmesan cheese and avocado slices in a large bowl.
10. Pour the dressing on top and mix.
11. Top the salad with boiled egg and serve.

Nutrition *Calories: 199; Carbs: 9.9g; Fats: 17.4g; Proteins: 2.4g; Sodium: 296mg; Sugar: 5.5g*

Dinner: Roasted Tofu
Serves: 4/Prep Time: 10mins

Ingredients:

- 2 (14 ounces) packages extra-firm, water-packed tofu, drained
- ⅔ cup coconut aminos
- ⅔ cup lime juice
- 6 tablespoons toasted sesame oil

Directions

1. Pat dry the tofu and slice into half inch cubes.
2. Mix all the remaining ingredients in a small bowl.
3. Marinate for 1 to 4 hours in the refrigerator.
4. Adjust the oven to 450 degrees F.
5. Spread the marinated tofu on a baking sheet and bake for 20 minutes.
6. Serve.

Nutrition *Calories: 104 Carbs: 6.7g Fats: 3.6g Proteins: 5.4g Sodium: 141mg Sugar: 1.4g*

Day 18

Breakfast: Cauliflower hash browns
Serves: 4/Prep Time: 10mins

Ingredients

- 15 oz. cauliflower
- 3 eggs
- ½ yellow onion, grated
- 1 tsp salt
- 2 pinches pepper
- 4 oz. butter, for frying

Directions

1. Grate the cauliflower in a food processor grinder to get fine rice.
2. Mix the cauliflower with all the remaining ingredients in a bowl. Let it sit for 10 minutes.
3. Take a large skillet and heat butter.
4. Spread a dollop of the cauliflower into the skillet to get a 4-inch round.
5. Cook for 3 minutes per side.
6. Use the entire batter to cook more hash browns.

7.   Serve and enjoy.

Nutrition *Calories: 109; Carbs: 6.2g; Fats: 9.6g; Proteins: 0.9g; Sodium: 227mg; Sugar: 1.8g*

Lunch: Colorful Roasted Sheet-Pan Veggies
Serves: 4/Prep Time: 5 minutes

Ingredients:

- 3 cups cubed carrots (1-inch)
- 3 tablespoons extra-virgin olive oil, divided
- 4 cups broccoli florets
- 2 red bell peppers, cut into squares
- 1 large red onion, diced
- 2 teaspoons Italian seasoning
- 1 teaspoon coarse kosher salt
- ¼ teaspoon pepper
- 1 tablespoon best-quality balsamic vinegar

Directions

1.   Adjust the oven to 425 degrees F.
2.   Toss carrots with oil and spread them on a baking sheet.
3.   Roast for 5 minutes.
4.   Toss all the remaining ingredients in a large bowl.
5.   Stir in roasted carrots and spread the mixture on the baking sheet.
6.   Bake for 5 to 7 minutes.
7.   Serve.

Nutrition *Calories: 124; Carbs: 6.4g; Fats: 13.4g; Proteins: 4.2g; Sodium: 136mg; Sugar: 2.1g*

Dinner: Korean Beef Brisket
Serves: 3/Prep Time: 10 minutes

Ingredients:

- 4 to 5 pounds beef brisket, diced into chunks
- 1 tablespoon sweet paprika
- ½ teaspoon red chili flakes
- 2½ teaspoon kosher salt
- ½ teaspoon freshly ground black pepper
- 1 to 3 tablespoons peanut oil, as needed
- 1 large onion, diced
- 4 garlic cloves, minced
- 1 tablespoon grated peeled fresh ginger
- 1 cup water
- ¼ cup Gochujang (Korean chili paste)
- 2 tablespoons sugar-free ketchup
- 2 tablespoons soy sauce
- 2 teaspoon Asian fish sauce
- 1 teaspoon toasted sesame oil

Directions

1.   Season the beef pieces with paprika, chili flakes, salt, and pepper.
2.   Heat oil in a large skillet and add beef to sear for 2 minutes per side.
3.   Transfer the beef to a plate.
4.   Add ginger, garlic, and onion to the skillet and sauté for 3 to 5 minutes.
5.   Add ketchup, soy sauce, fish sauce, sesame oil, water and water to the pan.
6.   Transfer the mixture to an electric pressure cooker along with the sautéed meat.
7.   Cover the lid and cook on high pressure for 90 minutes.

8. Release the pressure naturally for 20 minutes
9. Transfer the beef to a cutting surface and place a foil sheet on top.
10. Cook the remaining mixture in the cooker for 15 to 20 minutes on sauté settings.
11. Serve the beef with prepared sauce on top.

Nutrition *Calories: 196 Carbs: 13.4g Fats: 10.4g Proteins: 14.3g Sodium: 226mg Sugar: 1g*

Day 19

Breakfast: Keto Mexican scrambled eggs
Serves: 4/Prep Time: 10mins

Ingredients

- 6 eggs
- 1 scallion, chopped
- 2 pickled jalapeños, finely chopped
- 1 tomato, finely chopped
- 3 oz. shredded cheese
- 2 tbsp butter, for frying
- salt and pepper

Directions

1. Take a skillet and heat butter in the skillet.
2. Add scallions, tomatoes, and jalapenos. Sauté for 3 minutes.
3. Whisk eggs with salt and pepper.
4. Pour them into the skillet and cook for 2 minutes while scrambling it.
5. Top with cheese and serve.

Nutrition *Calories: 109; Carbs: 6.2g; Fats: 9.6g; Proteins: 0.9g; Sodium: 227mg; Sugar: 1.8g*

Lunch: Sheet Pan Chipotle Eye Round Roast
Serves: 6/Prep Time: 10 minutes

Ingredients:

- 1 tablespoon erythritol
- 1 tablespoon ground chipotle chile pepper
- 1 tablespoon paprika
- 1 tablespoon cumin powder
- Salt and pepper
- 1 (2.5-pound) eye round roast
- 3 tablespoons olive oil
- 1 white onion, chopped
- 1-pound Brussels sprouts halved

Directions

1. Adjust the oven to 425 degrees F. Layer a baking sheet with parchment paper.
2. Mix erythritol with paprika, cumin powder, and chipotle chile pepper in a small bowl.
3. Season the round roast with salt.
4. Toss Brussels sprouts with onion, salt, black pepper and 1 tablespoon oil in a large bowl.
5. Heat remaining 2 tablespoons oil in a flat skillet.
6. Place roast in the skillet and cook for 8 minutes until golden brown.
7. Transfer the roast to the baking sheet and top it with chipotle mixture.
8. Spread the vegetables around the roast in the baking sheet.
9. Bake for 25 minutes until al dente.
10. Spread the vegetables onto the same baking tray around the roast.

11. Slice the roast and serve.

Nutrition *Calories: 266 Carbs: 5.4g Fats: 26.4g Proteins: 0.6g Sodium: 455mg Sugar: 2g*

Dinner: Roasted Veggie Mason jar Salad
Serves: 1/Prep Time: 10mins

Ingredients:

- 2 tablespoons Creamy Vegan Cashew Sauce
- 1 cup roasted tofu
- 1 tablespoon pumpkin seeds
- 1 cup roasted vegetables
- 2 cups mixed greens

Directions

1. Layer a 4-cup jar with tofu, pumpkin seeds, vegetables, cashew sauce, and greens.
2. Cover the lid tightly.
3. Refrigerate up to 5 days.
4. Toss well before serving.

Nutrition *Calories: 191 Carbs: 7.1g Fats: 8.4g Proteins: 6.3g Sodium: 226mg Sugar: 0.1g*

Day 20

Breakfast: Low-carb baked eggs
Serves: 4/Prep Time: 10mins

Ingredients

- 3 oz. ground beef
- 2 eggs
- 2 oz. shredded cheese
- Salt and pepper, to taste

Directions

1. Adjust the oven to 400 degrees F.
2. Spread the beef in a baking dish and poke two holes using a spoon.
3. Crack one egg into each hole.
4. Sprinkle salt, pepper, and cheese on top.
5. Bake for 15 minutes.
6. Serve warm.

Nutrition *Calories: 109; Carbs: 6.2g; Fats: 9.6g; Proteins: 0.9g; Sodium: 227mg; Sugar: 1.8g*

Lunch: Lamb Shanks, Cauliflower Mash & Beans
Serves: 6/Prep Time: 10 minutes

Ingredients:
Lamb Shanks

- 6 Lamb Shanks
- 1 tablespoon olive oil
- 2 teaspoons salt
- 2 teaspoons pepper

- 2 carrots, roughly chopped
- 2 stalks celery, roughly chopped
- 1 brown onion, roughly chopped
- 1 tablespoon dried oregano
- 1 cup red wine

Cauliflower Mash

- 1 head cauliflower, broken into small florets
- 4 tablespoons salted butter

Green Beans

- 300 grams green beans, ends trimmed
- 1 tablespoon olive oil

- 1.5 cups chicken stock
- 1.5 tablespoons rosemary
- 1 400gram can have crushed tomatoes
- 3 Bay leaves

- 4 tablespoons heavy cream
- 1 teaspoon salt and pepper

- 1/2 teaspoon salt and pepper
- 1/2 teaspoon crushed garlic

Directions

1. Heat olive oil in a skillet over medium flame.
2. Sear the lamb shanks until brown from both the sides.
3. Season the lamb with salt and pepper. Set them aside.
4. Add vegetables to the same pan and sauté for 5 minutes.
5. Stir in red wine and bring the mixture to a boil then reduce the heat to low.
6. Let it simmer for 1 minute then transfer them to the slow cooker.
7. Add chicken stock, tomatoes, spices, and lamb shanks to the slow cooker.
8. Pour the prepared sauce over the shanks.
9. Cover the lid and cook for 4 hours on low settings.
10. Add cauliflower to a bowl along with a splash of water.
11. Microwave the cauliflower chunks for 9 minutes.
12. Blend all the ingredients for cauliflower mash along with cooked cauliflowers in a blender.
13. Meanwhile, sauté green beans in a skillet along with all the remaining ingredients.
14. Serve the lamb shanks with green beans and cauliflower mash.

Nutrition *Calories: 369; Carbs: 13.8g; Fats: 24.9g; Proteins: 31.9g; Sodium: 537mg; Sugar: 1.4g*

Dinner: Edamame Vegetable Bowl
Serves: 1/Prep Time: 10mins

Ingredients:

- ½ cup cooked cauliflower rice
- 1 cup roasted vegetables
- ¼ cup edamame
- ¼ avocado, diced

- 2 tablespoons sliced scallions
- 2 tablespoons chopped fresh cilantro
- 2 tablespoons Citrus-Lime Vinaigrette

Directions

1. Add cauliflower rice to the meal prep container or a bowl.
2. Top the rice with roasted veggies and edamame.
3. Add avocado slices, scallions and cilantro to the container.
4. Pour the vinaigrette over the vegetables.
5. Serve.

Nutrition *Calories: 142; Carbs: 3.4g; Fats: 8.4g; Proteins: 4.1g; Sodium: 346mg; Sugar: 1g*

Day 21

Breakfast: **Keto western omelet**
Serves: 4/Prep Time: 10mins

Ingredients

- 6 eggs
- 2 tbsp heavy whipping cream
- salt and peppers, to taste
- 3 oz. shredded cheese
- 2 oz. butter
- ½ yellow onion, finely chopped
- ½ green bell pepper, finely chopped
- 5 oz. smoked deli ham, diced

Directions

1. Beat eggs with cream, salt, and pepper until fluffy in a bowl.
2. Stir in half of the cheese and combine gently.
3. Take a frying pan and melt butter in it.
4. Add onion, ham, and pepper. Sauté for 4-5 minutes.
5. Pour in egg mixture and cook eggs until set.
6. Top the egg with remaining cheese then fold the omelet.
7. Serve warm.

Nutrition *Calories: 109; Carbs: 6.2g; Fats: 9.6g; Proteins: 0.9g; Sodium: 227mg; Sugar: 1.8g*

Lunch: **Garlic and Sage Rubbed Pork Tenderloin**
Serves: 4/Prep Time: 10 minutes

Ingredients:

- One 2-pound pork loin
- 2 cloves garlic, minced
- Zest of 1 lemon
- 2 tablespoons fresh sage, finely chopped
- 2 teaspoons Dijon mustard
- 2 teaspoon olive oil
- 1/2 teaspoon salt
- 1/4 teaspoon pepper
- Lemon slices

Directions

1. Adjust the oven to 375 degrees F.
2. Bake dry the paper towels and set it aside on a baking sheet.
3. Mix garlic with lemon zest, Dijon mustard, salt, oil, pepper and sage in a mixing bowl.
4. Rub the pork loin with mustard mixture.
5. Place the loin on the baking sheet and top it with lemon slices.
6. Roast for 30 to 35 minutes.
7. Turn the oven to broil setting on high temperature and broil for 3 minutes.
8. Transfer the pork to the cutting board and let it rest for 10 minutes.
9. Slice the pork into half inch slices.
10. Serve.

Nutrition *Calories: 213 Carbs: 4.5g Fats: 23.4g Proteins: 33.2g Sodium: 86mg Sugar: 2.1g*

Dinner: Citrus Lime Tofu Salad
Prep Time: 10 minutes/Serves: 3

Ingredients:

- 1 cup roasted vegetables, chopped
- 1 cup roasted tofu, cubed
- 1 tablespoon pumpkin seeds
- 2 tablespoons Citrus-Lime Vinaigrette

Directions

1. Add all the ingredients to a bowl.
2. Mix well.
3. Serve or refrigerate up to 5 days.

Nutrition *Calories: 79 Carbs: 5.8g Fats: 4.8g Proteins: 5g Sodium: 24mg Sugar: 2.3g*

Made in the USA
Middletown, DE
31 May 2019